Leveraging IoT and Machine Learning for Smart Urban Planning

Muneer Ahmad
University of Roehampton, UK

Rafia Mumtaz
National University of Sciences and Technology, Pakistan

Muhammad Ajmal Khan
National University of Sciences and Technology, Pakistan

IGI Global
Scientific Publishing
Publishing Tomorrow's Research Today

Vice President of Editorial Melissa Wagner
Managing Editor of Acquisitions Mikaela Felty
Managing Editor of Book Development Jocelynn Hessler
Production Manager Mike Brehm
Cover Design Phillip Shickler

Published in the United States of America by
IGI Global Scientific Publishing
701 East Chocolate Avenue
Hershey, PA, 17033, USA
Tel: 717-533-8845
Fax: 717-533-8661
Website: https://www.igi-global.com E-mail: cust@igi-global.com

Library of Congress Cataloging-in-Publication Data

Names: Ahmad, Muneer, 1977- editor. | Mumtaz, Rafia, 1981- editor. | Khan, Muhammad Ajmal, 1970- editor.
Title: Leveraging IoT and machine learning for smart urban planning / [edited by] Muneer Ahmad, Rafia Mumtaz, Muhammad Khan.
Description: Hershey, PA : IGI Global Scientific Publishing, [2025] | Includes bibliographical references and index. | Summary: "The objective of the book is to explore and demonstrate how advanced technologies like the Internet of Things (IoT) and machine learning can be applied to urban planning to make cities smarter, more efficient, and more sustainable"-- Provided by publisher.
Identifiers: LCCN 2024055947 (print) | LCCN 2024055948 (ebook) | ISBN 9798369390306 (hardcover) | ISBN 9798369390313 (paperback) | ISBN 9798369390320 (ebook)
Subjects: LCSH: Smart cities--Planning. | City planning--Technological innovations. | Internet of things. | Machine learning.
Classification: LCC TD159.4 .L49 2025 (print) | LCC TD159.4 (ebook) | DDC 307.1/416--dc23/eng/20250210
LC record available at https://lccn.loc.gov/2024055947
LC ebook record available at https://lccn.loc.gov/2024055948

British Cataloguing in Publication Data
A Cataloguing in Publication record for this book is available from the British Library.

Table of Contents

Detailed Table of Contents

Preface

INTRODUCTION

In an era where rapid urbanization and technological advancements are reshaping our world, the integration of smart technologies has become imperative for sustainable and efficient urban planning. *Leveraging IoT and Machine Learning for Smart Urban Planning* is a comprehensive exploration of how modern digital tools—specifically the Internet of Things (IoT) and machine learning—can revolutionize the way cities are designed, managed, and optimized for the benefit of their residents.

The primary objective of this book is to bridge the gap between theoretical understanding and practical implementation of these advanced technologies in urban environments. By delving into how IoT can collect valuable data from various city infrastructure components—such as traffic sensors, environmental monitors, and public utilities—and how machine learning can analyze this data to drive informed decision-making, we aim to provide a roadmap for creating smarter, more responsive cities. From predicting traffic congestion to optimizing energy consumption in buildings, the potential applications of these technologies are vast and transformative.

While existing research on smart cities has made significant strides, this book seeks to contribute new insights and practical frameworks for implementing IoT and machine learning in urban planning. Through detailed case studies, examples, and discussions of real-world applications, we present a resource that is both academically rigorous and practically relevant. Our goal is to push the boundaries of existing knowledge and encourage the widespread adoption of these technologies to enhance the sustainability and livability of urban spaces.

This book is tailored for a diverse audience, including urban planners, engineers, policymakers, and city officials who are actively engaged in shaping the future of cities. It also serves as a valuable reference for researchers, academics, and students in the fields of smart cities, urban studies, engineering, and technology. Additionally, technology developers and innovators working on IoT devices and machine learning applications will find this book beneficial in understanding the challenges and needs of urban environments, enabling them to design more effective and aligned solutions.

By exploring the convergence of IoT and machine learning in urban planning, we hope to inspire innovative approaches to city management that prioritize efficiency, sustainability, and quality of life. As editors, we extend our gratitude to the contributing authors whose expertise and research have enriched this book, and we invite readers to embark on this journey toward smarter, technology-driven urban development.

ORGANIZATION OF THE BOOK

Chapter 1: A Cyber-Physical Systems and the Smart City Vision: A Comprehensive Guide

The transformation of urban areas into smart cities through Smart Cyber-Physical Systems (SCPS) is among the most significant trends in modern urbanism. This chapter provides a comprehensive guide to SCPS, analyzing their integration within urban structures and their broader socio-economic impacts. By framing smart cities as interconnected systems that bridge the physical and digital realms, the chapter explores how SCPS enhance urban functions and improve the overall quality of life. The role of technological infrastructures in data collection, real-time analysis, and decision-making processes for efficient urban management is also examined, offering valuable insights for researchers and city planners alike.

Chapter 2: Citizen Engagement and Smart Governance

The evolution of smart governance is crucial in addressing urbanization challenges, resource constraints, and sustainability by fostering citizen engagement and participatory urban development. This chapter delves into theoretical frameworks such as social capital theory and the technology acceptance model to analyze community involvement in governance. Models like Arnstein's Ladder of Citizen Participation and the IAP2 Spectrum illustrate varying degrees of citizen influence in decision-making. The chapter also explores emerging trends, including gamified engagement, real-time data utilization, and augmented and virtual reality applications. Additionally, it emphasizes ethical frameworks, digital literacy initiatives, and equitable resource allocation to ensure inclusive and sustainable smart city development.

Chapter 3: Assessing Resident's Response Towards Smart Community Initiatives in Kota Belud

This chapter presents an empirical study assessing the response of Kota Belud residents to Smart Community initiatives implemented by the Malaysian government through MCMC. Employing a quantitative research methodology, self-administered questionnaires were used to collect data from 125 residents. The chapter provides a descriptive analysis of the community's engagement with ICT-based initiatives and evaluates their impact. Findings from the study inform policy recommendations aimed at enhancing smart community programs to foster digital empowerment and socio-economic development at the district level.

Chapter 4: Seasonal Prediction of Hybrid Renewable Energy Using Weighted Ensemble Algorithm with Optimal Allocation on Demand

Seasonal variations pose significant challenges to hybrid renewable energy allocation. This chapter introduces a novel weighted ensemble machine learning approach to optimize energy distribution across different seasons. Various algorithms, including Decision Trees, Random Forest, and

XGBoost, are evaluated for accuracy, with optimized allocation strategies using Particle Swarm Optimization, Grey Wolf Optimizer, and Lightning Search Algorithm. By integrating real-time environmental data, the proposed model enhances energy prediction accuracy and ensures efficient resource utilization, contributing to sustainable energy management.

Chapter 5: AirSense: An Integrated Air Quality Monitoring System

Air pollution remains a pressing public health issue in developing nations such as Pakistan. This chapter introduces AirSense, an IoT-based air quality monitoring system designed to address these challenges. Equipped with sensors and GPS tracking, AirSense collects real-time pollution data from urban areas and applies machine learning techniques for air quality forecasting. The results are made accessible via a public web platform, featuring heat maps and trend analyses to support informed policymaking and public awareness initiatives.

Chapter 6: Performance Evaluation of Various Machine Learning Models and Its Implications for Informed Air Policy Decisions: A Comparative Study for Delhi

Accurate air quality predictions are crucial for effective environmental policies. This chapter presents a comparative analysis of machine learning models for predicting Delhi's Air Quality Index (AQI). Regression models, including Random Forest, XGBoost, and CatBoost, are assessed using performance metrics such as RMSE and R^2. Findings indicate that Random Forest outperforms other models, achieving an R^2 of 0.932. The chapter concludes with policy recommendations, including urban greening initiatives and stricter vehicle emission regulations, to mitigate air pollution in Delhi.

Chapter 7: Ethical Considerations and Challenges of Leveraging IoT and Machine Learning in Smart Urban Planning

As IoT and machine learning technologies shape the future of smart cities, ethical and technical concerns emerge. This chapter explores these challenges through case studies, illustrating potential risks such as data privacy violations and algorithmic bias. It discusses modern tools and frameworks designed to mitigate these issues, emphasizing the importance of ethical AI practices and inclusive urban planning. By addressing these concerns, the chapter aims to foster responsible technology adoption for sustainable and equitable smart city development.

CONCLUSION

As we conclude this book, we reaffirm the transformative potential of IoT and machine learning in shaping the cities of the future. The insights, case studies, and frameworks presented herein underscore the urgency and necessity of leveraging these technologies for smarter urban management. With rapid advancements in digital solutions, it is essential that urban planners, engineers, policymakers, and researchers collaborate to harness these innovations for the benefit of society.

The journey toward intelligent, sustainable, and responsive cities is ongoing, and this book serves as a stepping stone in that direction. We encourage continued research, development, and implementation of IoT and machine learning strategies to address urban challenges effectively. By embracing these technologies, we can create urban environments that are not only efficient but also resilient and adaptable to future needs.

We thank our readers for engaging with this work and hope that the knowledge shared within these pages will inspire new ideas and meaningful contributions to the evolution of smart cities. The future of urban planning is here, and together, we can shape it for the better.

Chapter 1
A Cyber–Physical Systems and the Smart City Vision: A Comprehensive Guide

Khushboo Malik
https://orcid.org/0009-0005-3911-4122
Christ University, India

Kamal Upreti
https://orcid.org/0000-0003-0665-530X
Christ University, India

Onam Singh
Christ University, India

Pratham Tiwari
Christ University, India

Shreya Rathi
HSBC, India

Malika Ara
Saint Louis University, USA

ABSTRACT

The process of urban areas' transformation into smart cities with the help of smart cyber-physical systems (SCPS) is one of the most defining trends of modern urbanism. It requires a multifaceted perspective of smart cities, thereby evaluating the facets of SCPS intently concerning the complexities of their integration in urban structures while exploring their influence that transcends the domains of social sciences and economics, which has become crucial. In this context, smart cities are constructed as integrated

DOI: 10.4018/979-8-3693-9030-6.ch001

systems at the crossroads of the digital and the physical: they sustain, facilitate, and improve the performance of the city's functions and living environment. The importance of technological environments in orientation and close consideration of SCPS reveals the functions in gathering data, immediate analysis, and decision-making processes of urban management.

1. INTRODUCTION

In the rapidly urbanizing world, the smart city is a new important strategy to meet the complex challenges of urbanization. Smart cities make use of cutting-edge technologies in enhancing the quality of life of citizens, achieving sustainability, and bringing about operational efficiency in urban services. At the very epicentre of this transformative vision lies Smart Cyber-Physical Systems, which embeds computation and communication capabilities in physical processes in a bid to render environments smart and responsive. SCPS is at the heart of the paradigm of the smart city, facilitating real-time monitoring, data collection, and analysis that inform decision-making and efficient resource management. These are followed by the IoT, AI, big data analytics—of which these three, when combined, form the backbone for smart city infrastructure. SCPSs empower cities with seamless integration of technologies in order to optimize operations and reduce costs while enhancing the overall urban experience.

The relevance of smart cities and SCPS in contemporary urban planning is very high. In the process, as the population of the urban areas continues to surge, conventional methods of city management are proving inadequate to address issues such as traffic, pollution, energy supply, and resource supply. Smart cities present a proactive way of handling these emerging challenges by infusing technology into making urban spaces more livable, efficient, and sustainable. SCPS also falls within the trends of global digitization and sustainability of urban planning. The contribution to the broader goals—that is, mitigation of climate change, resilient economy, and social equity—is what these systems can do to support smart infrastructure development. SCPS can be used to bring greater adaptability to cities while ensuring a better quality of life for their residents.

1.1 SCPS Functions

SCPS, considered the backbone for smart cities, are used seamlessly to integrate any digital technology with their urban infrastructure in a seamless fashion. The entire functions of gathering data, online analysis, and automated decision can be summed together to improve operation and enhance lifestyles in the smart city.

A) Data Collection: The SCPS sensors are integrated within various urban items such as streetlights, cars, buildings, and environmental sensors. They read parameters like the consumption of energy, traffic movements, air conditions, and other weather conditions every time. This means that through smart meters that collect data of consumption in grids, sensors monitor and report vehicle activities and road situations in transportation networks.
B) Real-Time Analysis and Automated Decision-Making: SCPS process data in real-time through AI and big data analytics for proper patterns and trends to provide actionable insights. In transportation, real-time traffic is used for anticipating traffic congestion to recommend alternative routes and adjust the signal in a dynamic way. SCPS also allow for autonomous decision-making for timely and efficient response; for example, smart energy grids automatically vary the energy distribution according to the demand for public safety systems, and anomalies trigger emergency responses like dialing the emergency services.

1.2 Research Questions

RQ.1 What is the improvement in efficiency, sustainability, and resilience of smart city infrastructure that Smart Cyber-Physical Systems bring?
RQ.2 What are the key challenges to the integration of SCPS into urban environments and how should these be approached?
RQ.3 How will new technologies, including AI-enabled edge computing, blockchain, and digital twins, play a role in the evolution of SCPS for smart cities?

With current restraints in urbanization, resource scarcity, and environmental sustainability, integrating Smart Cyber-Physical Systems (SCPS) into urban environments has become of high relevance. Smart Cyber-Physical Systems constitute the backbone of smart cities by facilitating real-time monitoring of activities, efficient management of available resources, and data-driven decision-making to enhance the quality of living in cities. This chapter attempts to look at the technological, social, and economic dimensions of SCPS while also bringing into light their role in developing sustainable, inclusive, and resilient smart cities. It further goes on to provide an overall understanding through the practical applications, case studies, and challenges for the transformation of urban landscapes as SCPS could face in meeting future demands.

2. CONCEPTUAL FOUNDATIONS

2.1. Core Technologies in SCPS

Smart Cyber-Physical Systems will undergird the ambitions of smart cities. They will enable physical and computational processes to be intertwined in a synergistic fashion. The technologies driving SCPS are the Internet of Things, Artificial Intelligence, and Big Data Analytics.

IoT (Internet of Things): This is the network of physical devices basically embedded with sensors, software, and other associated technologies in connecting and exchanging data with other devices and systems via the internet. It facilitates real-time data collection, monitoring, and management. In this regard, it is critical to various smart city applications related to smart grids, intelligent transport systems, and environmental monitoring. For example, the smart grids collect consumption data through smart meters to rationalize energy distribution and reduce a whole range of wastages (Gubbi et al., 2013).

AI (Artificial Intelligence): It would improve SCPS's data input processing capability and ability to make decisions based on the same. It would automatically predict traffic patterns, work out public services, and augment security systems. For example, AI-based traffic management systems, with the integration of changing signal timings based on real-time traffic conditions, have reduced congestion and improved flow, according to (Kommineni et al., 2024).

Big Data Analytics: Big Data Analytics is a process to extract and analyze large data for the discovery of patterns and trends, which is used to gain meaningful insights. Smart city technologies are applied to improve urban services and operations. An array of datasets is harnessed from different sources, such as social media, sensors, and public records, for more efficient city planning and resource usage to predict future needs. Big Data Analytics helps officials to be more efficient and effective in cities, hence promoting data-driven decision-making (Manyika et al., 2011).

2.2. Integration of SCPS in Urban Infrastructure

SCPS forms the base for developing smart cities as far as integration into urban infrastructures is concerned. There are two major areas in which SCPSs are making their impacts: smart grids and intelligent transportation systems.

Smart Grids: SCPS makes it possible for smart grids to improve efficiency, reliability, and sustainability in electricity distribution networks. Such grids are enabled by IoT devices and artificial intelligence that monitor energy use in real time, detect outages, and predict maintenance needs. This facilitates the integration of renewable sources of energy into the grid, hence assisting a city in meeting its goals of sustainability. Dynamic balancing of supply and demand contributes to preventing the wastage of energy while at the same time offering stable power supply (Gungor et al., 2011).

Intelligent Transportation Systems: ITS implements SCPS to enhance safety and efficiency across transportation networks. IoT sensors gather information about vehicle movements, traffic flows, and road conditions. AI algorithms analyze this data to manage the traffic signals, provide real-time traffic updates, and optimize routes of public transport. As reported by Bifulco et al. in 2014, ITS can dramatically reduce times of travel, lower emissions, and generally improve the commuter experience and quality.

2.3. Data Management and Real-Time Analysis

Data management is an intrinsic part of SCPS, aside from real-time data analytics, which ensures that vast amounts of data are harnessed efficiently and securely.

Sensors and Data Collection: Smart cities have their data collected through a complex system of sensors embedded in many urban elements. According to the measurement, the information data the sensors collect refers to environmental conditions, health infrastructures, human activities, and many other parameters. Here, therefore, options have to be taken into consideration for ensuring the accuracy and reliability of the data given by sensors, so that SCPS work properly (Sundmaeker et al., 2010).

Data Privacy and Security: With the proliferation of data in smart cities, there is a high requirement for data privacy and security assurance. In this respect, robust encryption methods, secure solutions to store data, and stringent control on access are some of the aspects that can help protect sensitive information. On the other hand, some of the steps towards ensuring that the people's right to privacy is assured and goes a long way in enhancing public trust include adherence to protecting data regulations, such as GDPR (Zhang et al., 2018).

Autonomous Decision-Making: Such data insights could be autonomous in SCPS decision-making—no human intervention is required. This feature enables SCPS in response time, including critical situations like emergency management or even traffic control. Much support in making accurate and timely decisions by these systems is brought by AI and machine learning algorithms, further enhancing resilience and responsiveness of smart city infrastructure (Sarker et al., 2018).

3. APPLICATIONS OF SCPS IN SMART CITIES

3.1 Energy Efficiency

Smart Cyber-Physical Systems ensure much higher energy efficiency in cities by smart integration of such innovative technologies as IoT, AI, and big data analytics. IoT sensors and smart grids are able to detect and manage energy consumption in real-time so as to optimize its distribution and not lose any extra energy. As an example, smart grids can keep a tab on the balance of energy loads and integrate renewable sources of energy properly with the goal of reduction in GHG emissions. The AI algorithms predict the pattern of energy demand and modulate its distribution to minimize loss of energy and increase efficiency of the overall system (Khaleel et al., 2024).

3.2 Intelligent Transportation Systems

ITS implements SCPS to enhance safety and efficiency across transportation networks. IoT sensors gather information about vehicle movements, traffic flows, and road conditions. AI algorithms analyze this data to manage the traffic signals, provide real-time traffic updates, and optimize routes of public transport. As reported by Bifulco et al. in 2014, ITS can dramatically reduce times of travel, lower emissions, and generally improve the commuter experience and quality.

Figure 1. Application areas of SCPS in smart cities

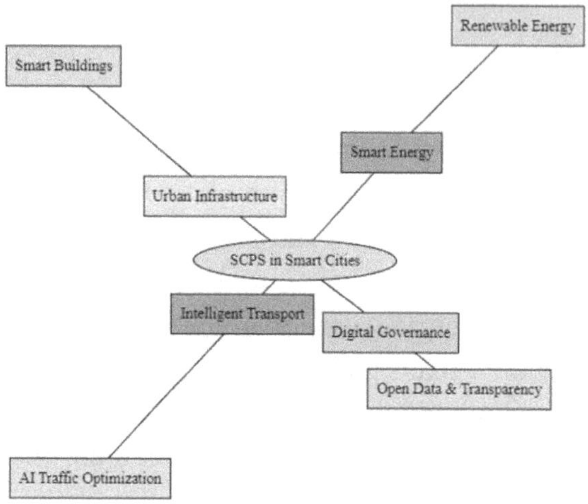

3.3 Data-Driven Urban Planning

The ability of smart cities to address global challenges such as climate change and rapid technological advancement is important because it ensures long-term sustainability. Data-driven urban planning makes more emphasis on sustainable development; its system utilizes advanced technologies such as IoT, AI, and big data analytics in optimizing resources, mitigating adverse environmental impact, and enhancing resilience. Adaptive infrastructure supported by insights from real-time data allow cities to respond preemptively to climate-related risks, protecting investments and making these cities appealing destinations for companies operating on the fundamentals of sustainability. Green technologies are incorporated into smart cities along with data-centric strategies such as mitigating environmental issues while placing the cities in a vanguard position regarding sustainable urban innovation (Albino et al., 2015).

4. CASE STUDIES OF SMART CITIES

i. Barcelona, Spain

Barcelona is one of the excellent examples in Europe that presents a Smart City Solution, making urban life more accessible and sustainable, aiming to achieve higher levels of energy efficiency by using smart lighting whose brightness automatically changes when it is noticed by the system because it does not notice movement. It makes use of the latest sensors on the flow of pedestrians or cars and therefore dim the lights on areas with less traffic, which has reduced the amount of energy consumption as well as their respective costs. As such, in the opinion of Navarro and Bousquet, 2015, the project not only reduced energy usage by over 30% but also costs relating to maintenance. One of the other important success factors in Barcelona is its intelligent parking system. There, the parking space floors are covered by sensors with real-time information being sent to a mobile application that can notify the driver of availability of vacant space nearby. This has eased traffic congestion and reduced the emission of pollutants that have further meant easier driving conditions, according to research done by Hernández-Muñoz et al. (2011).

Interoperability: Lack of Standardized Communication Protocols

Barcelona, Spain, is the epitome of addressing interoperability challenges in the adoption of smart city solutions. The smart grids put into place by integrating renewable energy and devices in IoT platforms are designed using ISO standards and protocols for easy data exchanges between systems, thereby minimizing operational inefficiency and demonstrating the value of standardization in system integration. However, broader global challenges remain since many smart city solutions lack interoperability due to fragmented communication frameworks. Cooperative efforts for developing global standards, such as IEEE's P2413, will be necessary in order to overcome these gaps. Such standards will provide a unified framework for communication protocols, thereby making the efficient, scalable, and interoperable CPS solution possible.

ii. Singapore Smart Nation Initiative: Data Privacy and Governance

In Asia, Singapore emerged as the leader of innovation for the smart city through the ambitious Smart Nation initiative; a well-integrated program aimed at creating an urban environment advanced in technology, enhancing quality of life for citizens. Singapore has developed an extensive network of sensors and cameras to monitor almost every aspect of the urban environment, from traffic flow to levels of air quality. With such an infrastructure, real-time data will be available so that public authorities can take quick decisions on matters in public transport, hazards to the environment, and even urban planning. According to Chourabi et al. (2012), because it uses the data-centric approach, Singapore was able to optimize its services and improve resources for its citizens, thus making greater resilience in its urban areas. This move has also included a smart transportation system that has reduced the time needed in commuting and unclogged roads, significantly improving the Singaporean's everyday life (Phang, 2013).

iii. New York City, USA: Public Safety and Scalability

New York City in North America is one of the examples doing fantastic work towards public safety through its smart city plan. The city says DAS consolidates data across multiple sources, including CCTV cameras, public safety sensors, and environmental monitors, in order to make it easier to prevent crime and respond quickly in case of emergencies. It aggregates data, using a series of machine learning algorithms to identify crime patterns, potential hazards, and enforce law enforcement in the right places. In this context, the sort of technology has led to a drastic decline in crime rates and ensured effective law enforcement. So, Saheb (2023) believes that effectiveness of the project would depend on the collaboration between the city governments and private tech firms with public safety agencies.

Scalability in CPS Solutions for Megacities - The case of New York City's use of Distributed Antenna Systems exemplifies how the scalability problem in CPS solutions can be addressed. The city created a flexible framework for integrating modular, AI-driven systems that promote monitoring in the city and crime reduction by reducing crime incidences. This modular approach sets a high potential for scalability of CPS solutions in addressing increasing demands in megacities. Developing similar frameworks across the globe can ensure smart cities remain nimble and supporting of large populations.

Ethical and Social Impacts of AI- One example is the New York City AI Surveillance System, through which smart city technologies are seen as raising deep ethical dilemmas. While it has made public safety sure by successfully preventing crime, there are debates over biases in AI algorithms and individual rights violated. Public forums have played a big role in airing concerns that require transparent algorithms and citizen oversight. Establishing ethical frameworks and conducting periodic audits will help reduce biases in society and ensure public equitability and responsibility through the application of AI technologies.

iv. Japan: Resilience to Natural Disasters

One of the good examples from Japan reveals that disaster management systems are a brilliant example of resilience in CPS solutions. The integrations of IoT and AI technologies within these systems provide early warnings for earthquakes and facilitate effective strategies to establish disaster response. It shows how systems need to be designed by implementing AI-driven predictive analytics and robust failover mechanisms to increase resilience against cyber and environmental threats. Expanding these practices worldwide can enhance the capacity of cities to remain operational during emergencies and continue to perform their core functions.

v. Copenhagen: Energy Efficiency and Green Practices

Other cities across the world have also adopted SCPS to ensure a greener environment. For instance, Copenhagen smart city strategies are geared at ensuring that the city is carbon neutral by 2025. This entails massive investments in smart grids, green building standards, and intelligent transportation systems (Krähmer et al., 2020). An example of one such innovation in Copenhagen is the smart lighting project, whereby adaptive street lighting is applied to make consumption of energy minimal; this is exemplary to other cities, according to Tunku et al. (2021).

The Copenhagen experience, among others, underlines the need for stakeholder collaboration in robust data management and innovation processes toward sustainability. Public-private partnerships and active citizen participation are considered essential ingredients in the successful implementation of SCPS. Moreover, all technologies need to be integrated seamlessly to avoid operational inefficiencies and maximize environmental gains (Cugurullo, 2018).

Sustainability: Energy-Efficient and Environmentally Friendly CPS Designs- Copenhagen has set a benchmark for sustainability through its smart lighting and transportation systems. These technologies contribute significantly to the city's goal of achieving carbon neutrality. For example, the integration of adaptive lighting and efficient public transportation systems has reduced energy consumption and emissions. The success of Copenhagen underscores the importance of combining AI with green technologies, such as smart grids and solar panels, to optimize urban resource utilization and reduce environmental impacts. Scaling such solutions to other cities could play a pivotal role in advancing global sustainability goals.

5. SOCIETAL IMPACTS AND ETHICAL IMPLICATIONS

5.1 Bridging the Digital Divide

The smart city vision unfortunately remains one of the utopian ideals of technological improvement for a better life quality for all citizens. This ideal is tempered with the realities of the so-called digital divide, or the gap between those who have access to modern information and communication technology and those who do not. That is to say, inadequate consideration of it might entrench already existing social inequities (Foth, 2017). Digital divide mitigation in smart cities is making sure that all citizens are on an even playing field by providing them with the basic requisite infrastructure: effective access to high-speed internet and developing digital literacy. Therefore, it should have in place digital literacy programs, cheap Internet packages, and universal device distribution. Besides, policies have to be directed toward the unserved population to avoid increasing digital divide (Van Dijk, 2020).

5.2 Accessibility and Affordability

Two of the most primal features that make inclusivity a taken characteristic within smart cities are accessibility and affordability. Ideally, 'accessibility' means more than just physical access to the digital infrastructure of a city; it further underscores the use of its digital services by persons with disabilities. Universal design principles will need to be embedded in smart cities so that technology remains usable by all, irrespective of their diverse abilities. Another critical point here is that of affordability, as the technology cost may prove prohibitive for the underprivileged. Subsidized internet services or public access in community centers and libraries are other ways of stemming such challenges. Additionally, policy frameworks need to have provisions for dealing with the result of smart city development that sees vulnerable populations being forced out because of the high cost of living (Gurstein, 2003).

5.3 Ethical Use of Data and Surveillance

5.3.1 Surveillance and Privacy

Large-scale data collection is often part and parcel of the integration of advanced technologies into smart cities, and it gives rise to important surveillance and privacy concerns. According to Lyon, such technologies of surveillance like CCTV cameras, sensors, and data analytics might, while improving security and efficiency, turn out as the pervasive control of citizens' activities. These technologies could be expected to serve ethical purposes with strong regulation in the sphere of data protection, transparency of data practices, and mechanisms of citizen oversight. People should be in control of their data, with insight into the way it is collected and stored, and for what purposes it is used.

5.3.2. Ethical Use of Data

Beyond privacy, the use of ethics in data encompasses consent, bias, and general miss-use of information. Algorithms and AI systems used in smart cities should be designed in a manner that avoids biases which have the potential to yield a host of disparate impacts, argues O'Neil in 2016. Transparent algorithms and accountability frameworks, with regular audits, are required with respect to fairness and justice in decisions arrived at through the use of big data. Moreover, informed consent should be at the forefront of data practices, thus in full realization of the role of the uses and purposes that citizens' data is serving (Floridi & Taddeo, 2016).

5.3.3. Digital Rights and Responsibilities

Smart cities also raise issues relating to articulating and protecting digital rights and responsibilities. Digital rights are those that guard the privacy, freedom of expression, and access to information for all citizens within the online space, (Hintz et al., 2018). On the other hand, digital responsibilities relate to the ethical use of digital tools and conformance to the rule of law and social norms in online behaviors. Digital literacy, rights, and responsibility education is key to having active and responsible participation in smart city ecosystems (Mossberger, Tolbert, & McNeal, 2007).

5.4 Digital Rights and Responsibilities

Smart cities also raise issues relating to articulating and protecting digital rights and responsibilities. Digital rights are those that guard the privacy, freedom of expression, and access to information for all citizens within the online space, (Hintz et al., 2018). On the other hand, digital responsibilities relate to the ethical use of digital tools and conformance to the rule of law and social norms in online behaviors. Digital literacy, rights, and responsibility education is key to having active and responsible participation in smart city ecosystems (Mossberger, Tolbert, & McNeal, 2007).

6. ECONOMIC AND FINANCIAL PERSPECTIVES

6.1 Economic Impact of SCPS

It has enormous economic impacts and is being driven by what have become developed to be "cutting-edge" technologies-such as IoT, AI, and big data analytics. All these change the urban economy, offer new jobs, and develop markets in cities (Mavikumbure et al., 2024). Smart cities directly influence or, rather, drive urban growth and competitiveness by their appeal to talent, businesses, and investments.

6.1.1 Job Creation and New Markets

It provides enormous employment opportunities in almost all domains as the smart city projects develop. IoT, AI, and data-driven services integration demand a competent workforce that encompasses knowledge in technology, data analysis, planning, and management of projects. For example, AI and machine learning knowledge holders of the algorithm play significant parts in large dimensions; those who develop systems that predict traffic flow or optimize energy consumption; data analysts decoding high volumes of city data for improved service delivery (Batty, 2018).

This necessitates new jobs in tech and support positions for IoT installation, maintenance, and big data analysis. In addition, start-ups and established firms continue to innovate solutions answering the needs unique to smart cities. New ventures cut across the sectors of transportation, healthcare, public safety, and energy, diversifying and enhancing the resilience of the urban economy (Caragliu et al., 2011). The results stimulate entrepreneurship, innovation of the economy, and an active urban career structure with a wider spectrum of employment opportunities.

6.1.2 Enhancing Urban Competitiveness

The city's competitiveness increases because smart city technologies enhance the urban region's operational efficiency and the quality of life enjoyed and its reputation as well. For example, traffic congestion decreases, commute becomes shorter, and consequently cuts pollution, making the cities livable and investable for residents and businesses as well. Smart city systems do contribute to improving the level of mobility that results in worker productivity and, of course, makes the attractiveness to talent in retaining as well as attracting a good employee even more relevant than access to business itself.

The effective energy management systems, typical of which are driven by artificial intelligence, reduce the costs of the public and private sectors undertaking the operations in the city. Through data-driven resource management, a better allocation of resources can be made to areas with high demand. Such benefits position a city on a higher level of performance, putting it on a competitive destination for tourism, investment, and human capital and thus allows sustainable economic development.

6.2 Investment and Financial Models

The large-scale amount of capital needed for such smart city projects makes it highly necessary to finance it innovatively with funding strategies and models for achieving economic sustainability.

6.2.1 Funding Strategies for Smart City Projects

There is mostly public and private funding put in the smart city projects, with PPPs usually at the helm. In such models, it will be mostly the private sector partners that will invest in technology and infrastructure, while it becomes the responsibility of governmental bodies to provide regulatory support and align the projects towards the benefits and interests of the public. The partnerships bring their expertise, share the risk profile, and leverage the resources on hand, meaning cities do not over-leverage their public budgets.

International financial institutions and development agencies provide grants and loans to especially brilliant city projects in developing countries, which the international community recognizes the value that cities add to global issues through resilience and sustainability. Cities take this further by finding creative ways of funding, such as local bonds or crowdsourcing from citizens, to sponsor particular projects (Anthopoulos et al., 2016). All this eases financial constraints and widens the pool of assets needed for the metamorphosis of cities into technologically advanced urban centers.

6.2.2 Cost-Benefit Analysis

Research work by Cavada et al. (2016) has pointed out that the high initial investments in technologies and infrastructural systems should be weighed against long-term benefits such as reduced running costs, greater efficiency, and a better life. Undoubtedly, such investments are justified by saving costs, especially those related to consumption and maintenance of energy. For instance, a smart grid can save energy by leaps and bounds, reducing actual consumption, thereby generating massive savings in the long run, making smart cities all the more economically attractive.

6.2.3 Economic Sustainability

Smart cities ought to be financially sustainable to avoid becoming liabilities on public budgets or increasing economic inequality. Smart cities need proper financial models for self-reliance and viability in the long term. For example, value capture financing bases the source of revenue on increased values for property that will be an effect of investments in smart cities to finance future developments-consequently, maintaining a stream of revenue needed to sustain improvements. This approach will make smart city benefits available to a large number of people, thereby supporting the economic inclusiveness and stability for all its urban residents.

6.3 Economic Resilience and Adaptability

Smart cities form part of a broader economic landscape, and they thrive on resilience and agility in the face of global challenges. As innovation centers, smart cities influence and are influenced by regional and international economies.

6.3.1 Economic Resilience

Economic resilience in smart cities can be defined as the capability of opposing or recovering from economic shock, such as a recession or natural disaster, or even something like a pandemic. The diversifying of economic activities and the integration of leading-edge technologies enable smart cities to react to an economic disturbance at a faster rate than any other city. For example, monitoring systems with real-time data can decisively respond to crisis situations with minimal financial loss and rapid recovery (Hollands, 2008). This agility helps keep smart cities stable and find investors even during volatile economic times.

6.3.2 Adaptability to Global Challenges

The ability of smart cities to adapt to global issues such as climate change and rapid technological shift is a prerequisite for their economic sustainability. Smart cities have, as a priority, sustainable urban planning and integration of green technology, making them leaders in solving the environmental woes of the world. Daptive strategies of change enhance the economic sustainability of cities. For instance, adaptive infrastructure that responds to climate risk is a form of protection for investments and attracts businesses that have a commitment to sustainability (Albino et al., 2015).

6.3.3 Impact on Local and Global Economies

This not only affects the local economy but also has regional and international influences on economies. Suitable smart city policies have catalytic models for regional development, promoting cooperation between cities and countries. As a central location for investments, talents, and innovations, smart cities add to the global economy, promoting economic integration and best practice sharing globally (Angelidou, 2014). The emergence of smart cities may provide an opportunity to develop a more connected and resilient global economy, since urban centers worldwide align their growth strategies with the principles of smart sustainable development.

Smart cities contribute to the transformation of local economies and shine as beacons of sustainable practices, hence supporting a global urban network that can stand together against economic and environmental challenges. Continuing growth and evolution, smart cities create a future-oriented global economic structure espousing resilience, sustainability, and inclusivity.

7. POLICY AND GOVERNANCE FRAMEWORKS

7.1 National and International Policies

National and international policies are very strong driving forces in the development process of smart cities and Smart Cyber-Physical Systems. Governments all around the world are exploiting the power of smart cities in mitigating urban challenges, improving quality life, and promoting sustainable development. Most of the countries have incorporated smart city strategies into their national agendas. For example, the Indian Smart Cities Mission has targeted the development of 100 smart cities by exploiting digital technology and infrastructural developments, as explained by Sharma in 2017.

At the international level, the United Nations' Sustainable Development Goals set a framework for the development of inclusive, safe, resilient, and sustainable cities in 2015. The European Union also supports smart city projects, through Horizon 2020, by funding innovation, energy efficiency, and sustainable mobility.

Yet, all the same, regulatory challenges are still a thorn in the way. Interoperability and standardization of technologies developed across different regions are very important. It requires quite stringent regulations for the balancing act between innovation, on the one hand, and privacy and security on the other. Indeed, efficient regulatory frameworks will not only protect citizens' rights but also stimulate innovation with ethical use of data.

7.2. Standardization and Interoperability

Standardization and interoperability of SCPS are fundamental in realizing smart cities, where diverse systems can be integrated for perfect functioning. If there are no uniform protocols developed in smart city solutions, fragmentation will cut down on their effectiveness. Global organizations, such as the International Organization of Standards and the Institute of Electrical and Electronics Engineers, comprise bodies that develop vital standards. ISO 37120 provides indicators for city services and quality of life, allowing cities to benchmark against global standards. On the other hand, interoperability amongst IoT devices and systems is encouraged by IEEE's P2413 standard.

Further, collaborative exercises like GSC3 directly support knowledge sharing for the creation of best practices that help in the creation of models for smart cities that are scalable and adaptable.

7.2.1 IEEE's P2413 and Other Standards

IEEE's P2413 is an integrated standard for the Internet of Things (IoT), with the aim to answer the challenge of interoperability, scalability, and system integration issues in IoT ecosystems that are basically a core of Smart Cyber-Physical Systems (SCPS). The standard provides integrated architecture with the ability to make diverse IoT devices and systems communicate coherently and efficiently for data exchange and integration across domains. P2413 helps in improving the reliability and scalability of IoT-based solutions in smart cities by defining key elements such as abstraction layers, data flow models, and security considerations.

Apart from IEEE's P2413, other standards provide the much-needed basis for interoperability and consistency within smart city deployments. For example, ISO 37120 concentrates on city service and quality of life indicators; it gives comparative benchmarks for sustainable urban development. Similarly, the ITU-T Y.4900 series gives an outline of the key performance indicators for smart sustainable cities to keep in line with international sustainability goals. These standards together promote harmonized approaches to smart city planning, foster cooperation, and ensure that all cities around the world can adopt scalable, secure, and interoperable technologies to address urban challenges.

7.3. Governance and Citizen Engagement

7.3.1. Participatory Governance Models

On the other hand, smart cities provide active citizen participation in effective governance. Nam and Pardo argue that participatory models of governance, whereby citizens take a more central role in decision-making, will improve transparency, accountability, and trust in public institutions. Typically, such models are technology-enabled and offer an opportunity for citizens to raise their concerns, contribute towards policy making, and engage in neighborhood projects collaboratively. These can be, among others, discussion forums created online, mobile applications through which people can file complaints, or digital platforms in terms of civic engagement. Models such as these make sure that benefits resulting from smart city initiatives are distributed equitably and policies address various needs of the population.

7.3.2. Public-Private Partnerships

PPPs are an integral part in developing and implementing smart city projects. This kind of partnership brings together two large players with their individual strengths—public sector oversight and private sector innovation and efficiency. This can provide the necessary funds, technical expertise, and innovative solution that may be beyond the single capacity of a public entity (Siemiatycki, 2013). However, equally significant is how such types of partnerships help secure transparency and accountability for clear role and responsibility definitions. Besides, the interests of partners in the private sector must serve the public for good, and it must ensure that profit intends do not undermine social equity and inclusion (Mazzucato, 2013).

8. CHALLENGES AND RISKS

Challenges arise in the integration of SCPS into urban environments. Cybersecurity risks are presented by the very nature of interconnectivity, which makes SCPS susceptible to attacks. Data privacy is a concern as SCPS gather enormous amounts of sensitive information. Interoperability issues also arise due to the lack of standardized protocols, which hinders the seamless integration of systems, and the digital divide exacerbates inequalities by limiting access to technology for marginalized populations. It faces challenges of scalability and sustainability, especially in cities growing rapidly, so it needs modular, energy-efficient, and adaptive solutions. Therefore, all these challenges have to be overcome for the effective and inclusive implementation of SCPS in smart cities. This section discusses three key challenges: cybersecurity threats, data privacy concerns, and the digital divide.

Figure 2. Challenges in SCPS integration

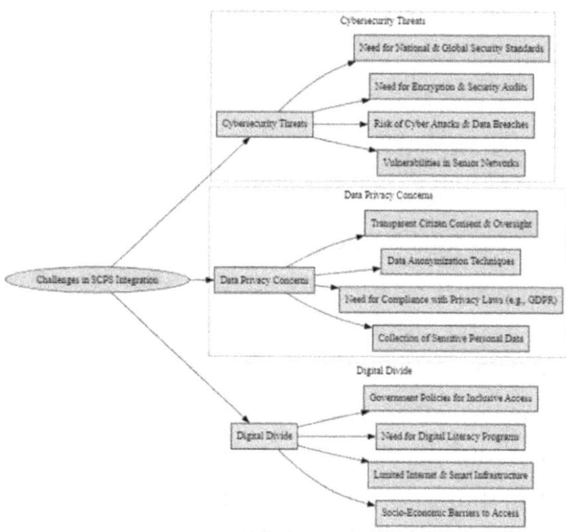

8.1. Cybersecurity Threats

Connectedness in the context of smart cities can be viewed as dependent; this can be seen from the deployment of sensor networks and IoT devices that collect, process, and then disseminate real-time data. Such dependence makes them vulnerable to cyber-attacks in which a breach in one component can cascade through an entire network with possibly severe disruptions. There are various entry points in SCPS technologies for cybercriminals. Alcaraz and Zeadally in (2015) suggest the SCPS infrastructure diverseness - as related to traffic management or power grids-is what increases the "attack surface" of their infrastructure, making cybersecurity that much tougher. As simple as data breaches, cyber-attacks can get quite complex by disrupting a whole city-endangering residents' safety.

Robust mitigation measures such as the use of encryption protocols, rigorous and regular security audits, and real-time threat monitoring are to be done to prevent breach events in real-time. Stakeholders would need awareness and regular training on cybersecurity in order to increase defence mechanisms against evolving threats. Adaptive or multi-layered frameworks need to be built says Roman et al. (2018) and it shall adapt itself according to new and emerging threats for continuous protection. To avoid cyber-attacks on such vital urban systems, governments and municipal authorities have a role to play in somehow collaboratively agreeing on national and international standards for the cybersecurity of infrastructures in smart cities.

8.2. Data Privacy Concerns

With the tremendous data processing involved in smart cities, there are severe privacy implications, as SCPS process a huge amount of personal and sensitive information. Citizens' data is being collected infinitely with various devices, sensors, and applications through which smart cities are exposed to misuse and breaches. Public trust relies on visible data management and the observance of privacy laws like GDPR with the high requirement of full protection of personal data. Binns (2018) posits that the SCPS should be designed with "privacy by design": that is, privacy protections are part of the core and should be well integrated from the beginning. This may prevent abuses in the exercise of power and ensure that privacy is treated as a critical feature of the smart city infrastructure.

Importantly, citizen identities can be anonymized through data methods such as the Gaussian method. Also, city officials should clearly point out well-informed citizen consent; citizens should be informed on how the data is being used, stored, and shared. The privacy policy shall be dynamic to change with time for novel technological advancement and threats. Strict compliance and development of public oversight can help create confidence in the hands of citizens; otherwise, they will resist the data collection, which is integral to SCPS.

8.3. Digital Divide

The digital divide is a core problem in smart cities. It creates obstacles for equal access and causes social differences. This is happening as the technology of smart city becomes the standard feature of urban life, thus separating people by income, education, and geographical location about their chances to participate and become effective users of these innovations. According to Van Deursen and van Dijk (2019), socio-economic inequalities restrict the access to digital services and may potentially exclude marginalized populations from the benefits of SCPS. For example, there is a low possibility that the respective poor neighborhoods will be introduced to cheaper, suitable, and abundant internet services. While this informs that such families will be limited in availing the necessary smart city services.

To this end, governments must prioritize enabling affordable internet access, digital device distribution, and digital skills training. As Norris (2001) cautions, unless such policy focus is available, smart cities will only serve to deepen social inequalities by favoring affluent and well-connected communities. Inclusiveness commitment obliges local governments to design policies to bridge gaps in access to digital and open the ways for all citizens to share in the benefits from digital transformation.

9. ENVIRONMENTAL SUSTAINABILITY AND CLIMATE ADAPTATION

9.1. Climate Change Mitigation and Adaptation

9.1.1. Smart City Solutions for Climate Resilience

SCPS is applied in smart cities to gain improved resilience in respect of climate change by adopting a few innovative solutions. Anticipating the events of natural disasters using real-time environmental conditions monitored from IoT sensors and using satellite imagery, through the adoption of appropriate response strategies, is carried out. For instance, a smart flood management system with the help of predictive analytics is capable of switching on the preventive procedures such as regulating the water level in the reservoir in order to mitigate the situation and even warn the residents about the risks of the flood phenomena (Anbarasan et al., 2019).

9.1.2. Green Technologies and Practices

Green technologies and sustainable practices have defined smart cities. Solar panels, besides efficient buildings, are integral constituents of the infrastructures in smart cities. Such elements help diminish the use of fossil fuels, thereby reducing carbon footprint. SCPS make smooth and effective integration of such technologies into urban infrastructures with respect both to their performance and environmental implications (Casini, 2017). The intelligent transport system also promotes using electric vehicles and public transport, therefore further reducing emissions.

10. LESSONS LEARNED AND RECOMMENDATIONS

10.1. Critical Success Factors

Other critical factors that can influence the sustainability of such a smart city project across different regions are governmental support, technological infrastructure, and public-private partnerships. It is through the launch of these factors that the smart city initiatives in Barcelona, Singapore, and New York City went perfectly well.

1. **Governmental Support and Policy Framework:** An effective policy framework together with pro-government involvement is one of the key factors. In the case of Barcelona, strong support by the city council spurred financing and regulatory support to move smart city projects forward (Navarro & Bousquet, 2015). Likewise, in Singapore, the government rendered substantial support and regulation in pushing for the Smart Nation initiative to ensure a well-coordinated plan in the investment areas towards infrastructure, IoT, and big data applications (Chourabi et al., 2012).
2. **Integration of Advanced Technologies:** The government has the ability to make real-time decisions on data-driven parameters through access to IoT, big data, and AI technologies. For example, in Barcelona's smart lighting and parking systems, IoT sensors will enable the city to decrease its cost of operations while improving efficiency, hence achieving greater resilience and sustainability (Hernández-Muñoz et al., 2011).
3. **PPPs:** Public-private collaboration is the only way to guarantee the efficient deliverability and upscaling of smart city projects. An example would be the relationship between New York City and private corporations, who involved the companies in developing novel solutions in public safety as well as sustainability. Instead of just access to leading-edge technology, partnerships also helped relief of financial burden to carry out these large smart city initiatives.

In a nutshell, findings through case studies have led to lessons that capture how customized approaches with specific technologies and robust collaborative frameworks can make smart city initiatives successful and sustainable across different contexts.

10.2 Differing Approaches and Outcomes

Although common to all successful smart city implementations are success factors, the approaches and outcomes sometimes differ significantly from one region to another. For instance, European cities, like Barcelona, place considerable emphasis on sustainability and social equity. Having a primary orientation toward reducing energy consumption and enhancing public services—hence improving the quality of life for all citizens—the smart city projects of Barcelona set a very good example.

On the other hand, the Asian cities like Singapore focus on economic growth and technological innovation. According to Phang, 2013, Smart Nation is a program aiming to make Singapore one of the leading technology and innovation hubs in the world so that to ensure economic competitiveness and woo investments. The move has overseen quite a massive infrastructural development of the urban infrastructure and public services but has also opened a can of worms regarding personal data privacy and surveillance.

City governments in North America, such as New York City, are more concerned with the issue of public safety and security. Although DAS implemented in New York has greatly enhanced counter crime and emergency prevention and response capabilities of the city, it also tends to raise surveillance issues and individual rights to privacy as stated by Saheb, 2023.

10.3. Recommendations for Policymakers and Planners

Case studies based on these kinds of aspects can be learned and utilized by policymakers and urban planners. First, securing public trust and safeguarding individual rights are considered highly essential, which would be captured through investment in good structure for data privacy and security. Second, finding public-private partnerships may bring onboard the necessary resources and expertise to ensure the delivery of successful smart city projects. The third is inclusiveness and equity in bridging the digital divide and promoting social equity (Chourabi et al., 2012).

Finally, smart city projects must be monitored and evaluated if errors are to be detected and long-term success is to be secured. Learning from experiences, especially in cities like Barcelona, Singapore, and New York, future smart city projects will be able to create much more sustainable, efficient, and inclusive urban environments by drawing on tested strategies and avoiding common mistakes.

11. CONCLUSION AND FUTURE DIRECTIONS

In a nutshell, Smart City is one of the most extreme changes introduced by urban development. Here, technology and data meet to bestow more efficient, livable, and sustainable urban space. To that end, the present chapter has comprehensively discussed integrating SCPS in dimensions of urban planning as technological, social, economic, and environmental. At the core of these SCPS are technologies such as IoT, AI, and Big Data Analytics that actually give impetus to the building of smart city processes through real-time capture, processing, and decision-making. They help make concrete certain smart urban infrastructures like smart grids and intelligent transportation systems that optimize resource usage and the quality of life in urban settlements.

The chapter has also brought to the fore how SCPS is useful in enhancing social equity, inclusion, and participatory governance. In like manner, the book has raised ethical and public concerns around data privacy, surveillance, and digital rights that challenge one for a balanced approach, so it respects individual liberty while fostering innovation. Smart cities contribute to job creation, urban competitiveness, and economic sustainability; at the same time, they are closely related with broader global economic systems. The dimension of environmental sustainability in smart cities, which is being driven by SCPS, looks at sustainability from the angle of energy efficiency, waste management, and climate change mitigation. Case studies and empirical data in the chapter strongly illustrate smart cities' potential for responding to contemporary urban challenges but also bring out their complexities and risks for implementation.

Such insights that one derives while going through this chapter impose huge importance on future urban planning because SCPS can be incorporated in the framework of a city only by adhering to an interdisciplinary dimension that involves not only technological development but also looks into the social, economic, and environmental contexts. Urban planners need to collaborate with technologists, policymakers, and indeed the citizen body in the design of smart cities that are not only efficient and sustainable but also equitable and inclusive.

Emerging technologies, including AI-powered edge computing for quick decision-making, blockchain for safe data management, and digital twins for optimized city planning, will define the future of Smart Cyber-Physical Systems (SCPS) in urban management. Improved communication between systems through 5G networks will make operations more responsive and efficient in urban contexts. In this context, SCPS will play a critical role in fostering resilience and sustainability for cities that are challenged by climate change and population growth. For them to be fully realized, inclusivity, ethical AI deployment, and bridging the digital divide must remain priorities in ensuring equitable and smart urban development.

REFERENCES

Albino, V., Berardi, U., & Dangelico, R. M. (2015). Smart cities: Definitions, dimensions, performance, and initiatives. *Journal of Urban Technology, 22*(1), 3–21. DOI: 10.1080/10630732.2014.942092

Anbarasan, M., Muthu, B. A., Sivaparthipan, C. B., Sundarasekar, R., Kadry, S., Krishnamoorthy, S., Samuel R, D. J., & Dasel, A. A. (2019). Detection of flood disaster system based on IoT, big data and convolutional deep neural network. *Computer Communications, 150*, 150–157. Advance online publication. DOI: 10.1016/j.comcom.2019.11.022

Angelidou, M. (2014). Smart city policies: A spatial approach. *Cities (London, England), 41*, S3–S11. DOI: 10.1016/j.cities.2014.06.007

Anthopoulos, L., Janssen, M., & Weerakkody, V. (2016). A unified smart city model (USCM) for smart city conceptualization and benchmarking. *International Journal of Electronic Government Research, 12*(2), 77–93. DOI: 10.4018/IJEGR.2016040105

Anttiroiko, A.-V. (2016). City-as-a-Platform: The rise of participatory innovation platforms in Finnish cities. *Sustainability (Basel), 8*(9), 922. DOI: 10.3390/su8090922

Caragliu, A., Del Bo, C., & Nijkamp, P. (2011). Smart Cities in Europe. *Journal of Urban Technology, 18*(2), 65–82. DOI: 10.1080/10630732.2011.601117

Casini, M. (2017). Green Technology for Smart Cities. *IOP Conference Series. Earth and Environmental Science, 83*, 012014. DOI: 10.1088/1755-1315/83/1/012014

Chourabi, H. (2012). Understanding Smart Cities: An Integrative Framework. 2012 45th Hawaii International Conference on System Sciences, 2289-2297. DOI: 10.1109/HICSS.2012.615

Clim, A., Toma, A., Zota, R. D., & Constantinescu, R. (2022). The Need for Cybersecurity in Industrial Revolution and Smart Cities. *Sensors (Basel), 23*(1), 120. DOI: 10.3390/s23010120 PMID: 36616718

Cugurullo, F. (2018). The origin of the Smart City imaginary: from the dawn of modernity to the eclipse of reason. Academic Press.

Goutam Mukherjee, A., Ramesh Wanjari, U., Chakraborty, R., Renu, K., Vellingiri, B., & George, A., C R, S. R., & Valsala Gopalakrishnan, A. (2021). A review on modern and smart technologies for efficient waste disposal and management. *Journal of Environmental Management, 297*, 113347. DOI: 10.1016/j.jenvman.2021.113347 PMID: 34314963

Gurstein, M. (2003). Effective use: A community informatics strategy beyond the Digital Divide. *First Monday, 8*(12). Advance online publication. DOI: 10.5210/fm.v8i12.1107

Hernández-Muñoz, J. M. (2011). Smart Cities at the Forefront of the Future Internet. In Lecture Notes in Computer Science: Vol. 6656. *The Future Internet. FIA 2011*. Springer. DOI: 10.1007/978-3-642-20898-0_32

Jaeger, P. T. (2012). *Disability and the Internet: Confronting a digital divide*. Lynne Rienner Publishers.

Khaleel, , Yusupov, , Alfalh, , Güneşer, , & Nassar, , & El-Khozondar. (2024). *Impact of Smart Grid Technologies on Sustainable Urban Development*. Academic Press.

Kommineni, M., & Baseer, K. K. (2024). An Architecture and Review of Intelligence Based Traffic Control System for Smart Cities. *EAI Endorsed Transactions on Energy Web, 11*. Advance online publication. DOI: 10.4108/ew.4964

Krähmer, K. (2020). Are green cities sustainable? A degrowth critique of sustainable urban development in Copenhagen. *European Planning Studies, 29*(7), 1272–1289. DOI: 10.1080/09654313.2020.1841119

Lyon, D. (2014). Surveillance, Snowden, and Big Data: Capacities, consequences, critique. *Big Data & Society, 1*(2). Advance online publication. DOI: 10.1177/2053951714541861

Mansur, T., Nizar, T. M., Ali, R., Baharudin, N., & Ananda-Rao, K. (2021). Performance analysis of smart lighting control system for sustainable campus operation. *International Journal of Advanced Technology and Engineering Exploration.*, *8*(74), 54–63. DOI: 10.19101/IJATEE.2020. S2762179

Mavikumbure, H. S., Cobilean, V., Wickramasinghe, C. S., Drake, D., & Manic, M. (2024, July). Generative AI in cyber security of cyber physical systems: Benefits and threats. In 2024 16th International Conference on Human System Interaction (HSI) (pp. 1-8). IEEE.

Mishra, A., Jha, A. V., Appasani, B., Ray, A. K., Gupta, D. K., & Ghazali, A. N. (2023). Emerging technologies and design aspects of next generation cyber physical system with a smart city application perspective. *International Journal of System Assurance Engineering and Management*, *14*(S3, Suppl 3), 699–721. DOI: 10.1007/s13198-021-01523-y

Mossberger, K., Tolbert, C. J., & McNeal, R. S. (2007). *Digital Citizenship: The Internet, Society, and Participation*. MIT Press. DOI: 10.7551/mitpress/7428.001.0001

Norris, P. (2001). *Digital divide: Civic engagement, information poverty, and the Internet worldwide*. Cambridge University Press. DOI: 10.1017/CBO9781139164887

Saheb, T. (2023). Ethically contentious aspects of artificial intelligence surveillance: A social science perspective. *AI and Ethics*, *3*(2), 369–379. DOI: 10.1007/s43681-022-00196-y PMID: 35874304

Sharma, A. (2017). India's Smart Cities Mission: Smart for Whom? *Cities (London, England)*, *91*, 70–78.

Smuha, N. A. (2021). From a 'race to AI' to a 'race to AI regulation': Regulatory competition for artificial intelligence. *Law, Innovation and Technology*, *13*(1), 57–84. DOI: 10.1080/17579961.2021.1898300

Talaminos-Barroso, A., Reina-Tosina, J., & Roa, L. M. (2022). Adaptation and application of the IEEE 2413-2019 standard security mechanisms to IoMT systems. *Measurement. Sensors*, *22*, 100375.

Van Dijk, J. (2020). *The Digital Divide*. Polity Press.

Yigitcanlar, T. (2014). Smart cities: An effective urban development and management model? *Australian Plants*, *52*(1), 27–34. DOI: 10.1080/07293682.2015.1019752

Zhang, K., Shi, Y., Karnouskos, S., Sauter, T., Fang, H., & Colombo, A. W. (2022). Advancements in industrial cyber-physical systems: An overview and perspectives. *IEEE Transactions on Industrial Informatics*, *19*(1), 716–729.

Chapter 2
Citizen Engagement and Smart Governance

Amitava Podder
https://orcid.org/0009-0004-9268-3781
University of Engineering and Management, India

Piyal Roy
https://orcid.org/0009-0007-5378-2789
Brainware University, India

Shivnath Ghosh
https://orcid.org/0000-0001-7368-7139
Brainware University, India

Saptarshi Kumar Sarkar
https://orcid.org/0009-0004-1786-8284
Brainware University, India

Rajashri Roy Choudhury
Brainware University, India

ABSTRACT

Evolution of smart governance addresses challenges of urbanization, resource constraints, and sustainability by prioritizing citizen engagement

DOI: 10.4018/979-8-3693-9030-6.ch002

and inclusive urban development. This chapter examines the integration of participatory governance models, emphasizing theoretical frameworks such as social capital theory and the technology acceptance model to explore dynamics of community involvement. Models like Arnstein's Ladder of Citizen Participation and the IAP2 Spectrum highlight the varying levels of citizen influence in decision-making. Emerging trends such as gamified engagement, real-time data utilization, and the use of augmented and virtual reality reshape citizen participation. The chapter emphasizes the significance of ethical frameworks, digital literacy initiatives, and equitable resource allocation for sustainable smart city development, providing practical insights for policymakers and researchers.

1. INTRODUCTION

The term "smart cities" has recently gained currency as metropolitan areas around the world undergo significant technological transformations. A smart city, at its core, optimizes urban development through the use of current technology and data-driven approaches to improve effectiveness, environmental sustainability, and overall quality of life. This evolution encompasses the integration of technological advances, such as the Internet of Things (IoT), as well as the analysis of data within urban infrastructure, leading to a fundamental shift in how cities are developed and managed.

1.1. Background

The intelligent integration of technology for communication and information (ICTs) optimizes various urban activities, including travel, energy consumption, waste disposal, and public services, distinguishing smart cities. Smart city efforts have evolved as strategic responses to the problems faced by an increasing population, resource constraints, and environmental concerns.

The adoption of smart city technology promises the potential for better resource management, improved public services, and increased economic competitiveness. However, the success of these programs is significantly dependent on community engagement and meaningful public participation in the conception, execution, and assessment of smart city projects.

1.2. Rationale

The importance of community engagement and citizen participation in smart city initiatives cannot be overstated. While technological advancements serve as the foundation of smart cities, the human element is crucial in ensuring the relevance, acceptance, and sustainability of these initiatives (Townsend, 2013). Engaging the community fosters a sense of ownership, inclusivity, and shared responsibility, leading to more responsive and people-centric urban development.

Furthermore, citizen participation acts as a valuable source of diverse perspectives, local knowledge, and innovative ideas. Without active involvement from residents, smart city projects risk overlooking critical contextual factors and may encounter resistance or skepticism from the very communities they aim to benefit.

1.3. Objectives

This review work is motivated by two basic goals. Firstly, it aims to critically examine the existing literature on community engagement and citizen participation within the context of smart city initiatives. This includes synthesizing significant data, detecting trends, and analyzing the different models and frameworks used to encourage community engagement in smart city project development and implementation.

Second, the article aims to identify the problems, opportunities, and success factors associated with community participation in smart cities. By shedding light on these aspects, the review provides insights that can inform policymakers, urban planners, and researchers on strategies to enhance the effectiveness and sustainability of smart city initiatives through active community involvement.

2. METHODOLOGY

2.1. Criteria for Acceptance and Exclusion

Criteria for acceptance and exclusion were established to maintain credibility, transparency, and thoroughness. Literature deemed relevant to the intersection of smart city initiatives, community engagement, and citizen involvement was considered eligible. The research was limited to authoritative reports, peer-reviewed journal articles, and conference papers, with a preference for recent publications to reflect the present-day landscape.

The screening process ensured that the chosen literature aligned with the review's objectives by excluding irrelevant works, non-English pieces, and research that did not meet standards. These criteria were meticulously applied to focus on the review's goals (Ruhlandt, 2018).

2.2. Data Extraction

To gain useful insights from the identified sources, the data extraction procedure was thorough. A standardized data extraction form was created, which included crucial information such as the author(s), publication year, study methodology, major results, and conceptual frameworks used. This methodical approach facilitated a systematic evaluation of various studies, providing a comprehensive understanding of the current state of the literature.

During the extraction procedure, both qualitative and quantitative information were evaluated. This entailed synthesizing numerical data, thematic substance, and any previously published models or frameworks. The analysis followed known principles for systematic reviews of literature, which improved both the validity and reliability of the synthesized data (Putnam, 2020).

3. CONCEPTUAL FRAMEWORK

Establishing a coherent conceptual framework is critical in the realm of smart city efforts for grasping the numerous links between essential ideas. This section goes into the fundamentals of community involvement, participation by the public, and smart city efforts by explaining important concepts and addressing theoretical viewpoints.

3.1. Definitions

The vocabulary related to community involvement, participation by the public, and smart city projects is diverse in the fast-expanding environment of smart cities. It is critical to develop precise definitions to manage this complexity.

3.1.1. Community Engagement

Community participation is a dynamic, ongoing process that entails forming alliances and collaborating with government agencies, corporate participants, and the community to solve mutual challenges and capitalize on opportunities. It encompasses a broad range of activities, from information exchange to active engagement in decision-making processes, all aimed at making towns more inviting, responsive, and egalitarian.

3.1.2. Citizen Participation

Citizen engagement is defined as citizens actively participating in decision-making processes that impact their communities (Dinda, 2008). It goes beyond simply disseminating information and includes tools for individuals to offer ideas, voice concerns, and engage in the collaboration of policies and services. Citizen involvement in smart cities includes harnessing technology to improve accessibility and inclusiveness of participatory procedures (Simonofski et al., 2017).

3.1.3. Smart City Initiatives

Smart city efforts use modern technology, statistical analysis, and digital networks to optimize urban services, increase long-term viability, and enhance the general level of life (Dinda, S., 2008). These efforts use cutting-edge technologies like the IoT, AI, and sensor networks to address urban concerns and convert cities into more efficient, habitable, and resilient environments (Figure 1).

By clarifying these definitions, a solid knowledge of the major words is formed, paving the way for a more in-depth examination of their interaction in the larger context of smart cities (Tene & Polonetsky, 2013).

Figure 1. Smart city initiatives

3.2. Theoretical Perspectives

In the context of smart cities, the theoretical foundations of community engagement and public involvement provide a prism through which to analyze and evaluate their dynamics. The section that follows looks at key theoretical frameworks that help us comprehend these events.

3.2.1. Social Capital Theory

According to social capital theory, a community's networks and ties contribute to its general well-being and performance. Social capital is critical for smart cities to boost community involvement and citizen participation. Strong social relationships and networks can promote information flow, foster trust, and boost collective efficacy, fostering an atmosphere conducive to cooperative decision-making and solution-finding Innes (Margerum, 2011).

3.2.2. Democratic Governance Theory

To maintain the legitimacy and efficacy of governance systems, democratic governance theory emphasizes the significance of incorporating citizens in decision-making processes (Moher et al., 2010). Where technology combines with urban government in smart cities, democratic rule becomes a guiding concept for making sure that technological improvements correspond with residents' beliefs, needs, and ambitions. This idea emphasizes the significance of accessible and participatory techniques in determining the course of smart city efforts (Roy et al., 2025a).

3.2.3. Planning Theory

Planned theory, especially cooperative and communicative planning techniques, elucidates how urban planning procedures may include community viewpoints and local knowledge (Schryen, 2015). Planning theory emphasizes the need for inclusive planning in the context of smart cities, which involves multiple stakeholders, including people, in the collaborative development of urban areas. This approach is consistent with the idea of smart city programs, which combine technological integration with a people-centric focus.

The Technology Acceptance Model (TAM) is frequently used to study the elements that influence technology uptake and acceptance. TAM can give insight into the elements that influence individuals' desire to participate with digital mediums and technology in participatory processes in the context of smart cities. In creating technology-enabled citizen engagement platforms, perceived simplicity of use, perceived utility, and other TAM components become critical concerns.

To understand how technology and data may be utilized for urban innovation, urban informatics investigates the interface of technology for information, the study of cities, and social sciences. Urban informatics provides an academic foundation for analyzing the function of data in promoting community involvement in the context of smart cities. It emphasizes the need to use responsibly and ethically to empower residents and enhance urban living circumstances.

Civic technology and open government ideas both emphasize the use of technology to improve openness, accountability, and citizen engagement in governance (Townsend, 2013). These ideas drive the establishment and execution of online platforms that allow citizens to obtain government information, engage in making decisions, and contribute to the co-creation of municipal policies and services in the context of smart cities.

By delving into these theoretical views, we may gain a full grasp of the underlying structures that determine community involvement and public involvement in smart city programs. These theories give a prism through which to examine the complexity and subtleties of important stakeholders' relationships in the changing terrain of smart cities.

In conclusion, this section clarified essential concepts and investigated theoretical views to create a solid theoretical foundation for understanding community involvement, citizen participation, and intelligent city efforts. The next parts will expand on this foundation, diving into community involvement strategies, variables impacting participation, and real-world cases to present a comprehensive perspective of the growing smart city scene.

4. MODELS OF COMMUNITY ENGAGEMENT

Effective community participation models are critical for guaranteeing the effectiveness, long-term viability, and relevancy of urban development programs in the complex terrain of smart cities. This section digs into three main kinds of community interaction within smart city projects: participation by stakeholders, collaborative leadership, and technology-mediated engagement.

4.1. Stakeholder Involvement

The stakeholder mapping carried out during the design stage, based on the reintegration program's strategic objectives and the selection of relevant stakeholders, requires the lead reintegration organization to define an engagement and communications strategy for the various groups of mapped stakeholders. Engagement strategies describe how a given stakeholder is approached and how relationships are managed over time. The strategy needs to be tailored to the specific profiles of stakeholders, as well as to their expected roles in the program. In particular, engaging with local authorities at an early stage is crucial, considering their in-depth knowledge of local services and their direct connection to returnees and their communities.

Engagement strategies can be classified into the following three categories, based on the stakeholder's level of interest in the reintegration program and their level of influence over the reintegration process (Figure 2).

Figure 2. Gradient engagement model

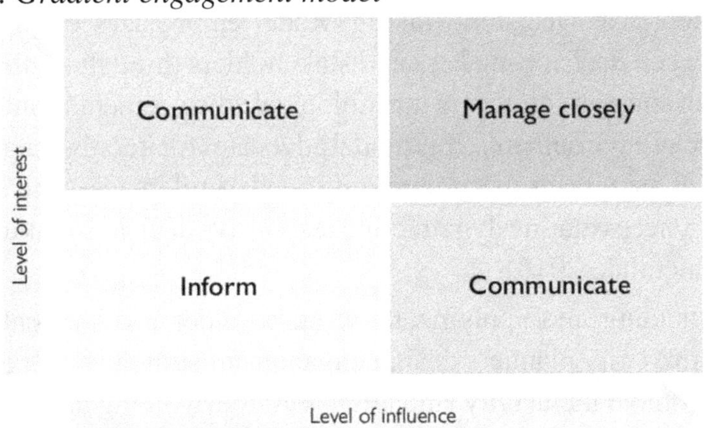

4.1.1. Arnstein's Ladder of Citizen Participation

Arnstein's Ladder provides a nuanced perspective on the levels of citizen participation, ranging from non-participation to degrees of citizen power (Townsend, 2013). In the context of smart cities, this model encourages stakeholders to move beyond tokenistic involvement and towards active participation and shared decision-making. For instance, citizens might progress from being merely informed about smart city projects to having substantial control in shaping those initiatives.

4.1.2. The IAP2 Spectrum of Public Participation

The IAP2 Spectrum offers a flexible framework, allowing smart city planners to tailor their engagement strategies based on the desired level of public influence. By categorizing participation into stages such as Inform, Consult, Involve, Collaborate, and Empower, the spectrum guides the selection of appropriate methods for community engagement. This model proves valuable in aligning engagement efforts with the specific objectives of smart city projects.

4.1.3. Interactive Decision-Making Model

The Interactive Decision-Making Model emphasizes ongoing interaction between decision-makers and stakeholders throughout the project lifecycle. In smart cities, where technological advancements continuously reshape urban environments, this model advocates for iterative engagement processes. It recognizes that community needs, preferences, and concerns may evolve, necessitating dynamic and responsive decision-making mechanisms (Salemink, 2016).

Understanding and applying these stakeholder involvement models can help smart city planners design engagement strategies that empower citizens, promote inclusivity, and align with the evolving nature of urban development.

4.2. Collaborative Governance

4.2.1. Co-Production Model

The co-production model revolves around citizens actively participating in the creation and delivery of public services (Phang et al., 2018). In smart cities, this translates to residents contributing their local knowledge and skills to enhance the design and execution of urban services. Co-production fosters a sense of shared responsibility, ensuring that smart city initiatives are tailored to the specific needs of the community.

4.2.2. Network Governance

Network governance models advocate for collaborative networks involving diverse stakeholders working collectively to address complex urban challenges. In smart cities, this approach breaks down traditional silos, promoting cross-sector collaboration among government agencies, businesses, and community organizations. Network governance improves community engagement by enabling collective problem-solving and building a comprehensive grasp of urban concerns.

4.2.3. Participatory Budgeting

Citizens are empowered by participatory budgeting because it allows them to have an impact on the allocation of government funds for specific initiatives (De Lange & De Waal, 2017). This strategy democratizes the budgeting process in smart cities, allowing inhabitants to prioritize projects based on what they require. Participatory budgeting improves transparency and responsibility in resource distribution, increasing community ownership and trust.

These collaborative governance approaches highlight the significance of shared accountability and cooperation in the creation and implementation of smart city projects. These strategies help the establishment of more welcoming, responsive, and successful urban settings by actively incorporating individuals and promoting cooperation.

4.3. Technology-Mediated Engagement

4.3.1. Citizen Sensing and Crowdsourcing

Citizen scanning and crowdsourcing projects use technology to engage individuals in data-gathering and monitoring procedures (De Lange & De Waal, 2017). Citizens outfitted with smartphones and sensors in smart cities may provide real-time data on the surroundings, patterns of traffic, and other urban phenomena. This methodology improves environmental stewardship and increases community involvement by providing useful, localized data that informs decision-making.

4.3.2. Online Participatory Platforms

Online participatory platforms, such as websites that are interactive and mobile applications, enable digital places for residents to submit ideas, provide comments, and participate in debates about smart city initiatives. Physical obstacles are addressed by these platforms, allowing a larger proportion of the public to participate in the process of decision-making. They promote a dynamic and inclusive interaction process by facilitating ongoing contact and feedback loops.

4.3.3. Social Media Engagement

Social media networks have emerged as important instruments for altering community participation dynamics in the context of smart cities. This type of digital contact breaks down old barriers, offering dynamic avenues for individuals to take an active role, express their thoughts, voice concerns, and work on urban issues. We dive into social media's complex function in supporting community involvement, explaining its influence on real-time interaction, the exchange of knowledge, and the establishment of virtual communities (Simonofski et al., 2017).

Social media sites like Twitter, Facebook, Instagram, and LinkedIn provide smart city people with rapid and direct communication channels (Figure 3). Citizens can stay updated about ongoing activities, events, and announcements related to smart city efforts in a world where immediate notifications are crucial. This rapid communication provides a more interconnected and aware populace, encouraging participation in the growing urban scene.

Figure 3. Smart community

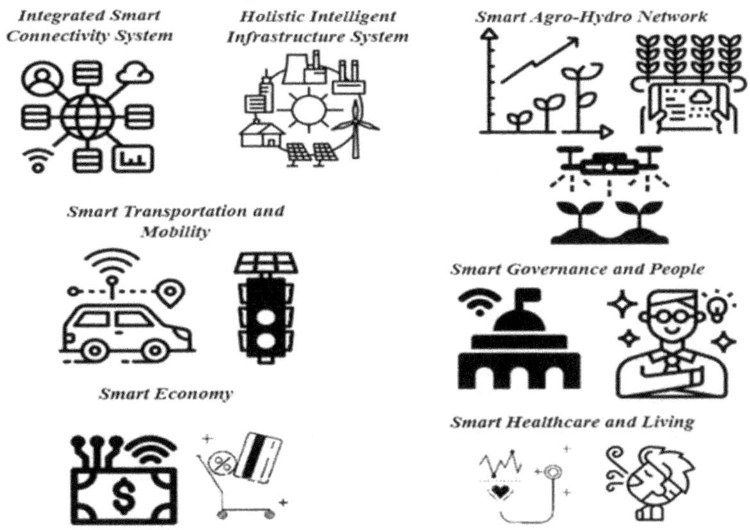

Residents may share their views, experiences, and significant local news on social networking sites, which works as an extensive reservoir of information. Social media platforms serve as a centralized hub for information exchange, whether it is about local projects, environmental concerns, or community events. The democratization of data allows citizens to participate in urban discourses as more informed participants, enhancing accountability and community awareness (O'Reilly, 2011).

One of the most innovative aspects of smart cities is the ability of social networking sites to facilitate community creation. Citizens may communicate, discuss similar interests, and collaborate on civic issues through online clubs, discussions, and sites focused on local topics. These online communities transcend physical barriers, enabling people from diverse backgrounds to contribute to the city's community conversation about its future (Perera et al., 2017).

Social media serves as a democratizing force, amplifying the voices of citizens who would otherwise be disenfranchised from traditional decision-making processes. It makes civic participation easier and more affordable by allowing individuals to convey their ideas, circumstances, and concerns directly to decision-makers. This direct line of communication enhances the response of local leaders to community needs (Horgan & Dimitrijević, 2019).

Social media, unlike conventional methods of communication, allows for two-way contact between citizens and decision-makers. These platforms may be used by government agencies and authorities to collect public input, run surveys, and reply to requests in real-time. This participatory method turns social networking sites into a virtual common square, where the interchange of thoughts and views influences the evolving story of the smart city.

While social media has many advantages, it is not without its drawbacks. Misinformation, digital disparities, and privacy issues must all be addressed carefully. It is crucial to ensure that the information posted on social media is accurate and credible, and efforts should be made to bridge the digital gap and involve residents who may have limited access to internet platforms.

Blockchain technology opens up new avenues for public engagement in smart cities (Perera et al., 2017). Blockchain enables individuals to govern and safely access their data by offering secure and transparent solutions (Figure 4). It may be used to ensure the authenticity of citizen-contributed data, secure voting systems, and transparent transactions. Blockchain technology leads to a more responsible and democratic approach to urban governance.

While these technology-mediated interaction models have the potential to be transformational, obstacles such as digital disparities, worries about data security, and the need for effective cybersecurity must be properly addressed. Striking a balance between technical innovation and inclusion is crucial for maintaining the success and ethics of these methods in smart city programs (Ahmad et al., 2021).

Figure 4. Blockchain for citizen empowerment

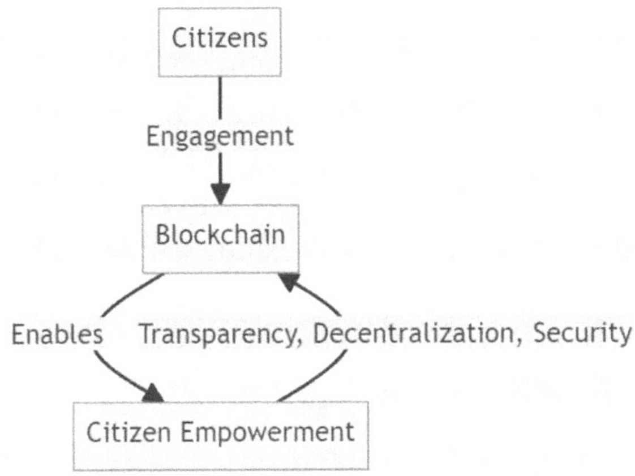

5. FACTORS INFLUENCING COMMUNITY ENGAGEMENT

A variety of factors influence the involvement of communities in the broader context of smart city development, shaping the form and scope of their participation. This section explores two key aspects: cultural and social influences and technological limitations. A thorough understanding of these characteristics is necessary to develop inclusive solutions that cater to the diverse needs and circumstances of smart city citizens (Roy et al., 2025).

5.1. Cultural and Social Factors

Community participation is inextricably linked to a community's cultural and social fabric. Cultural diversity, social frameworks, and historical contexts all influence how residents connect with and engage with smart city initiatives.

5.1.1. Cultural Diversity

Cultural variety is a distinguishing feature of many metropolitan environments, and it has a considerable impact on how people interact with smart city growth. Social conventions, languages, and communication methods influence the success of engagement tactics. Understanding and valuing diversity is critical for establishing culturally appropriate and inclusive programs.

5.1.2. Social Structures and Hierarchies

Within a society, social structures and hierarchy can impact the allocation of influence and authority in the process of decision-making. Established social systems may promote certain groups while marginalizing others in particular instances. Recognizing these relationships is critical for promoting equitable involvement and ensuring that all community members' perspectives are heard (Dommett et al., 2024).

5.1.3. Historical Context

A community's collective memory, events, and views on urban growth are shaped by its historical background. Injustices from the past, such as discriminatory laws or exclusionary practices, might influence faith in government endeavors. Recognizing and dealing with historical context is critical for establishing trust and engaging meaningfully with historically marginalized people (De Lange & De Waal, 2017).

5.1.4. Case Studies and Best Practices

Barcelona, a leader in smart city efforts, has included cultural inclusion methods in its projects. The city understands the value of interacting with various cultural populations and uses festivals and other cultural activities as forums for conversation. This strategy guarantees that smart city efforts are both technologically advanced and culturally relevant (Goodman et al., 2020).

Singapore, renowned for its diverse language landscape, has adopted a bilingual approach to community engagement in smart city development. By providing information in numerous languages and using various communication methods, residents from different languages can access and take part in smart city conversations.

Understanding and dealing with cultural and social aspects is critical for developing effective and inclusive community involvement initiatives. In the next portion, we will look at how technology impediments might stymie citizen participation in smart city construction (Anttiroiko et al., 2014).

5.2. Technological Barriers

The integration of technology in smart city initiatives holds immense potential for transforming urban living. However, technological barriers can hinder the widespread adoption and accessibility of digital platforms, potentially excluding certain community groups. Analyzing these challenges is crucial for devising strategies that bridge the digital divide and ensure equitable participation (Batty, 2013).

5.2.1. Analysing Technological Barriers

Disparities in digital literacy skills pose a significant barrier to community engagement in smart city initiatives. Some residents may lack the necessary skills to navigate digital platforms, limiting their ability to access information, participate in online discussions, or utilize technology-enabled services (Dommett et al., 2024). Bridging this gap requires targeted efforts to enhance digital literacy across diverse communities.

Unequal access to technology, including smartphones, computers, and high-speed internet, can create disparities in engagement opportunities. Residents without access to these resources may be excluded from digital platforms, hindering their ability to participate in online consultations or access information about smart city projects. Addressing this barrier necessitates strategies to improve digital infrastructure and provide technology access to underserved communities.

Concerns about personal information privacy and security might hinder people from actively participating in smart city programs. Concerns may arise regarding the monitoring or exploitation of sensitive information from the collection and utilization of citizen data for decision-making and planning purposes. Building trust and resolving privacy issues both require strong privacy rules and open data practices.

5.2.2. Case Studies and Best Practices

To eliminate technical hurdles and promote digital fairness, New York City has created a Digital Inclusion Plan. The initiative focuses on enhancing internet connectivity, digital skills learning, and device access for persons in underprivileged locations. By removing these obstacles, the city aims to ensure that all citizens actively engage in New York City's digital environment.

The creation of inclusive online spaces for citizen interaction has been prioritized in Amsterdam. These platforms are built with accessibility features to ensure that people of all abilities may participate. Furthermore, efforts have been made to provide alternative channels of interaction for individuals without internet access, thereby increasing their inclusion in smart city-making decisions.

Mitigating technical hurdles necessitates a holistic approach that tackles infrastructural limitations as well as digital literacy issues. Smart cities may foster equitable involvement and enable all inhabitants to actively participate in urban development by making technology accessible and user-friendly (Bon et al., 2020).

6. SUCCESS STORIES AND CASE STUDIES

Successful smart city efforts rely on community involvement and public participation. This section examines best practices and lessons learned from real-life instances, offering insights into the elements that contribute to successful community participation, as well as the valuable lessons derived from both successes and failures.

6.

6.1. Best Practices in Community Engagement

Community engagement in smart city projects can take various forms, and successful examples often share standard best practices. Examining these practices provides a blueprint for designing effective strategies that resonate with diverse communities (Horgan & Dimitrijević, 2019).

6.1.1. Highlighting Successful Examples

Barcelona stands out as a global leader in citizen engagement within smart city projects. The city has successfully implemented co-creation strategies that involve residents in shaping their urban environment. Notable initiatives include the "Superblocks" project, which transforms neighborhoods into pedestrian-friendly zones through input from local communities. Barcelona's commitment to involving citizens in decision-making processes has fostered a sense of ownership and pride among residents (KIM, 2022).

Co-Creation Workshops: Barcelona conducts workshops where citizens, along with urban planners and policymakers, collaboratively design and envision urban spaces.

Digital Platforms for Input: The city utilizes digital platforms to gather input and feedback from residents, ensuring a broad participation process.

Amsterdam has embraced inclusive digital platforms to enhance citizen participation in smart city initiatives. The city's digital platforms are designed with accessibility features, ensuring that individuals with diverse abilities can engage effectively. Additionally, efforts have been made to provide alternative engagement methods for those without internet access, emphasizing inclusivity in smart city decision-making City of Amsterdam (Bon et al., 2020).

Accessible Design: Amsterdam's digital platforms prioritize accessibility, considering the diverse needs of users, including those with disabilities.

Offline Engagement Options: Recognizing the digital divide, the city offers offline engagement options, such as community workshops and physical suggestion boxes (Roy et al., 2025).

The multilingual approach to community involvement reflects Singapore's commitment to language diversity. Singapore distributes information on smart city initiatives in several languages, recognizing the city-state's linguistic variety. This guarantees that persons from all linguistic backgrounds can engage in debates, resulting in a more inclusive process for making decisions.

Multilingual Communication: Smart city project information is made available in several languages so that language obstacles do not prevent participation.

Diverse Communication Channels: To reach a wide audience, Singapore uses a variety of communication channels, such as community gatherings and public forums.

Several recommended practices arise from the examination of these successful cases. Co-creation workshops, accessible digital platforms, and bilingual engagement tactics may help ensure that community participation is not just successful but also accessible and accessible.

6.2. Lessons Learned from Successes and Failures

While success stories provide valuable insights, lessons learned from both successful and unsuccessful cases are equally important. Analyzing these lessons helps refine strategies, avoid pitfalls, and foster continuous improvement in future smart city initiatives.

6.2.1. Discussing Lessons Learned

Toronto's Quayside project, led by Sidewalk Labs, faced challenges related to privacy concerns and data governance. Despite ambitious plans for a sensor-driven smart neighborhood, the project was met with resistance from citizens concerned about data collection and surveillance. The lessons learned from this case highlight the importance of transparent data practices and robust privacy frameworks in gaining public trust.

Transparency is Paramount: Communicating transparently about data collection practices and addressing privacy concerns is crucial for fostering trust.

Proactive Community Engagement: Proactively engaging the community in discussions about data governance helps build understanding and mitigate potential opposition.

Songdo, South Korea, was envisaged as a smart city of the future. However, the city encountered social integration issues. The early vision undervalued the significance of social and cultural problems, resulting in a lack of liveliness in the neighborhood. The lessons learned emphasize the importance of social interactions in smart city development.

Cultural Sensitivity is Important: To promote a sense of community and vibrancy, smart city development should recognize and respect the community's cultural and social fabric.

Smart city designs should be adaptive and enable natural development, enabling the community to create its own identity over time.

San Francisco, a technology innovation hotspot, has encountered unexpected repercussions of tech-driven gentrification. The rapid entry of tech businesses has led to increasing housing costs and social inequities, underscoring the need for an equitable and inclusive strategy for smart city development that considers the more significant social impacts (Komninos, 2019).

Equitable Urban Planning: Smart city initiatives must prioritize equitable urban planning to avoid exacerbating existing social disparities.

Inclusive community engagement is crucial in ensuring that the benefits of smart city development are shared by all residents. Analyzing lessons learned from both successes and failures emphasizes the importance of a holistic approach to smart city development. Transparency, cultural sensitivity, and equitable urban planning emerge as recurring themes, underscoring the need for comprehensive and community-centric strategies (Salemink, 2016).

7. CHALLENGES AND OPPORTUNITIES

Obtaining meaningful community participation in smart city programs is a difficult task that brings both problems and possibilities. This section digs into those obstacles to participation, finding frequent problems in encouraging active engagement. Following that, it looks at areas for development, suggesting various solutions for overcoming these obstacles and increasing public engagement.

7.1. Barriers to Participation

Community involvement in initiatives related to smart cities might face several challenges that limit the success of programs. Identifying these barriers is essential for devising targeted strategies that address the root causes and promote inclusive participation.

7.1.1. Identifying Common Barriers

The digital gap, in which some parts of the population either lack access to information or face challenges to digital literacy, is a serious concern. Because of this gap, some citizens are unable to engage in online platforms or get information on smart city initiatives.

Many residents may be unaware of ongoing smart city initiatives or lack sufficient information to understand the potential impact on their communities. This lack of awareness can result in disengagement and a perception of exclusion from decision-making processes.

Tokenistic engagement, where citizens are involved superficially or symbolically, can lead to a perception of power imbalances. When community input is not genuinely considered in decision-making processes, residents may become disillusioned and disengaged.

Concerns about the collection and use of personal data for smart city projects can create apprehension among citizens. Fears of privacy breaches and data misuse may deter individuals from actively participating in initiatives that involve data sharing (Phang et al., 2018).

Cultural and linguistic diversity within urban populations can present challenges in communication and engagement strategies. Failure to address these barriers may result in the exclusion of specific cultural or linguistic groups.

Insufficient resources and funding can impede the development and implementation of robust community engagement strategies. This barrier may disproportionately affect marginalized communities with fewer resources to participate (Salemink, 2016) and act more actively.

Resistance to change, often rooted in fear of displacement or disruptions to established routines, can hinder community engagement efforts. Overcoming resistance requires addressing concerns and emphasizing the positive impacts of smart city initiatives.

7.1.2. Case Studies and Examples

Kansas City faced challenges related to the digital divide, particularly in underserved areas of the city. The city implemented the "Connecting for Good" initiative, which provides affordable internet access and digital literacy training to bridge the technological gap.

Manchester, UK, recognized the importance of inclusive engagement forums. The city established community forums that actively involve residents in decision-making processes related to smart city projects. This approach addresses barriers such as tokenistic engagement and lack of representation (Bryson et al., 2014).

Identifying and understanding these challenges is crucial for formulating effective strategies to enhance community engagement in smart city initiatives. The following section explores opportunities for improvement and strategies to overcome these barriers.

7.2. Opportunities for Improvement

While challenges exist, numerous opportunities for improvement in community engagement strategies within smart city projects also exist. Exploring these opportunities can guide the development of practical approaches that maximize citizen participation.

7.2.1. Exploring Potential Strategies

Addressing the digital divide requires proactive initiatives to ensure universal access to technology and digital literacy. Cities can invest in digital inclusion programs, offering affordable internet access, providing devices to underserved communities, and offering training to enhance digital skills.

To overcome the lack of awareness and information, cities can implement targeted education and awareness campaigns (Ghosh et al., 2025). Informing residents about ongoing projects, their benefits, and how to participate creates a more informed and engaged community City of Amsterdam.

To combat tokenistic engagement and power imbalances, empowering local community leaders is crucial. Cities can establish mechanisms to amplify community voices, engage residents in decision-making processes, and promote collaboration between local leaders and city officials.

Addressing privacy and data security concerns requires incorporating privacy-by-design principles into smart city initiatives. Cities can implement transparent data practices, clearly communicate how data will be used, and ensure robust security measures to protect citizen information.

Recognizing and addressing cultural and linguistic barriers involves tailoring engagement strategies to meet the needs of diverse communities. Offering information in multiple languages, employing culturally sensitive communication, and involving community leaders from different cultural backgrounds can enhance inclusivity (Goodman et al., 2020).

To overcome limited resources and funding challenges, cities should prioritize equitable allocation of resources. Ensuring that marginalized communities receive adequate support for engagement initiatives promotes inclusivity and mitigates disparities in participation.

Involving residents in collaborative planning and co-creation processes can address resistance to change. Cities can organize workshops, design charrettes, and participatory planning sessions to allow citizens to contribute ideas and shape the development of smart city projects (Salemink, 2016).

7.2.2. Case Studies and Examples

Barcelona's success in co-creating urban spaces involved hosting workshops that facilitated co-creation. These workshops brought together diverse stakeholders, including residents, urban planners, and policymakers, to collaboratively design and shape the city's development (Angelidou et al., 2018).

Singapore's approach to collaborative planning involves engaging citizens in the development of urban solutions. The city actively seeks public input through consultations, workshops, and participatory forums, ensuring that residents play a role in shaping the smart city agenda.

Identifying and capitalizing on these opportunities for improvement can transform challenges into catalysts for meaningful community engagement. By adopting these strategies, cities can foster inclusive and participatory environments that empower citizens in the development of smart cities.

8. FUTURE DIRECTIONS

The prospects of community engagement in smart city programs are fluid and ever-changing. This section delves into the developing themes impacting the environment of community participation in the larger context of smart cities. It also identifies research gaps, identifying areas where further study is needed to increase knowledge and improve the efficacy of community involvement methods.

8.1. Emerging Trends in Community Engagement

Several new factors are shaping the course of community participation as technology advances and smart city efforts mature. Examining these trends reveals information on the changing nature of public engagement in influencing the urban environment.

8.1.1. Discussing Current Trends

The digital gap continues to be a serious concern, but rising trends show a commitment to more comprehensive digital inclusion measures. Cities are expanding their investments in programs that provide low-cost internet connection, distribute gadgets to marginalized areas, and give targeted digital literacy training (O'Reilly, 2011).

The combination of augmented reality (AR) and virtual reality (VR) technology is changing how individuals interact with smart city initiatives. These immersive technologies enable citizens to see and engage with proposed projects in unique ways, increasing knowledge and involvement.

Real-time data is increasingly being used for decision-making. Sensors, which are IoT devices, as well as data analytics, are being used by cities to get insights into urban processes. This real-time data allows for more responsive decisions and offers citizens current information for meaningful involvement.

Participatory budgeting, a practice that enables residents to actively influence how public funds are allocated, is gaining favor in smart city programs. Cities are looking at methods to include citizens in choices about how financial resources are distributed to projects related to smart cities to develop a feeling of responsibility and ownership (Roy et al., 2025b).

To make community interaction more participatory and pleasant, gamification approaches are being used. Cities want to enhance engagement and sustain ongoing involvement by introducing game features such as prizes, tournaments, and collaborative projects (Walczak et al., 2023).

There is a growing emphasis on inclusion in smart city design, with a focus on accessibility for all people, including those with disabilities. Cities are using universal design concepts to guarantee that smart city programs are accessible to people from all walks of life.

8.1.2. Case Studies and Examples

The MyHelsinki service in Helsinki is an example of improved digital inclusion tactics. The city offers a comprehensive web platform with up-to-date information on municipal services, events, and transportation. The platform is designed to be simple to use and accessible to individuals with varying levels of technological literacy.

Singapore's Virtual Singapore project showcases the integration of AR and VR technologies. The project creates a 3D digital twin of the city, allowing residents to explore and engage with proposed developments virtually. This immersive experience enhances public understanding and input in the planning process. These emerging trends demonstrate a shift towards more inclusive, interactive, and technologically advanced approaches to community engagement in smart city initiatives. As cities embrace these trends, the potential for fostering a deeper connection between residents and the urban environment becomes increasingly promising.

8.2. Research Gaps in Community Engagement in Smart Cities

Despite advances in community participation in smart city initiatives, significant research gaps remain that need to be addressed. It is crucial to identify these gaps to inform future research efforts and enhance our understanding of how to effectively optimize community involvement techniques.

8.2.1. Identifying Areas for Further Research

While digital inclusion programs are becoming increasingly common, comprehensive evaluations are necessary. The success of these programs in closing the digital divide, promoting digital literacy, and providing fair access to smart city efforts should be studied (Walczak et al., 2023).

The use of virtual reality (VR) and augmented reality (AR) in community involvement is still in its early stages. Further research is needed to clarify the user experience, acceptability, and effectiveness of these technologies in enhancing public awareness and engagement in smart city initiatives.

The growing reliance on real-time information for decision-making presents ethical concerns. The moral implications of collecting, evaluating, and exploiting real-time information in smart city programs should be examined, particularly with privacy, consent, and potential biases.

While collaborative budgeting is gaining popularity, there is an urgent need to examine the long-term effects on empowering communities, fostering trust in the administration, and allocating resources to meet diverse community needs. The research should look at the long-term viability and sustainability of participatory budgeting methods in smart cities.

Gamification in community participation is a growing trend, although its long-term effectiveness and impact on sustained involvement require further research. Gamification should be studied to understand its impact on citizen behavior, motivation, and the overall effectiveness of community involvement programs.

Further research should be conducted to investigate the inclusive design concepts used in smart city programs. This involves measuring the success of these concepts in meeting the needs of various groups, including individuals with disabilities, as well as their overall impact on community well-being.

8.2.2. Case Studies and Examples

As part of the Quayside task, Toronto's Sidewalk Labs could serve as a case study for evaluating the impact of digital, inclusive programs. The impact of efforts such as affordable internet access and instruction in digital literacy on closing the digital gap might be studied.

Stockholm's real-time information strategy, particularly its moral structure, provides a case study for scholars investigating the moral consequences of utilizing real-time data to make choices. Examining the impact on public trust and privacy may aid in the development of a more thorough understanding of sustainable data practices.

Closed research gaps will lead to a complete and more based-on-evidence approach to community participation in smart cities. It will help to shape tactics that are not just technologically sophisticated but also ethical, inclusive, and sensitive to the requirements of various groups.

9. CONCLUSION

This chapter presents a comprehensive review of community engagement in smart city projects as part of an inclusionary and holistic row. It shows the interaction of stakeholders involvement, administrative leadership, and a technology-mediated interaction that promotes collaboration between citizens and decision-makers. The study also shows that cultural and social factors, as well as technological barriers, affect community engagement. Best-practice review of community engagement in smart city initiatives is presented in Barcelona, Amsterdam, and Singapore.

We are identified as having significant challenges when it comes to bridging the participation gap: the digital divide, lack of awareness, and a willingness to be engaged. Improvement opportunities include digital inclusion initiatives, education campaigns, and participatory budgeting. There are also new trends in community engagement, including digital inclusion strategies, the use of AR and VR technologies, and the gathering of real-time data for decision-making.

There will be a need among policymakers, urban planners, and researchers to focus on digital inclusion, the responsible use of emerging technologies, participatory budgeting, inclusive design, and collaborative planning. To better serve the communities in which they exist, digital inclusion programs (such as those featured in Norm), participatory budgeting models, emerging technologies, and increasingly prevalent smart city initiatives should be the subject of comprehensive impact assessments by researchers and pursued in an ongoing dialogue.

REFERENCES

Ahmad, R. W., Salah, K., Jayaraman, R., Yaqoob, I., & Omar, M. (2021). Blockchain for waste management in smart cities: A survey. *IEEE Access : Practical Innovations, Open Solutions*, *9*, 131520–131541. DOI: 10.1109/ACCESS.2021.3113380

Angelidou, M., Psaltoglou, A., Komninos, N., Kakderi, C., Tsarchopoulos, P., & Panori, A. (2018). Enhancing sustainable urban development through smart city applications. *Journal of Science and Technology Policy Management*, *9*(2), 146–169. DOI: 10.1108/JSTPM-05-2017-0016

Anttiroiko, A. V., Valkama, P., & Bailey, S. J. (2014). Smart cities in the new service economy: Building platforms for smart services. *AI & Society*, *29*(3), 323–334. DOI: 10.1007/s00146-013-0464-0

Batty, M. (2013). Big data, smart cities and city planning. *Dialogues in Human Geography*, *3*(3), 274–279. DOI: 10.1177/2043820613513390 PMID: 29472982

Bon, A., van den Nieuwenhuijzen, D., Akkermans, H., de Bour, W., Edoga, C., Hegeman, M., & Werdervoort, M. (2020). *Digital Divide, Citizenship and Inclusion in Amsterdam*. Pangea.

Bryson, J. M., Crosby, B. C., & Bloomberg, L. (2014). Public administration's final exam: Integrating empirical research on public engagement. *American Review of Public Administration*, *44*(2), 225–241.

De Lange, M., & De Waal, M. (2017). Owning the city: New media and citizen engagement in urban design. In *Urban land use* (pp. 109–130). Apple Academic Press. DOI: 10.1201/9781315365794-5

Dinda, S. (2008). Social capital in the creation of human capital and economic growth: A productive consumption approach. *Journal of Socio-Economics*, *37*(5), 2020–2033. DOI: 10.1016/j.socec.2007.06.014

Dommett, K., Barclay, A., & Gibson, R. (2024). Just what is data-driven campaigning? A systematic review. *Information Communication and Society*, *27*(1), 1–22. DOI: 10.1080/1369118X.2023.2166794

Ghosh, S., Sarkar, S. K., Roy, P., Roy, B., & Podder, A. (2025). Role of Libraries in Promoting Digital Literacy and Information Fluency. In Navigating AI in Academic Libraries: Implications for Academic Research (pp. 77-108). IGI Global.

Goodman, N., Zwick, A., Spicer, Z., & Carlsen, N. (2020). Public engagement in smart city development: Lessons from communities in Canada's Smart City Challenge. *The Canadian Geographer. Geographe Canadien*, *64*(3), 416–432. DOI: 10.1111/cag.12607

Horgan, D., & Dimitrijević, B. (2019). Frameworks for citizens participation in planning: From conversational to smart tools. *Sustainable Cities and Society*, *48*, 101550. DOI: 10.1016/j.scs.2019.101550

KIM, S. J. (2022). A Study on the Development Plan of Smart City in Korea. The Journal of Economics. *Marketing and Management*, *10*(6), 17–26.

Komninos, N. (2019). *Smart Cities and Connected Intelligence: Platforms, ecosystems and network effects*. Routledge. DOI: 10.4324/9780367823399

Margerum, R. D. (2011). *Beyond consensus: Improving collaborative planning and management*. Mit Press. DOI: 10.7551/mitpress/9780262015813.001.0001

Moher, D., Liberati, A., Tetzlaff, J., & Altman, D. G.Prisma Group. (2010). Preferred reporting items for systematic reviews and meta-analyses: The PRISMA statement. *International Journal of Surgery*, *8*(5), 336–341. DOI: 10.1016/j.ijsu.2010.02.007 PMID: 20171303

Mora, L., Bolici, R., & Deakin, M. (2017). The first two decades of smart-city research: A bibliometric analysis. *Journal of Urban Technology*, *24*(1), 3–27. DOI: 10.1080/10630732.2017.1285123

O'Reilly, T. (2011). Government as a Platform. *Innovations: Technology, Governance, Globalization*, *6*(1), 13–40. DOI: 10.1162/INOV_a_00056

Perera, C., Qin, Y., Estrella, J. C., Reiff-Marganiec, S., & Vasilakos, A. V. (2017). Fog computing for sustainable smart cities: A survey. *ACM Computing Surveys*, *50*(3), 1–43. DOI: 10.1145/3057266

Phang, S. Y., Phang, S. Y., & Pacey, R. (2018). *Policy innovations for affordable housing in Singapore*. Springer International Publishing. DOI: 10.1007/978-3-319-75349-2

Putnam, R. D. (2015). Bowling alone: America's declining social capital. In *The city reader* (pp. 188–196). Routledge.

Roy, P., Ghosh, S., Podder, A., & Sarkar, S. K. (2025). Opportunities and Challenges of Artificial Intelligence (AI) in the Banking and Finance Sector. Shaping Cutting-Edge Technologies and Applications for Digital Banking and Financial Services, 120.

Roy, P., Ghosh, S., Sarkar, S. K., Podder, A., & Paul, S. (2025). AI-Driven Ambient Intelligence Systems for Mental Health Monitoring and Proactive Intervention. *Cuestiones de Fisioterapia*, *54*(3), 2743–2752.

Ruhlandt, R. W. S. (2018). The governance of smart cities: A systematic literature review. *Cities (London, England)*, *81*, 1–23. DOI: 10.1016/j.cities.2018.02.014

Salemink, K. (2016). Digital Margins: How spatially and socially marginalized communities deal with digital exclusion. Academic Press.

Schryen, G. (2015). Writing qualitative is literature reviews—Guidelines for synthesis, interpretation, and guidance of research. *Communications of the Association for Information Systems*, *37*(1), 12. DOI: 10.17705/1CAIS.03712

Simonofski, A., Asensio, E. S., De Smedt, J., & Snoeck, M. (2017, July). Citizen participation in smart cities: Evaluation framework proposal. In 2017 IEEE 19th conference on business informatics (CBI) (Vol. 1, pp. 227-236). IEEE.

Tene, O., & Polonetsky, J. (2013). Big data for all: Privacy and user control in the age of analytics. *Northwestern Journal of Technology and Intellectual Property*, *11*(5), 239–273.

Townsend, A. M. (2013). *Smart cities: Big data, civic hackers, and the quest for a new utopia*. WW Norton & Company.

Walczak, R., Koszewski, K., Olszewski, R., Ejsmont, K., & Kálmán, A. (2023). Acceptance of IoT edge-computing-based sensors in smart cities for universal design purposes. *Energies*, *16*(3), 1024. DOI: 10.3390/en16031024

Chapter 3

Assessing Resident's Response Towards Smart Community Initiatives in Kota Belud

Normalini Md Kassim
https://orcid.org/0009-0007-5971-3186
Universiti Sains Malaysia, Malaysia

Jasmine Yeap Ai Leen
Universiti Sains Malaysia, Malaysia

Nor Hazlina Hashim
https://orcid.org/0000-0003-4265-0557
University of Malaya, Malaysia

Saravanan Nathan Lurudusamy
Telekom Malaysia Berhad, Malaysia

T. Ramayah
https://orcid.org/0000-0002-7580-7058
Universiti Sains Malaysia, Malaysia

Jin Kai
https://orcid.org/0009-0007-5971-3186
Sichuan Technology and Business University, China

ABSTRACT

This chapter assesses the Kota Belud community on their response towards Smart Community initiatives implemented by the Malaysian government through MCMC with the aim of empowering communities at district levels through ICT adoption and usage. A quantitative research method was

DOI: 10.4018/979-8-3693-9030-6.ch003

employed where self-administrated questionnaires consisting of different sections with both open and close-ended questions were developed to gather information from the residents in Kota Belud. A total of 125 forms were distributed in different locations within the Kota Belud smart community site. A descriptive analysis of the residents' response towards the Smart Community initiatives implemented in Kota Belud was carried out, and subsequently, recommendations were suggested at the end of the chapter.

INTRODUCTION

The growth of urbanization has been dramatic in the past decade. Indeed, according to Lierow (2014), it is expected that More than six billion people, or seventy percent of the global population, are projected to consider urban areas homes by 2050. Therefore, cities need to become smart if they are to continue serving as the platforms that promote financial, social, and environmental well-being. This rate has increased the pressure for adjusting the actual infrastructures and investing in new ones to support the flow of goods and people, as well as to minimize the associated impact related to environmental degradation, quality of life, and others (Caragliu et al., 2009). Additionally, Zhang (2023) emphasized that urbanization not only expands consumption scales but also drives structural upgrades in service-oriented economies, aligning with the need for smart community frameworks. Therefore, it is highly necessary to know the criteria and prerequisites for community involvement and participation in a Smart Community in the Malaysian context. Hence, recommendations were made for criteria for Smart Community engagement, participation and processes based on the evaluation and impact study conducted in this research.

The concept can be emulated easily across communities within Malaysia in ensuring long term sustainability, meeting community needs by moving at an adaptable speed by the community, where these initiates are replicable, scalable and reachable. The application of technology within communities is considered a key element to move forward into the future. Kota Belud, as one of the sites selected for the deployment of smart community, has its own problems which ICT can help to solve. Technology has significantly reduced the risk where people are alerted when the water level is increasing and precautions and evacuation could be taken much earlier ahead. For Kota Belud, where floods occurred frequently after the earthquakes that happened in 2015, the landscapes changed, and the river bed is getting shallow by the dropping stones from the hillsides. IoTs are fixed along the river banks and integrated with Security and Integrated Flood Operation Network (S.A.I.F.O.N.) to monitor the water levels.

While many are stressing the development of a smart city, it is believed that the presence of a smart community needs to be first established. One of the ultimate objectives is aiming to the next level in establishing a smart community which could sustain itself with the ICT infrastructure provided. The smart community's initiatives are "tailor-made" to suit the needs of different communities, and so to be the reason of this research is important to evaluate the impacts and adoption level of the local community towards the initiatives provided. Hence, improvements could take place to enhance the infrastructure and its functionality.

Under the purview of the Malaysian Communications and Multimedia Commission (MCMC), the Smart Community project was developed with the primary aim of empowering communities at district levels through ICT adoption and usage. Building a digitally smart and savvy community in smaller districts is a challenge as much as a necessity for smaller districts. Migration of the young from smaller districts to the city has been on the rise in recent years simply because better opportunities can be found in the cities. In addition to being focal areas of economies, cities are vibrant and have far better systems to facilitate one's lifestyle. The catalyst behind the development of such urban areas is ICT. In this manner, ICT enables the growth of smart communities which can eventually pave the way towards smart cities. With this realization, MCMC, via smart community initiatives, aspires to improve the lives of the community in the smaller, rural districts.

Kota Belud, located in Sabah, is one of the areas within Malaysia which was selected to deploy the Smart Community initiatives. Various initiatives have been carried out under the Smart Community project in Kota Belud ranging from the enhancement of infrastructure, provision of ICT-related and entrepreneurship training, development of digital applications as well as other initiatives. Table 1 shows the description of MCMC Smart Community Initiatives in Kota Belud.

Table 1. Description of MCMC smart community initiatives in Kota Belud

Key term	Description
Pusat Internet	Pusat Internet (PI) is an initiative which will provide collective broadband access in rural and sub-urban areas. The center is aimed as a local transformation platform for the community to learn ICT.
Data Services	Data services is Internet content delivered to most of the time mobile devices such as smartphones and tablets over a wireless cellular connection. Cellular providers have offered mobile data through a number of different technologies, including GSM (in 1G, 2G, 3G UMTS and 4G LTE Advanced), CDMA and TDMA.
Dashboard	Aiming to facilitate communication among the community, this application complements the facilities that allow the community to get local information at their fingertips.
VHF (Very High Frequency)	Very high frequency (VHF) is the International Telecommunication Union (ITU) designation for the range of radio frequency electromagnetic waves (radio waves) from 30 to 300 megahertz (MHz), with corresponding wavelengths of ten to one meter. The implementation of a VHF Radio Communication Network is intended to provide an alternative communication medium during the disaster.
ICT Training	Training is provided to individuals and communities to improve their digital literacy and become smart digital citizens.
Entrepreneurship	Training aims to enhance the capacity and willingness of business people to develop, organize, and manage their business ventures.
MyCrib Booking	A Smart Tourism Web Portal & App that empowers homestay/guesthouse entrepreneurs / attractive package / rental car operators to manage business and reservation in a complete system with a payment gateway and monthly sales monitoring.
S.A.I.F.O.N.	S.A.I.F.O.N. is a monitoring system that is equipped with a centralized monitoring center. There were three sensors installed at major rivers while twelve closed-circuit televisions (CCTVs) were installed at strategic location in Kota Belud town to help local agencies, especially the District Office and Angkatan Pertahanan Awam (APM), to monitor, plan and take action effectively in ensuring the safety of the community during emergency. The system is being monitored by a centralize monitoring center developed at Kota Belud APM's office.
E-Magazine	This tool is aimed at generating creativity and innovation among teachers and students in using ICT.

(Authors, 2025)

In accordance with MCMC's aspiration of improving and empowering lives in rural districts, much remains to be known about the state of the smart community project. The impact of the initiatives needs to be determined from time to time to determine the project's effectiveness on the residents of Kota Belud. Thus, this study was carried out with the goal of assessing the residents' response towards the Smart Community initiatives implemented in Kota Belud.

LITERATURE REVIEW

Information and Communications Technology (ICT)

The phrase "information and communication technologies" has been used by academic researchers since the 1980s. Information and communications technology (ICT) is an extensional term for information technology (IT) that stresses the role of unified communications and the integration of telecommunications (telephone lines and wireless signals) and computers, as well as necessary enterprise software, middleware, storage and audiovisual, that enable users to access, store, transmit, understand and manipulate information (Murray, 2011). It includes computing technologies like servers, laptop computers, and software applications, as well as the wired and wireless communication technologies that support telephones, the Internet, the Internet of Things (IoT), and the metaverse. The goal of ICT is to improve access to information and make human-to-human, human-to-machine, and machine-to-machine (M2M) communication easier and more efficient (Margaret, 2024).

The convergence of computer networks, telephone networks, and audiovisual networks via a single cable or connection system is often referred to as ICT. There are strong financial incentives to combine the computer and phone networks into a single, unified system for administration, distribution, and cabling. Any communication equipment, including radios, televisions, mobile phones, computers, network hardware, satellite systems, and so forth, as well as the myriad services and appliances that go along with them, such as video conferencing and distance learning, are all included under the broad category of information and communication technology, or ICT. Analog technology, including paper communication, and any modality that conveys communication are also included in ICT (Ozdamli, 2015).

The concept of ICT can be traced back to the 19th century with the development of the telegraph and the telephone. These two inventions revolutionized the way people worked and interacted socially by making it possible for one person to communicate with another person in a different location in real or near-real time (Margaret, 2024). ICT is a large topic with constantly changing notions. It includes any products that may electronically store, retrieve, alter, process, transmit, or receive data in a digital format (e.g., personal computers, including smartphones, email, digital television, or robots). One of the various approaches for outlining and overseeing the competencies required of ICT workers in the twenty-first century is the Skills Framework for the Information Age. ICT has changed the dynamics of the workforce and the global economy. For instance, by facilitating smooth cross-border transactions and interactions, e-commerce has supported globalization by opening up new options for both consumers and enterprises. By utilizing IT and communication technologies to enhance public services, transportation, and municipal infrastructure, smart cities are enhancing urban living. In summary, ICT has had a significant impact on management, communities, and business. Technology has become an essential component of both contemporary businesses and communities, from improving decision-making and simplifying operations to opening up new company models and encouraging international cooperation (Margaret, 2024).

Internet of Things

Kevin Ashton is sometimes called the "Inventor of IoT" since the first used the term in 1999 to describe a system where the Internet is connected to the physical world via ubiquitous sensors. In 1999, Kevin introduced the concept of the Internet of Things (IoT) as a means of communication via radio-frequency identification (RFID) tags. These two concepts are currently driving the Internet of Things, allowing any living or dead thing to connect and communicate with one another (Chin et al., 2019). IoT has evolved over the past 20 years and is now used in a variety of industries.

Because no accepted definition of IoT has yet been created, it is, therefore, impossible to define this concept accurately (Sidek & Ali, 2019).

Defining the IoT is hard for many reasons. One reason is that the IoT has a large number of applications, from monitoring supply chains to stopping trains and lighting homes, which involves all economic and social aspects of daily life and changes the way humans interact with the world around them. Another reason is that the IoT involves software and hardware, a variety of protocols and standards, devices and networks, storage, analytics, automation, and many other topics such as Artificial Intelligence (AI), Big Data, Machine Learning, and Augmented Reality (AR), which makes it even harder to understand the IoT itself. Furthermore, concepts generally included in the IoT vision strongly relate to visions under other names such as Web of Things, Web of Goods, Internet of Everything, and Cloud of Things, while other concepts, including Cyber-Physical Systems (CPS), Industry 4.0, Machine to Machine Communications (M2M), and System of Systems (SoS) relates to IoT but should be considered as part of or complementary to the IoT (Lapenna, 2022).

IEEE defines the Internet of Things in a broad sense, which is an IoT system starting from the level where a single "thing" is identified using a unique global identifier and can be accessed from anywhere, anytime (IEEE, 2015). According to Abdur et al. (2017), the Internet of Things facilitates communication and data sharing between a vast number of computers, people, and utilities. The following two definitions of IoT have been heavily used and linked to this research in several research publications. Things of the Internet of Things (IoT) were previously viewed as dynamic participants in the information, industry, and social systems in which they may interact and link, according to a cluster of European research initiatives. When these gadgets respond to and shape activities in the physical world on their own, they communicate data with the environment through operational procedures that can function with or without human intervention (Gubbi et al., 2013). The ITU Telecommunication Standardization Sector (ITU-T) has defined IoT as "a global infrastructure for the information society, enabling advanced services by interconnecting (physical and virtual) things based on existing and evolving interoperable information and communication technologies" (ITU, 2015).

The Internet of Things can be further explained using the two definitions mentioned above. Imagine an environment in which billions of creatures can perceive, read, interact, and exchange pertinent data via Internet protocol (IP) networks. Information used in decision-making, management, processing, and frequent intervention are all included in these integrated frameworks (Gupta & Gupta, 2016). All of these are made feasible by the development of the Internet of Things (IoT), which is a conglomeration of several hardware and software advances rather than a single technology. It seeks to link objects at any time, anywhere, and with anybody. This can be regarded as an entity in the Internet of Things; it's either a dumb, non-communicating item or a communication device. As a result, everything may engage in online communication, whether it is a bottle of water, a tree leaf (Aazam et al., 2015) or an intelligent gadget. The Internet of Things' data-driven approach to everyday tasks can streamline our lives and make cities or industries run more effectively.

AI in Smart City

Smart cities could become even smarter with the increased application of AI, both in infrastructure development and analysis of data. Enhancing safety, sustainability, quality of life and resident experience are key benefits of urban areas becoming more AI-powered (Zoe, 2024). When AI skills are applied to new or current information or streams, smart cities can benefit from the use of AI. IoT apps gather data, but AI analytics can identify trends, forecast outcomes, merge data streams (data fusion), and improve the quality of the data. The use cases that arise from analyzing the AI + IoT (AIoT) equation differ depending on the application and the city. In addition to historical research and prescriptive insight into metrics like demand forecasts and planned resource usage, several IoT application vendors provide AI analytics in their insights for clients. AI governance, data quality and employee data literacy are chief considerations to make before procuring and deploying AI applications and a full-scale AI strategy within a city (Zoe, 2024). Cities globally have begun to establish smart city offices and directorates with dedicated staff resources and budgets to support projects and initiatives. Countries have established smart city challenges to spur innovation and allocated funding to support project establishment and scale. Smart cities are at a crossroads. Cities of all sizes and locations may undergo a digital revolution if IoT data collecting is combined with AI analytics and insights. However, these technologies are not risk-free, even if they have the potential to address some of the most urgent sustainability and safety concerns facing the public sector. When governments and municipalities implement smart city programs and collaborate with vendors in the field, data openness, community involvement, and digital fairness should be given top priority (S&P Global, 2024).

Sustainable Development

Sustainable development is an approach to growth and human development that attempts to fulfill current demands without compromising future generations' ability to meet their own needs (United Nations, 1987). The goal is to create a civilization in which living circumstances and resources fulfill human needs without jeopardizing ecological integrity (Mensah, 2019). The Brundtland Report, published in 1987, helped to popularize the notion of sustainable development. Sustainable development seeks to strike a balance between economic, environmental, and social concerns.

The normative concepts of sustainability and sustainable development are related. The normative concepts of sustainability and sustainable development are related (Purvis et al., 2019). The idea of sustainable development has gained international attention as a result of the Rio Process, which started with the 1992 Earth Summit in Rio de Janeiro. In 2015, the 2030 Sustainable Development Goals were accepted by the United Nations General Assembly (UNGA). Global issues, including poverty, climate change, biodiversity loss, and peace are addressed by these development goals.

Smart City vs Smart Community

With global rapid change impacting cities and communities across the world, there is a need for leaders to increase their agility and responsiveness to meet and exceed the growing needs of communities. Leaders need to be equipped with the right tools to make smart decisions, ensuring the best outcomes for society, the economy and the environment. A smart community is one that uses information technology, innovation and data to be more efficient, solve problems, and create new opportunities for people, businesses, and organizations (ASCS24, 2024). A smart community enables improved service delivery, economic development, and liveability with a reduced environmental footprint. The "Smart Community" will provide comprehensive solutions encompassing energy, water, and medical systems in order to realize a synergetic balance between environmental considerations and comfortable living. ITU-T Focus Group on Smart Sustainable Cities established a concrete definition for smart sustainable cities, which can be used worldwide. They reviewed 116 definitions of smart sustainable cities from different sources such as academic, government, and corporate. In their report, smart community and smart city are considered as the same term. Similarly, Albino et al. (2015) did not differentiate the terms smart city and smart community, and they treat these two terms with the same meaning.

They clarified the meaning of the word "smart" in the context of cities through an approach based on an in-depth literature review of relevant studies as well as official documents of international institutions. However, a smart city initiative needs to create a community where all citizens can engage more easily and effectively (Paskaleva, 2009). Ishida and Isbister (2000) debated some similar terms such as digital community, smart community, digital city, information city and e-city. Tanabe, van den Besselaar, and Ishida (2003) considered all of those alternative terms to refer to a connected community that combines broadband communications infrastructure. The geographical dimension (space) of smart communities is varied; it can be extended from a city district up to a multimillion metropolis (Besselaar & Koizumi, 2005). Harrison et al. (2010) agreed that Instrumented, Interconnected and Intelligent were the three fundamental factors for a smarter city.

A smart city is an urban area that uses digital technology to collect data and operate / provide services (Goldsmith, 2021). Smart cities integrate information and communication technology (ICT) and devices connected to the Internet of Things (IoT) network to optimize city services and connect to citizens. While as referring to Nam and Pardo (2011), in their study that attempts to conceptualize a smart city with multi-dimensions, stated that there are various definitions of smart city, and the majority of them focus on hardware development by providing infrastructures and services such as education, health care, transportation and etc. which congruent with other existing literature. Eger (2005) pointed out that the key factor in a smart community is all about collaboration and connectivity, where the internet, knowledge creation and innovation and the core elements of the community. Apparently, these presented the distinctiveness between smart city and smart community through definitions, and a gap exists between these concepts that require further clarifications, which is agreed by researchers as well (Stratigea, 2012). And it is notable to take note as how it is defined will determine the development path. Malaysia has developed policies and strategies for Smart Cities recognized as the Malaysia Smart City Framework. Malaysia has been actively advancing the creation of Smart Cities in recent years. Some of the cities are meticulously designed as integrated and sustainable smart, focusing on eco-friendly technology and communal living. It incorporates an array of Smart City features and technologies, such as a fiber-optic network, an intelligent traffic management system, and a centralized security system (Salma et al., 2024)

Smart City Threats and Issues

Cities are the most complex objects created by humans. Modern cities face the challenge of combining competitiveness and sustainable urban development simultaneously. The notion of a "smart city" came into our lives in 2006. When talking about smart cities, we immediately witnessed the concerns of citizens that smart cities effectively create an environment of total surveillance and control and push towards unwelcome intrusion into personal life. Gurstein (2014) argued that the current trend of developing more and more smart cities has deviated from its original objectives that attempt to improve the quality of life. As for now, many smart city development plans are emphasizing installing edge-cutting technology rather than shifting their attention to educating innovative citizens and empowering them in community development projects. Eger (2005) agreed that it should not just be about technology and ICTs, it should be concerning jobs, dollars and quality of life. And emphasizes not just deploying technology as it is but understanding how the local citizens perceive the infrastructure and facilities in their daily lives and works, which acts as one of the objectives of this study in measuring the impacts of ICT implementation initiatives. Besides, Gurstein (2014) criticized on current imbalance situation where politicians and major technology corporations utilize "smart city" as a PR tool and mainly focus on urban and desirable areas and tend to ignore rural and less attractive suburbs, particularly in less developed countries, where the living standard of the citizen were barely reach the basic requirement, and government initiative to develop towards "smart cities" is equal to transferring the resources from the poor to the rich as many resources is putting on installing high technology and expensive devices, whereas there are still people who has limited access to basic living facilities such as health care, environmental management and security.

Incontestably, providing critical and basic infrastructure is essential. While it could be said that a smart city development plan should separate into several stages, the first priority is the provision of basic facilities, including healthcare, education, transportation and security, which is particularly important for developing countries in order to develop a smart city it should first fulfil the requirement to be a city and thereafter high technology infrastructure such as IoT, broadband and other ICT initiative could only take place on top of the fundamental and act as catalyst to drive smarter development (Nam & Pardo, 2011). Hence, there are opinions stating that the development direction should focus on producing a smart community rather than a smart city, and the ultimate goals of a smart community should not just rely on high technologies and hardware while nurturing the smarter citizens that could ensure these infrastructure and facilities able to optimize their daily life and work and at the same time the community itself able to sustain by its own as they have acquired the knowledge and are well prepared to be part of the smart community (Eger, 2005).

Characteristics of Smart Community

Smart Citizen

Evidently, it shows the need to shift to developing a smart community rather than a smart city where social inclusion, enabling citizens, and supporting community should be included in the city development agenda (Gurstein, 2014). Wongbumru and Dewancker (2014)'s study focuses on how next-generation technology could be utilized and integrated into the community, particularly through improving citizen innovation and participation in reaching the goal of improving quality of life, demonstrating example from Japan that not only focuses on smart energy management but going further to smart community by involving all the stakeholders and aims towards behavioral change through lifestyle innovation. Moreover, the author pointed out the challenges where there is a situation where although infrastructure on smart energy system is provided, citizen shows a lack of participation and concluded that bringing up "smart citizen" should be put as a priority before succeeding a smart community (Wongbumru & Dewancker, 2014).

A smarter city should be treated as an organic system - as a network, as a linked system, and smart citizen is part of it (Nam & Pardo, 2011). In order to enable this part of the "smart citizen" to be fully integrated into the entire system, first, the citizens should be educated in a way to "infuse" themselves in the smart system. Without the knowledge, it could not maintain the sustainable cycle of the system, and it will become a huge hinder to long-term sustainable development. If only a smart and innovative citizen acts as a motivator for the entire system to ensure a smooth network and linkage among the smart initiatives, they themselves could only be the beneficiaries of the smart system. Various authors have started to explore the implied roles of citizens in relation to smart city visions and practices. Foth (2017) has described in the debate on smart cities that the relationships between city governments and citizens have been reconfigured a number of times. Whereas their relationship was originally conceived of one between administrator and residents (Cities 1.0), this has been reconceived as the relation between 'service provider' and 'consumer' (Cities 2.0), 'facilitator' and 'participants'(Cities 3.0) and now is increasingly understood as one between 'collaborator' and 'co-creator' (Cities 4.0) (Foth, 2017; de Waal et al., 2017)

Training

Stratigea (2012)'s work focuses on relating the smart cities concept to community development, adapting the concepts from the Intelligent Community Forum (ICF) that demonstrated the critical success factors for cities "going smart" and presented in a pyramid structure. As Broadband infrastructure acts as the first fundamental base, a knowledge-based workforce is the second level from the bottom, proving that apart from infrastructure and facilities, it is important to educate a skilled workforce to support further development. It is agreed by Eger (2005) as well that internet and broadband access is just the first step and an integrated intelligent community is a catalyst to economic growth (Hughes & Spray, 2002). Undoubtedly, the installation of internet and broadband could offer citizens the accessibility to be linked and connected with each other as well as with the government and businesses, stimulating local growth in terms of both economy and society (Nam & Pardo, 2011). Moreover, introducing innovative energy systems, information and communication technology could encourage and support private companies, governments and SMEs in providing various services to the community (Wongbumru & Dewancker, 2014).

Smart Governance

Apart from installing ICTs in the city, the citizens should introduce a new decision-making mechanism which incorporates the community into the city planning (Eger, 2005). Hollands (2008) emphasize that the way citizen interacts and become a member of society is the goal of succeeding in a smart community, and information technology plays a role not just as a physical infrastructure that drives towards smart cities but also offers opportunities to empower and educate "smart citizen". Frost and Sullivan (2014), a consulting and research firm, identifies eight key aspects that define a smart city and smart citizen to be part of it, which acts as the main role in building a smart community (Singh, 2014).

Besides, the argument exists, according to (Gurstein, 2014), that the current situation was a centralized and top-down approach, and the voices and opinions of the citizens were put as the lowest priority when it comes to city development. While in the process of development towards a smarter community, all stakeholders from every segment of society should be included, and each party should assume the responsibility and attention as none of the segments should be neglected. Public-private partnerships to involve locals and realize a connected society are an example (Hughes & Spray, 2002). A smart community that should focus on cooperation and emphasize shared governance and participation of the citizens is essential to include the voice and opinions of the community in local development. The role of government and policy in providing governance to the city is strong support for smart city initiatives (Nam & Pardo, 2011). Besides, their study of conceptualizing a smart city with dimensions pointed to the element of institutional factors, which includes integrated and transparent governance, strategic and promotional activities, networking and partnership. Other than that, the launch of e-government in many smart cities as one of the initiatives encourages the participation of citizens in more community development projects. In such a way, the government should be more transparent and accountable for sharing information with a citizen so they can voice their opinion and be part of the decision-making process which affects their daily lives. Smart governance is set to be the cornerstone of a smart city. Therefore, partnership and collaboration could prove as an effective approach to connecting the public, private and individuals towards structuring an effective bottom-up mechanism, which is the key step in transforming citizens towards a smarter way.

Implementation of Smart Cities in the World

China

Smart city development is favorable by governments and developers as to its benefits that have been proven with the help of ICT it could improve the quality of life for the people. For instance, many smart city projects have been carried out around the world while different developing models have been implemented, and various initiatives have been introduced to achieve respective targets. In China, smart community planning took place in Yishanwan, Jiangxia District, Wuhan. The community was developed alongside a comprehensive framework to achieve the targets of construction of infrastructure, establishing a sharing platform, developing and researching an application system and developing a service portal (Anrong et al., 2016). In the development plan, the synchronous development of informatization, new industrialization, agricultural modernization and new urbanization act as the core of developing the smart community. The authority especially emphasizes agricultural modernization as it plays an important role in rural areas and acts as fundamental for the suburban area to develop through urbanization. (Strong et al., 2016) agreed that it is insufficient to improve only infrastructure but also stress the innovation ability of society by integrating the concept of sustainability into city development (Chourabi et al., 2012).

United States

As part of its smart city pilot program in 2020, New York City has deployed and tested hundreds of smart sensors and technology across its several districts. In order to improve the efficiency of services like trash management and collection, the software gathers data. In addition, smart hubs, including WiFi, contactless technologies, and online charging stations, have replaced phone booths in New York. In the Big Apple, car-sharing programs are also quite popular and contribute to lower overall emissions and traffic congestion. New York City hosts an annual competition for applications that make the best use of the city's open data sets, offering a substantial cash prize in an effort to foster more local viewpoints and innovation.

The Netherlands

In 2009, Amsterdam's smart city initiative encompassed over 170 distinct activities around the city. Whether it's using renewable energy for electric garbage trucks, putting in solar-powered bus stops, billboards, and lights, or building floating villages to alleviate overcrowding and offer an alternative to land reclamation, Amsterdam's ability to remain innovative is what really stood out. Smart meters, ultra-low energy LED lights, automatically dimming light switches, and energy-efficient roofing insulation have already been installed in hundreds of operational homes and businesses around the city.

Finland

Helsinki has established a goal to become carbon neutral by 2035, and they are showing signs of progress toward that objective. Even in 2017, the city was able to reduce emissions by 27% compared to 1990. With initiatives like converting the whole fleet of municipal buses to electric vehicles and growing its Metro and electric vehicle charging networks, Helsinki is also aiming to reduce transportation emissions by 69% in three decades by 2035. Since more than half of Helsinki's emissions come from heating, the city is concentrating on adding more renewable energy to its buildings and executing energy-efficient renovations that could cut building emissions by 80%.

Singapore

Singapore was ranked 7th in the world's smartest cities, according to the 2019 Cities in Motion Index (CIMI), issued by the IESE Business School. The index ranks across nine dimensions, including human capital, social cohesion, the economy, governance, the environment, mobility and transportation, urban planning, international outreach, and technology (Esri Singapore, 2022). A digital twin for planning in Singapore is Urban challenge, innovation process, solution and continuity. Singapore has long faced challenges whilst planning for the built environment. Innovations in housing, mobility, and land use have been key priorities of the government. In 2013, 3D modelling was an emerging technology, and the state recognized its potential in offering planners a more comprehensive and accurate medium to design and pilot urban solutions. With access to live real-time monitoring data from IoT sensors, decision-making and urban interventions are better informed by accurate spatial data and real-life human behaviour. Some of the applications of virtual Singapore include flood risk analysis, opportunities for solar panels and green roofs, and examining the impact of wind load on vegetation (UNDP, 2022)

Malaysia

Medini Smart City in Iskandar Puteri, Malaysia, was chosen to be the pilot for smart city projects, which focuses on three areas, economy, environment and social and promotes six dimensions: smart economy, smart governance, smart environment, smart mobility, smart people and smart living (Ghazali et al., 2016). This is a project collaborating with the university and regional development agency. The objective of this project was to focus on infrastructure provision and change of quality of life and environment as long-term targets by developing smart living through engaging local citizens for sustainable development. However, Gil and Navarro (2013) argued that in terms of governance and policy context, which were some of the factors in analyzing smart city initiatives, the participation of locals seems lacking from the technology partnership. While there was a noticeable effort from the aspect of education where there are few internationally well-known universities, such as the University of Newcastle, plan to open up campus in Medini.

METHOD

Sampling and Data Collection

A quantitative research design has been employed whereby the local residents in the Kota Belud smart community project sites are the main targeted respondents for this study. A purposive sampling method was used to distribute survey forms. Respondents were selected based on their living area, which must be located within the Smart Community project site where MCMC's initiatives are implemented.

At Kota Belud, 150 survey forms have been distributed within the Kota Belud district including Usukan, Tempasuk and Kadamaian. As most of the population was focused on Usukan where this area covered the district capital Kg. Pekan Kota Belud, Kg. Bobot, Kg. Pirasan, and Kg. Ambong, 90 survey forms were distributed in these places. While 45 survey forms have been distributed at Tempasuk, which covered Kg. Tempasuk, Kg. Taun Gusi, Kg. Jawi-Jawi, Kg. Gundins, Kg. Tamai and Kg. Rampayan. Equally, 45 survey forms were distributed at Kadamaian, including Kg. Malangkap, Kg. Taginambur and Kg. Tamu Darat.

At survey sites, one or more enumerators were appointed to assist in distributing survey forms to the target respondents. They have been briefed and trained by the researchers regarding the content of the survey forms as well as guidance to be given to the respondents. Out of the 150 survey forms distributed, only 125 questionnaires were completed and used for data analysis. Respondents were asked about their demographic, technological profiles and their awareness of MCMC's initiatives.

DATA ANALYSIS

Respondent Profile

There is a rather equal representation of both males (56.1%) and females (43.9%) among the respondents, with the males slightly outnumbering the females (See Table 1). Most of the respondents were either from the 20-29-year-old group (30.4%) or the 30-39-year-old group (22.4%), given that those two age ranges had the majority number of persons. A large number of respondents were Bumiputeras/natives of Sabah (92.6%), followed by the Malays (3.3%), the Chinese (3.3%) and Indians (0.8%).

The majority of the respondents had a modest educational background, having either SPM or an equivalent level of educational qualification (37.6%) or a Certificate or Diploma (32%). There was still a band of respondents who only had a primary school education, became a secondary school dropout or even had no formal education at all (4.8%). In terms of employment, most of the respondents were self-employed (20.3%). For most of them, their monthly income ranged between RM 1001 to RM 3000 (33.6%).

Respondents who are married (61.6%) far outnumber the single (37.6%) and widowed (0.8%). For those who are married, having two children seemed to be the norm (14.9%). A high percentage of the respondents surveyed did not have any children (38%), mainly due to the fact that they are still single/unmarried.

Table 2. Respondents' demographic profile – Kota Belud

Variable	Category	Frequency	Percentage*
Gender	Male	69	56.1
	Female	54	43.9
Age	<20	16	12.8
	20-29	38	30.4
	30-39	28	22.4
	40-49	24	19.2
	>50	19	15.2
Race	Malay	4	3.3
	Chinese	4	3.3
	Indian	1	0.8
	Bumiputra	112	92.6
Education	SPM Or Equivalent	47	37.6
	STPM Or Equivalent	16	12.8
	Certificate/Diploma	40	32.0
	Bachelor's Degree	12	9.6
	Master's or PhD Degree	4	3.2
	Others	6	4.8
Occupation	Professional/Management	15	12.2
	Teacher	12	9.8
	Housewife/Husband	10	8.1
	Technical Staff	16	13.0

continued on following page

Table 2. Continued

Variable	Category	Frequency	Percentage*
	Self-Employed	25	20.3
	Admin/Clerical Staff	12	9.8
	Retired/Pensioner	8	6.5
	Student	17	13.8
	Others	8	6.5
Income	Not Working	30	24.0
	RM1000 or below	21	16.8
	RM1001-RM3000	42	33.6
	RM3001-RM5000	21	16.8
	RM5001-RM7000	8	6.4
	RM7001 and above	3	2.4
Marital Status	Single	47	37.6
	Married	77	61.6
	Widowed	1	0.8
Number of	0	46	38.0
Children	1	8	6.6
	2	18	14.9
	3	12	9.9
	4	9	7.4
	5	12	9.9
	6	6	5.0
	7	6	5.0
	8	3	2.5
	10	1	0.8

*Note: n=125; *valid percentages are used which were calculated by excluding missing cases.

(Authors, 2025)

Almost all the respondents surveyed owned a smartphone (97.6%) (See Table 2). The brands of smartphones owned were predominantly Samsung (41.3%). Besides smartphones, the majority of the respondents also own a laptop (47.2%) and a tablet (21.6%). The average number of years of internet usage experience among the respondents was 9 years (std. dev.=5.79). The responses were varied with some being very new to the internet (1 to 5 years) to those who are experienced users (> 15 years).

95.2% of the respondents subscribed to a mobile data plan, with Digi (48.3%) and Celcom (30.5%) being the major service providers preferred by respondents. 44.1% of the mobile data plan subscribers were happy and rated the mobile data service quality as good. Those who were not satisfied with the quality of mobile data service (rated bad and terrible = 11.8%) mentioned reasons such as 'limited coverage', 'signal is not strong enough' and 'not being able to see much value in the data plan packages'.

For the home broadband plan, a large percentage of the respondents (64.2%) did not subscribe to it. Among those who subscribed to the home broadband plan, TM was the preferred choice (88.6%). The majority were happy with the quality of the home broadband service, with 47.7% of respondents rating the service as good. For the few respondents who were not satisfied with the broadband service (rated bad = 11.4%), they cited reasons such as the 'speed not living up to expectations', the 'exorbitant price' and 'slow connection'.

Table 3. Respondents' technological profile – Kota Belud

Variable	Category	Frequency	Percentage
Own A Smartphone	Yes	122	97.6
	No	3	2.4
Smartphone Brand	Samsung	50	41.3
	Apple	21	17.4
	Huawei	13	10.7
	Xiaomi	3	2.5
	Others	34	28.1
Other Device Ownership	Laptop	59	47.2
(upon 100)	Desktop	17	13.6

continued on following page

Table 3. Continued

Variable	Category	Frequency	Percentage
	Tablet	27	21.6
	Others	4	3.2
	None	33	26.4
Subscribe mobile data plan	Yes	118	95.2
	No	6	4.8
Mobile data plan brand	Digi	57	48.3
	Celcom	36	30.5
	Maxis	11	9.3
	UMobile	8	6.8
	Others	6	5.1
Mobile data service quality	Excellent	25	21.2
	Good	52	44.1
	Mediocre	27	22.9
	Bad	11	9.3
	Terrible	3	2.5
Subscribe broadband plan	Yes	44	35.2
	No	79	64.2
Broadband plan brand	TM	39	88.6
	Maxis	3	6.8
	Others	2	4.5
Broadband service quality	Excellent	9	20.5
	Good	21	47.7
	Mediocre	9	20.5
	Bad	5	11.4

continued on following page

Table 3. Continued

Variable	Category	Frequency	Percentage
Years of using the Internet	Mean = 9.00		
	Std. deviation = 5.79		

(Authors, 2025)

Descriptives for MCMC's Initiatives in Kota Belud

As many as 74.4% of respondents surveyed were aware of Kota Belud being a Smart Community project area. The various initiatives carried out by MCMC under the Smart Community project were grouped under three broad overarching themes, namely Infrastructure, Content Training and Digital Services (See Table 3).

Awareness of two initiatives, namely Pusat Internet (PI) and telecommunication (telco) data services such as Maxis/DiGi/Celcom/UMobile, was the highest at 94.4% and 90.9%, respectively, followed by ICT training and Entrepreneurship training workshops at 75.8% and 68.9% respectively. Usage of the initiatives was the highest for telco data services (85.1%), followed by PI (82.9%), ICT training workshops (45.4%), S.A.I.F.O.N, a flood monitoring and alerting system (37.3%) and the entrepreneurship training workshops (31.6%).

Table 4. Respondents' awareness and usage of the smart community initiatives – Kota Belud

Initiatives	Aware (%)	Not aware (%)	Use (%)	Don't use (%)
Infrastructure				
1. Pusat Internet	**117(94.4)**	7(5.6)	**102(82.9)**	21(17.1)
2. Data Services	**110(90.9)**	11(9.1)	**103(85.1)**	18(14.9)
3. Dashboard	**28(23.9)**	89(76.1)	**9(8.3)**	100(91.7)
4. VHF	**10(8.8)**	104(91.2)	**1(0.9)**	111(99.1)

continued on following page

Table 4. Continued

Initiatives	Aware (%)	Not aware (%)	Use (%)	Don't use (%)
Content Training				
1. ICT Training	**94(75.8)**	30(24.2)	**54(45.4)**	65(54.6)
2. Entrepreneurship	**84(68.9)**	38(31.1)	**37(31.6)**	80(68.4)
Digital Services				
1. MyCrib Booking	**56(45.9)**	66(54.1)	**29(24.6)**	89(75.4)
2. S.A.I.F.O.N	**73(59.3)**	50(40.7)	**44(37.3)**	74(62.7)
3. E-Magazine	**34(28.3)**	86(71.7)	**11(9.6)**	104(90.4)

**Note: n=125*
(Authors, 2025)

In terms of the frequency of usage for infrastructure initiatives, there were varied responses among the respondents regarding PI, whereby there were some who answered that they use to a lesser degree, to those who use moderately and a large degree (mean=3.92, std. dev = 2.08) (See Table 4). Nevertheless, out of all the responses, the majority reported that they used PI to a large extent (mode=7). Similarly, for data services, although the frequency of usage varied among the respondents (mean=4.57, std. dev = 2.18), the majority reported that they used data services to a large extent (mode=7). On the other hand, the community dashboard (mode=1; mean=1.27, std. dev. = 0.92) and VHF (mode=1.00, mean=1.01, std. dev. = 0.10) were either not used much or not used at all by the respondents.

The rest of the initiatives, namely ICT training, entrepreneurship, My-Crib, S.A.I.F.O.N, and e-magazine, did not gain much usage among the respondents (mean for the stated initiatives ranged from 1.35 to 2.50). In fact, the majority responded that they do not use all of these initiatives (mode=1). However, for those who did use ICT training (mean=2.50, std. dev. =1.81), entrepreneurship training (mean=2.05, std.dev.=1.63), S.A.I.F.O.N (mean=2.05, std. dev.= 1.63) and MyCrib (mean=1.84, std. dev. = 1.57), their usage was somewhere between slight to moderate use.

Table 5. Descriptives for usage frequency of the smart community initiatives – Kota Belud

Initiatives	Mode	Mean	Median	Std. Deviation
Infrastructure				
1. Pusat Internet	7.00	3.92	4.00	2.08
2. Data Service	7.00	4.57	5.00	2.18
3. Dashboard	1.00	1.27	1.00	0.92
4. VHF	1.00	1.01	1.00	0.10
Content Training				
1. ICT Training	1.00	2.50	1.00	1.81
2. Entrepreneurship	1.00	2.05	1.00	1.63
Digital Services				
1. MyCrib Booking	1.00	1.84	1.00	1.57
2. Saifon	1.00	2.05	1.00	1.61
3. E-Magazine	1.00	1.35	1.00	1.05

*Note: N=125; Items were measured on a scale 1=not at all to 7=a large extent
(Authors, 2025)

For the respondents who used the initiatives, generally, they felt satisfied with the initiatives, as seen from the mean scores of all the initiatives which ranged from 5.14 to 5.60 except for VHF and e-magazine (See Table 5). Upon closer inspection, the majority of the respondents were very satisfied with PI, data services, ICT training and MyCrib (mode for the stated initiatives = 7). Satisfaction levels for the dashboard (mode=5) and entrepreneurship training (mode=6) were also on the high side. However, there is probably some room for improvement for initiatives like S.A.I.F.O.N (mode=4) and e-magazine (mode=4), as most of the respondents were only moderately satisfied with the initiatives.

Table 6. Descriptive for satisfaction with usage of the smart community initiatives – Kota Belud

Initiatives	Mode	Mean	Median	Std. Deviation
Infrastructure				
1. Pusat Internet	7.00	5.60	6.00	1.42
2. Data Services	7.00	5.40	6.00	1.59
3. Dashboard	5.00	5.17	5.00	1.27
4. VHF*	2.00	2.00	2.00	-
Content Training				
1. ICT Training	7.00	5.59	6.00	1.20
2. Entrepreneurship	6.00	5.53	6.00	1.37
Digital Services				
1. MyCrib Booking	7.00	5.14	5.00	1.53
2. Saifon	4.00	5.34	5.00	1.41
3. E-Magazine	4.00	4.60	4.00	1.84

*Note: N=125; Items measured on a scale 1=very dissatisfied to 7=very satisfied.
*Scores were calculated for those who use the initiatives.
*There was only 1 user of VHF, hence std. Dev. was not applicable.
(Authors, 2025)

DISCUSSION

In terms of the infrastructure initiatives in Kota Belud, the community has come to rely much on the infrastructure. On the other hand, having the necessary conditions like time, effort, and knowledge would facilitate the community's participation in content training along with a perceived notion that ICTs improve their daily lifestyle routine (performance expectancy). As for digital services in the likes of MyCrib app, SAIFON app and e-magazine makers, how innovative the community is would affect the extent to which these digital services are used. Innovativeness is also essential in determining the usage of infrastructure initiatives and participation in content training activities. For those who are more innovative, the easier it is to understand and apply the knowledge gained from the ICT and entrepreneurship training programs, the higher the possibility of attending and learning further from other training programs in future because the more innovative users in the community are considered as pioneers in technology who would be interested in integrating ICTs in their lifestyles.

Overall, the community of Kota Belud rated impact from the informational aspect as the highest, where the MCMC's initiatives improved their capacity to use different forms of ICTs, such as smartphones and laptops. Besides that, due to the ability to use these ICT devices, they could communicate easily with family members and friends. Impacts from psychological, social and political were high too while cultural and economic were among the lowest, where they received lesser impact from these aspects and required improvement and encouragement from MCMC.

RECOMMENDATIONS

Local Content and Application Development

Low digital service participation is fundamentally attributable to a significant misalignment between available digital infrastructures and community needs, compounded by the absence of systematic digital governance frameworks and effective cross-sector coordination. The deployment of community applications needs to be improved. The process by which information is initially intended to be made available for the public's use via an application has not been deployed to the community this way, but somehow, it was justified that the information required by the community is being broadcast to them via other means such as WhatsApp communication or SMS. This breach has to be overcome, and based on our qualitative interview with stakeholders, the community here welcome the idea to able to self-service from the community applications, as the information-pull factor applies. Apart from that, locations of common facilities such as Pusat Internet need to be positioned at strategic locations to ensure public participation is appreciated.

Role of Local authorities, institutions and local champions.

The lack of robust communication and collaboration among local authorities, academic institutions, and private stakeholders further undermines the sustainable development and adoption of community-centric digital solutions. Federal and state authorities should give full support to smart community initiatives. Apart from that, public and private agencies should put their hands together to ensure this program and initiatives are successfully implemented and sustainable in the long run. Collaboration with public and private agencies really helps to improve existing initiatives. Higher institutions for each respective area can collaborate together. For example, the Kemaman Smart community project has collaborated with Universiti Technology Malaysia for some of the waste projects on the Internet of Things (IoT). We might need some sponsors for certain devices, but for the software or the solution to the system, we may invite higher education or individual experts to share the knowledge to develop the software, and it can benefit the community.

Local champions need to discuss and work closely with the researcher. Besides, the local champions should establish good relationships with the local district officer for each area and not only for selected areas. We found that local champions are not aware and communicate with the district office and local community. This is very useful to help us to understand the respective research area. Most of the time, we visited the research area by ourselves and met with the respective district officer team, and other arrangements were made with the help of the Pusat Internet Manager and community leader.

ACKNOWLEDGMENT

The authors acknowledge all reviewers for their comments on this manuscript and are grateful to the committee members of the International Journal of Entrepreneurship for organizing a beneficial conference that provided a good platform for research. This article is supported by the Malaysian Communication and Multimedia Commission Research Grant (No: 304/PMGT/650865/M147).

REFERENCES

Aazam, M., Huh, E. N., St-Hilaire, M., Lung, C. H., & Lambadaris, I. (2015). Cloud of Things: Integration of IoT with Cloud Computing. *Robots and Sensor Clouds*, *36*, 77–94. DOI: 10.1007/978-3-319-22168-7_4

Abdur, M., Habib, S., Ali, M., & Ullah, S. (2017). Security Issues in the Internet of Things (IoT): A Comprehensive Study. *International Journal of Advanced Computer Science and Applications*, *8*(6), 383–388. DOI: 10.14569/IJACSA.2017.080650

Anrong, D., Li, G., Li, J., & Kong, X. (2016). Research on Smart Community Planning of Yishanwan, China towards New Urbanization. *International Review for Spatial Planning and Sustainable Development*, *4*(1), 78–90. DOI: 10.14246/irspsd.4.1_78

ASCS24. AUSTRALIAN smart communities association. (2024). What is a Smart Community? https://www.australiansmartcommunities.org.au/smart-communities

Caragliu, A., Del Bo, C., & Nijkamp, P. (2009). Smart Cities in Europe, Series Research Memoranda 0048. VU University Amsterdam, Faculty of Economics, Business Administration and Econometrics.

Chin, J., Callaghan, V., & Ben Allouch, S. (2019). The Internet-of-Things: Reflections on the Past, Present and Future from a User-Centered and Smart Environment Perspective. *Journal of Ambient Intelligence and Smart Environments*, *11*(1), 45–69. DOI: 10.3233/AIS-180506

Chourabi, H., Nam, T., Walker, S., Gil-Garcia, J. R., Mellouli, S., Nahon, K., Pardo, T. A., & Scholl, H. J. (2012). Understanding smart cities: An integrative framework. Paper presented at the System Science (HICSS), 2012 45th Hawaii International Conference on System Sciences. DOI: 10.1109/HICSS.2012.615

de Waal, M., & Dignum, M. (2017). The citizen in the smart city. How the smart city could transform citizenship. it -. *Información Tecnológica, 59*(6), 263–273. Advance online publication. DOI: 10.1515/itit-2017-0012

Eger, J. M. (2005). Smart communities, universities, and globalization: Educating the workforce for tomorrow's economy. *Metropolitan Universities, 16*(4), 28–38.

Foth, M. (2017). Some thoughts on digital placemaking. In Media Architecture Compendium? Digital Placemaking.DOI: 10.7238/d.v0i12.915.31

Gao, W., Fan, L., Ushifusa, Y., Gu, Q., & Ren, J. (2016). Possibility and Challenge of Smart Community in Japan. *Procedia: Social and Behavioral Sciences, 216*, 109–118. DOI: 10.1016/j.sbspro.2015.12.015

Ghazali, M., Okamura, T., Abdullah, T., Sunar, M. S., Mohamed, F., & Ismail, N. (2016). In the Quest of Defining Smart Digital City in Medini Iskandar Malaysia, Iskandar Puteri, Malaysia. Proceedings of the SEACHI 2016 on Smart Cities for Better Living with HCI and UX.

Gil, O., & Navarro, C. (2013). Innovations of Governance in Cities and Urban regions: Smart Cities in China, Iskandar (Malaysia), Japan, New York and Tarragona (Spain). Paper presented at the EURA Conference: Cities as Sheedbeds for Innovation.

Goldsmith, S. (2021). As the Chorus of Dumb City Advocates Increases, How Do We Define the Truly Smart City? datasmart.ash.harvard.edu

Gubbi, J., Buyya, R., Marusic, S., & Palaniswami, M. (2013). Internet of Things (IoT): A Vision, Architectural Elements, and Future Directions. *Future Generation Computer Systems, 29*(7), 1645–1660. DOI: 10.1016/j.future.2013.01.010

Gupta, R., & Gupta, R. (2016). ABC of Internet of Things: Advancements, Benefits, Challenges, Enablers and Facilities of IoT. *Symposium on Colossal Data Analysis and Networking* (pp. 1–5). DOI: 10.1109/CDAN.2016.7570875

Gurstein, M. (2014). Smart cities vs. smart communities: Empowering citizens not market economics. *The Journal of Community Informatics, 10*(3). Advance online publication. DOI: 10.15353/joci.v10i3.3438

IEEE. (2015). Towards a definition of the Internet of Things (IoT). https://iot.ieee.org/images/files/pdf/IEEE_IoT_Towards_Definition_Internet_of_Things_Revision1_27MAY15.pdf

ITU. (2015). The Internet of Things: data for Development. https://www.itu.int/en/ITU-D/Statistics/Documents/bigdata/MIS2015_Chapter5.pdf

Lapenna, S. (2022). What is Internet of Things (IoT)? 139+1 definitions since 1999. https://www.rtsrl.eu/blog/what-is-internet-of-things-iot/

Lierow, M. (2014). B2City: the next wave of urban logistics. Academic Press.

Mahajan, V., Muller, E., & Bass, F. M. (1995). Diffusion of new products: Empirical generalizations and managerial uses. *Marketing Science, 14*(3, supplement), G79–G88. DOI: 10.1287/mksc.14.3.G79

Margaret, R. (2024). Information and Communication Technology (ICT). https://www.techopedia.com/definition/24152/information-and-communications-technology-ict

Mbah, T. B. (2010). The Impact of ICT on students study habits. Case study: University of Buea, Cameroon. *International Journal of Science and Technology Education Research, 1*(5), 107–110.

Mensah, J. (2019). Sustainable development: Meaning, history, principles, pillars, and implications for human action: Literature review. *Cogent Social Sciences, 5*(1), 1653531. DOI: 10.1080/23311886.2019.1653531

Murray, J. (2011). Cloud network architecture and ICT - Modern Network Architecture. TechTarget =ITKnowledgeExchange.

Nam, T., & Pardo, T. A. (2011). Conceptualizing smart city with dimensions of technology, people, and institutions. *Proceedings of the 12th annual international digital government research conference: digital government innovation in challenging times.* DOI: 10.1145/2037556.2037602

Ozdamli, F., & Ozdal, H. (2015). Life-long Learning Competence Perceptions of the Teachers and Abilities in Using Information-Communication. Technologies. *Procedia: Social and Behavioral Sciences*, *182*, 718–725. DOI: 10.1016/j.sbspro.2015.04.819

Purvis, B., Mao, Y.k & Robinson, D. (2019). Three pillars of sustainability: in search of conceptual origins. Sustainability Science, 14(3), 681–695. DOI: 10.1007/s11625-018-0627-5

Salma, Rahman, & Liyana. (2024). Future of smart cities: integrating health, well-being and productivity in residential building design. https://smart.cidb.gov.my/article/future-of-smart-cities-444

Shih, C. F., & Venkatesh, A. (2004). Beyond adoption: Development and application of a use-diffusion model. *Journal of Marketing*, *68*(1), 59–72. DOI: 10.1509/jmkg.68.1.59.24029

Shih, E., Venkatesh, A., Chen, S., & Kruse, E. (2013). Dynamic Use Diffusion Model in a Cross-National Context: A Comparative Study of the United States, Sweden, and India. *Journal of Product Innovation Management*, *30*(1), 4–16. DOI: 10.1111/j.1540-5885.2012.00982.x

Sidek, N., & Ali, N. (2019). Internet of Things-Based Services Implementation and Challenges in Malaysia: An Inquiry. *Test Engineering and Management*, *81*(11–12), 3219–3231.

S&P Global. (2024). The Rise of AI-Powered Smart Cities. https://www.spglobal.com/en/research-insights/special-reports/ai-smart-cities

United Nations. (2022). *The 17 Goals*. Sustainable Development Goals. UN.

United Nations General Assembly. (1987). Report of the World Commission on Environment and Development: Our Common Future; Transmitted to the General Assembly as an Annex to document A/42/427 – Development and International Co-operation: Environment; Our Common Future, Chapter 2: Towards Sustainable Development; Paragraph 1. United Nations General Assembly.

Venkatesh, V., Thong, J. Y., Chan, F. K., Hu, P. J. H., & Brown, S. A. (2011). Extending the two-stage information systems continuance model: Incorporating UTAUT predictors and the role of context. *Information Systems Journal, 21*(6), 527–555. DOI: 10.1111/j.1365-2575.2011.00373.x

Zhang, F. (2023). Urbanization and consumption structure upgrade: Perspectives from China. China City News. Retrieved from https://www.chinadailyhk.com

Zoe, R., & Melissa, I. (2024). The Rise of AI-Powered Smart Cities. https://www.spglobal.com/en/research-insights/special-reports/ai-smart-cities

Chapter 4
Seasonal Prediction of Hybrid Renewable Energy Using Weighted Ensemble Algorithm With Optimal Allocation on Demand

Tirth Vishalbhai Dave
https://orcid.org/0009-0000-2538-4766
Vellore Institute of Technology, Chennai, India

Sajidha S. A.
https://orcid.org/0000-0003-4771-3131
Vellore Institute of Technology, Chennai, India

M. Nivedita
https://orcid.org/0000-0003-3104-0497
Vellore Institute of Technology, Chennai, India

Aakif Mairaj
https://orcid.org/0000-0001-6699-2039
Indiana University, Kokomo, USA

DOI: 10.4018/979-8-3693-9030-6.ch004

ABSTRACT

Numerous amounts of work towards optimal hybrid energy allocation using PSO, HG-PSO, GA, HOMER-Pro-Software, multi-objective PSO, and many algorithms have been effectively applied. Challenges posed by seasonal variations in solar and wind power generation have not been addressed so far. A novel method of seasonal prediction of hybrid energy and optimal allocation using weighted ensembled ML models and optimization algorithms is proposed. Algorithms such as Decision Trees, Random Forest, K-Nearest Neighbors, XG Boost, Lasso Regression, and Ridge Regression are evaluated for accuracy based on which they are allocated weights and then ensembled for prediction of the renewable energy for each season. Utilization of user-input parameters, reflective of real-time environmental data on the ensembled model predicts the hybrid renewable power. Both the predicted values and the stated energy needs are required for optimal allocation with minimal deficit using algorithms: Particle Swarm Optimization, Grey Wolf Optimizer, and Lightning Search Algorithm for each season has been achieved.

I. INTRODUCTION

The global shift towards renewable energy sources is driven by growing awareness of the environmental impacts associated with traditional methods of energy generation, primarily those that rely on fossil fuels such as coal, oil, and natural gas. These traditional energy sources are major contributors to air pollution, greenhouse gas emissions, and climate change, prompting urgent calls for sustainable alternatives. Renewable energy, derived from natural processes that are continuously replenished, offers a viable solution to these environmental challenges, providing cleaner, and more environmentally friendly options.

The importance of renewable energy extends beyond environmental benefits; it also encompasses economic and security aspects. Economically, it reduces dependency on imported fuels, which can be volatile in price and availability, thus enhancing the energy security of a nation. Furthermore, the renewable energy sector has been a significant driver of job creation and technological innovation worldwide. Socially, it can improve public health by reducing pollution-related diseases and providing energy access in remote areas through off-grid solutions. Furthermore, renewable energy contributes to sustainable development by offering a stable and secure energy supply. As these technologies become more cost-effective and storage solutions more efficient, the predictability and reliability of renewable sources continue to improve, aligning closely with global energy demands.

Nations like Germany, China, and the United States are leading the transition, each having implemented ambitious policies to support renewable energy development. Germany, for instance, under its "Energiewende" initiative, aims to cut greenhouse gas emissions by 80-95% by 2050 (Federal Ministry for the Environment, 2020). China, currently the world's largest producer of solar power, aims to reach 35% of its total energy consumption from renewable sources by 2030 (National Development and Reform Commission., 2021). The United States, through various federal and state initiatives, continues to increase its capacity in both solar and wind energy sectors (U.S. Energy Information Administration, 2022). Despite the rapid growth and adoption of renewable energy sources, one of the primary challenges remains their variability and intermittency. Solar and wind energies, which constitute the major share of renewables, are dependent on weather conditions and time of day, thereby raising issues related to reliability and consistent supply. This variability necessitates the development of sophisticated prediction and management techniques to ensure an optimal energy supply that meets fluctuating demands.

Hybrid renewable energy systems (HRES) is one of the commonly studied topics amongst researchers nowadays. The study (Ammari, 2022) provides a comprehensive literature review of recent research on HRES for power generation. By replacing traditional energy sources with renewables, nations can achieve greater ecological balance, economic stability, and social well-being, paving the way for a sustainable and prosperous future. This research paper aims to further explore these benefits by focusing on the seasonal optimal prediction of hybrid renewable energy, enhancing the integration and optimization of renewable energy into our daily lives and industrial processes.

To build upon the foundational understanding of hybrid renewable energy systems, it is essential to review existing research and methodologies. The next section provides a comprehensive literature survey, highlighting advancements, challenges, and gaps in renewable energy optimization.

II. LITERATURE SURVEY

Researches are happening in this field with the use of different tools and technologies. HRES is one of the commonly studied topics. In their 2020 paper, (Ha, 2020) propose a hybrid genetic particle swarm optimization (HG-PSO) approach to optimize distributed generator allocation in power distribution networks. This method aims to improve network voltage control and reduce losses by effectively distributing generators. By integrating particle swarm optimization and genetic algorithms, the approach combines their strengths within the same population. The study introduces a methodology for multi-objective optimization, ensuring unbiased decision-making. The paper (Mahesh, 2020) reviews the enhanced best sizing approach employing Genetic Algorithm (GA) and a new energy filter algorithm for a grid-connected solar PV-wind-battery hybrid system. The study focuses on minimizing the total cost of a hybrid energy system while ensuring reliability. Key considerations include the complementary nature of photovoltaic (PV) and wind systems, power grid fluctuations, and battery state of charge (SOC).

An off-grid hybrid renewable energy system (HRES) intended to supply power to three Indian villages is the subject of an investigation (Suresh, 2020). It assesses HOMER Pro Software and Genetic Algorithm (GA), two optimization techniques. The study also emphasizes how susceptible the system is to yearly changes in wind speed and the price of biomass fuel.

(Roy, 2022) review recent advancements in wind-solar hybrid renewable energy systems (HRES) for power generation. The paper discusses power architectures, mathematical modeling, converter topologies, and optimization techniques. It also explores coupling technologies for hybrid energy storage systems, power converters, and control strategies. However, it lacks detailed comparisons of HRES configurations, cost analysis, and consideration of social, economic, and environmental aspects.

Additionally, (Jia, 2023) explore large-scale hybrid renewable energy systems (HRES), integrating wind power, solar photovoltaics, gas turbines, hydrogen energy storage, and electrochemical energy storage, with a focus on optimizing system configuration and power dispatch strategies. In the realm of microgrids (MG), economic analysis is essential, prompting the use of optimization techniques for optimal operational efficiency. Particle swarm optimization (PSO) emerges as a preferred method, offering valuable insights into practical applications for enhancing the economic viability and sustainability of microgrid systems.

Additionally, (Gabbar, 2020) explore optimal planning for a nuclear-renewable micro-hybrid energy system (N-R MHES) integrating a micro-nuclear reactor and renewable sources, aiming to minimize net present cost (NPC) while ensuring system reliability amidst varying renewable energy source (RES) availability and load characteristics.

The study by (Zhang, 2020) proposes an enhanced cuckoo search (CS) method and a hybrid self-recurrent support vector regression (SVR) model with variational mode decomposition (VMD) to predict electric load. By incorporating various techniques such as the Tent chaotic mapping function, the VMD approach, and the CS algorithm, the study aims to develop a reliable forecasting model. Novel neighbor operators are introduced to improve the solution, along with a semi-conducted starting population theorem. The paper concludes by suggesting that this model could be a valuable tool for enhancing Malaysia's renewable energy industry and providing alternative sustainable energy sources.

(Abdolrasol, 2021) propose an innovative method that combines artificial neural networks (ANN) with particle swarm optimization (PSO) to optimize renewable energy resources (RESs) within a virtual power plant (VPP) system. The study aims to enhance microgrid (MG) energy scheduling by prioritizing sustainable resources over conventional grid power. By integrating PSO with ANN, the research seeks to improve the performance of the ANN, particularly comparing it with the original Binary Particle Swarm Optimization (BPSO) technique.

The paper (Jumin, 2021) offers a case study of a solar radiation forecast based on data obtained in Malaysia and discusses the solar radiation prediction using boosted decision tree regression (BDTR) model for power production and renewable carbon-free energy industry. The study aims to create a reliable prediction model using the BDTR algorithm, a recent artificial intelligence technique. It compares BDTR's performance with that of traditional regression methods like linear regression and neural networks. Additionally, the paper investigates the impact of different normalization techniques, splitting sizes, and input parameters on model accuracy. Sensitivity and uncertainty analyses validate the proposed model, demonstrating that BDTR achieves superior accuracy compared to other algorithms.

A case study of a grid-connected hybrid PV/wind turbine system that provides energy to a rural community in Egypt is presented in the paper by (Barakat,2020), which also reviews the multi-objective optimization of grid-connected PV-wind hybrid systems for power generation and environmental sustainability. The project aims to minimize the cost of energy (COE) and the likelihood of power supply failure (LPSP) while optimizing the renewable energy b percentage (REF) in response to fluctuating weather conditions. The best solutions are classified into three categories: economic, renewable energy, and environmental using multi-objective particle swarm optimization (MOPSO).

These studies have laid a robust foundation by demonstrating effective methodologies for managing hybrid energy systems. However, they primarily focus on static conditions without adequately addressing the impact of seasonal variations that significantly affect solar and wind power generation. Based on the insights gleaned from the literature survey, this research aims to advance the field of hybrid renewable energy management by focusing on the seasonal prediction and optimal allocation of resources.

The contributions of this work can be listed as follows:

· Develop a Weighted Ensemble Machine Learning Model: Integrate and enhance multiple machine learning models, including Decision Trees, Random Forest, K-Nearest Neighbors, XG Boost, Lasso Regression, and Ridge Regression, and assign performance-based weights for improved prediction accuracy.

· Implement Seasonal Prediction of Hybrid Energy Supply: Utilize the developed weighted ensemble model to accurately predict the availability of renewable energy sources, such as solar and wind, for each season, to ensure relevance and accuracy.
· Optimize Energy Allocation Using Advanced Algorithms: Employ optimization algorithms, including Particle Swarm Optimization, Grey Wolf Optimizer, and Lightning Search Algorithm, to optimally allocate the predicted hybrid renewable energy to meet energy demands with minimal deficits throughout the seasons.
· Contribute to Sustainable Energy Management: Provide a novel tool that aids policymakers, energy planners, and stakeholders in making informed decisions about energy distribution and utilization, thereby supporting sustainable development goals and reduce reliance on non-renewable sources.

Research shows that seasonal variations significantly affect hybrid renewable energy efficiency (Mahesh, 2020; Suresh, 2020). Solar power output can drop by up to 30% in winter due to shorter daylight hours, while wind energy tends to increase by 25% in colder months due to stronger winds. Studies also indicate that failing to account for these variations in energy optimization can lead to a 15% rise in winter energy deficits. This highlights the importance of incorporating forecasting models like SOREAM to improve energy distribution and reduce deficits, strengthening the study's real-world relevance.

The existing literature provides valuable insights into hybrid renewable energy systems, yet challenges such as seasonal variations and optimal energy allocation remain. The following section outlines the methodology used in this study, detailing the data sources, machine learning models, and optimization techniques employed to address these challenges.

III. METHODOLOGY

The Dataset Description for this study focuses on two critical datasets obtained from Kaggle: the solar dataset and the wind dataset, both of which are instrumental in modeling and predicting renewable energy outputs for their respective sources. These datasets form the foundation of the study's analysis by providing the necessary parameters for accurate and reliable energy forecasting across multiple seasons. Both datasets are segmented quarterly to account for the significant seasonal variations that impact energy generation, ensuring that the developed models are highly adaptable to changing weather conditions throughout the year.

The solar dataset contains several key parameters, including the date, hour, wind speed, sunshine duration, air pressure, solar radiation, air temperature, relative humidity, and system production. These variables are essential for assessing the solar energy potential at any given time and place. The parameter "system production" specifically captures the amount of solar energy generated, while variables like "solar radiation" and "sunshine duration" provide insight into the environmental conditions influencing energy generation. Additionally, factors like air pressure and air temperature are crucial in determining the efficiency of solar energy systems, while wind speed can affect cooling mechanisms and performance. Conversely, the wind dataset comprises parameters such as the date, time, LV active power, wind speed, theoretical power curve, and wind direction. These attributes are essential for evaluating wind energy production. LV active power represents the amount of power generated by the wind turbine, while wind speed is the critical factor driving wind energy production. The theoretical power curve serves as a reference point for determining how much power the turbine is expected to produce under specific wind conditions, and wind direction helps optimize turbine orientation to maximize energy capture. The solar dataset includes over 8,700 instances, providing a robust dataset for assessing solar energy potential across a wide range of environmental conditions. The wind dataset, on the other hand, contains more than 50,000 instances, making it substantially larger and offering a rich set of data points for analyzing wind energy generation. These large datasets enable the models to capture complex patterns and relationships between environmental variables and energy output, resulting in more accurate and reliable predictions.

To account for seasonal variability, both datasets are segmented into quarterly subsets—a crucial step in addressing the significant seasonal impacts on renewable energy generation. By breaking the data down into four quarters in Fig.1. the analysis can better capture the differences in solar and wind energy potential across different times of the year. For example, in Quarter 1 (January to March), sunshine duration is generally lower compared to wind speed, which means that wind energy may play a more prominent role in energy generation during this period. In Quarter 2 (April to June), the pattern shifts, with sunshine duration increasing and wind speed becoming less significant, making solar energy the dominant contributor to renewable energy production during these months.

In Quarter 3 (July to September), wind speed again becomes more prominent, often surpassing the impact of sunshine duration. This shift suggests that wind energy would be the more reliable source of power during this quarter. Finally, in Quarter 4 (October to December), wind speed remains the dominant factor, continuing to exceed sunshine duration, which indicates that wind energy will once again be the primary resource for energy generation in these months.

This quarterly analysis highlights the dynamic nature of renewable energy sources and the importance of adapting energy generation strategies to seasonal changes. By segmenting the data in this way, the study can develop models that are fine-tuned to account for the changing contributions of solar and wind energy across different seasons. This approach not only improves the accuracy of the energy forecasts but also enhances the model's ability to optimize energy distribution strategies based on real-world seasonal conditions. Thus, the segmentation of the solar and wind datasets into quarters is a crucial step in ensuring that the models developed are responsive to seasonal variations and capable of effectively managing renewable energy resources throughout the year.

Figure 1. Monthly variations in wind speed and sunshine

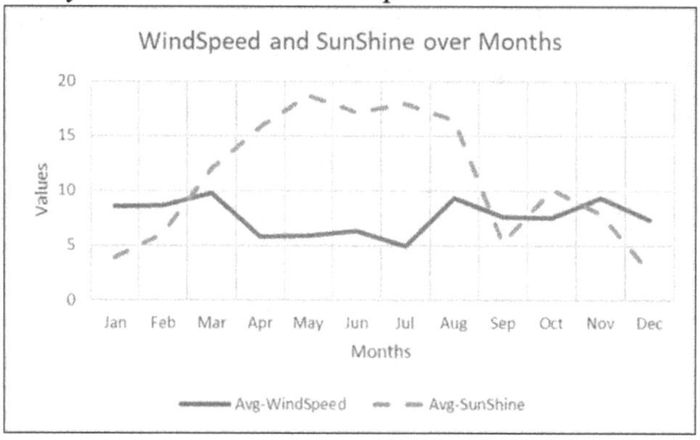

The development of this model is divided into 3 main phases. Phase 1 consists of preparation of data and initial model training. The next phase deals with integration of trained models using weighted ensembling method. Also, the hybrid renewable energy powers are predicted using the weather parameters provided by user. Further in phase 3 these predicted powers along with energy demand are used for optimal allocation of Wind and Solar Energy using different optimization techniques.

Phase 1. Data Preparation and Initial Model Training

The foundational phase of the project, as depicted in Figure 2, focuses on the critical steps of dataset segmentation, data preprocessing, and initial model training for both solar and wind energy data. These steps are essential to ensure that the models are trained on clean, well-structured data, allowing for more accurate predictions and optimization.

Dataset Segmentation

The first step in the foundational phase is the segmentation of the dataset. This is done by dividing the data according to quarters, such as Quarter 1 (Q1), Quarter 2 (Q2), Quarter 3 (Q3), and Quarter 4 (Q4). This segmentation aligns the analysis with seasonal variations, which is crucial for renewable energy systems where environmental factors like sunlight and wind patterns fluctuate throughout the year. By segmenting the data this way, the model can better capture these seasonal differences, improving its predictive power and accuracy for each period. For example, solar energy generation may peak during certain months, while wind energy may be more prominent in others. By tailoring the models to each quarter, the project ensures that the system is sensitive to these environmental variations, enhancing its ability to allocate energy effectively.

Data Preprocessing

Once the data is segmented, the next step is data preprocessing. This stage is essential for ensuring the quality and reliability of the data that will be used to train the models. In the preprocessing phase, several key actions are performed:

· Outlier Removal: Outliers, or data points that deviate significantly from the rest of the dataset, are identified and removed. These outliers can skew the results and lead to inaccurate predictions if not handled properly. For instance, an unusually high or low solar energy reading due to a rare weather event could distort the model's learning process if left untreated.

· Null Value Handling: Missing or null values are also addressed during preprocessing. This might involve imputing missing values with statistical estimates, such as the mean or median, or removing incomplete records altogether. Proper handling of null values is crucial, as leaving them in the dataset can cause issues during model training, leading to incorrect predictions.

· Feature Scaling and Normalization: To ensure that all input features contribute equally to the model's learning process, features are scaled and normalized. This step is especially important when working with different types of data, such as temperature, wind speed, and solar irradiance, which may have different units and ranges. Overall, the goal of the preprocessing phase is to clean and prepare the data, ensuring that it is free of errors and inconsistencies before being used in the machine learning models.

Data Splitting and Model Training

Once the data has been preprocessed, the next phase involves splitting the data and training the machine learning models. For each quarter (Q1-Q4) and for both solar and wind energy datasets, the data is split into a training set and a testing set in an 80-20 ratio. The training set consists of 80% of the data and is used to train the machine learning models, while the remaining 20% of the data is reserved for testing and evaluating the models' performance.

To further enhance the robustness of the model, the training set is subdivided into six distinct sets with randomization. This technique, known as cross-validation, helps prevent overfitting, a situation where the model learns too much from the training data and performs poorly on unseen data. By training the models on multiple subsets of the data, the project ensures that the model generalizes well to new, unseen data and is not overly reliant on any one portion of the dataset.

Six different machine learning models are trained for each dataset and quarter. These models include:

1. Decision Tree: A simple, tree-based model that makes decisions based on splitting the data into subsets according to the most significant features.
2. K Neighbors: A model based on the K-Nearest Neighbors algorithm, which makes predictions based on the most similar instances in the dataset.
3. Random Forest: An ensemble model that builds multiple decision trees and combines their outputs to improve accuracy and reduce overfitting.
4. XGBoost: A powerful gradient-boosting algorithm that builds models sequentially, where each new model corrects the errors made by previous ones.
5. Lasso: A linear regression model with L1 regularization that helps reduce overfitting by penalizing large coefficients.
6. Ridge: A linear regression model similar to Lasso, but with L2 regularization, which also helps prevent overfitting by shrinking the coefficients.

Training these six distinct models with multiple randomized datasets enhances the robustness of the overall system. This approach allows the models to adapt to various data scenarios and ensures that they are capable of making accurate predictions across different environmental conditions. By employing a diverse set of models, the project can mitigate the risk of poor performance due to model-specific weaknesses and build a stronger ensemble system in later stages.

Figure 2. Proposed architecture of phase 1 (solar/wind)

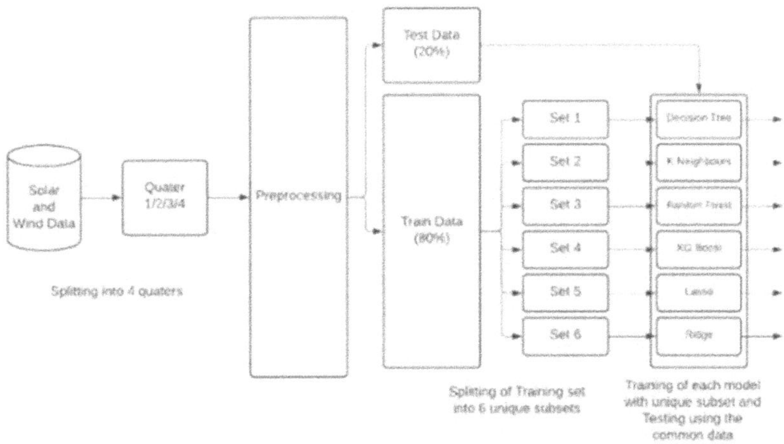

Phase 2. Model Integration and Weighted Ensembling

The subsequent phase of the project, as illustrated in Figure 3, involves the strategic integration of outputs from six independently trained models through a weighted ensembling technique for both solar and wind data. This phase is essential for synthesizing the unique strengths of each predictive model into a singular robust output that enhances the reliability and accuracy of energy forecasts for both solar and wind power.

Figure 3. Proposed architecture of phase 2 (solar/wind)

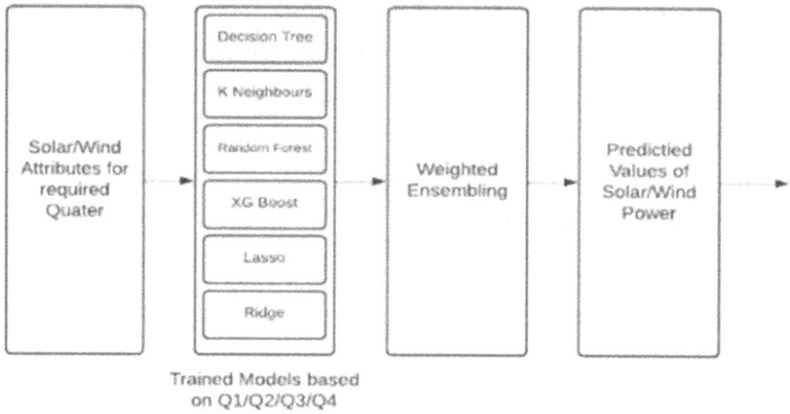

Model Input Processing is a crucial stage in the project that ensures the six trained machine learning models receive the most relevant and accurate data for each specific quarter. This targeted, quarter-based approach is essential in the context of renewable energy prediction, where environmental conditions such as solar radiation and wind speed vary significantly throughout the year. Each quarter—Q1 through Q4—represents a distinct set of environmental factors that influence energy production, and by tailoring the input data to reflect these seasonal variations, the models can make more precise predictions. During this stage, the models are fed a set of input attributes that have been carefully curated during the data preparation and preprocessing phases. These inputs include a wide range of variables directly tied to renewable energy generation, such as:

Wind Speed: A critical factor for wind energy production, wind speed varies across different seasons and geographic locations, making it an important predictor for wind-based energy models.

Solar Radiation: Solar energy generation is highly dependent on the amount of sunlight received, which fluctuates throughout the year, particularly between summer and winter months. Accurate measurements of solar radiation allow the models to predict solar energy output effectively.

Air Temperature: Temperature can impact both solar and wind energy efficiency, as it affects equipment performance and energy transfer rates.

Additional Predictors: Other environmental factors like humidity, cloud cover, and atmospheric pressure, identified during data exploration, may also be included in the input set for a more comprehensive understanding of the environmental context.

By aligning the input data with seasonal conditions specific to each quarter, the models are better equipped to learn from the most current and relevant information, ensuring that their predictions reflect the actual environmental conditions experienced during that time of the year. This level of customization not only enhances the accuracy of the models but also strengthens their ability to adapt to the diverse and often unpredictable nature of renewable energy systems.

Weighted Ensembling: The weighted ensembling technique is applied once all individual models have generated their predictions.

1. Compute the sum of the accuracies of the models

$$\sum_{j=1}^{N} R_j^2 \tag{1}$$

2. Compute relative accuracy(weight) of each model

$$w_i = \frac{R_i^2}{\sum_{j=1}^{N} R_j^2} \tag{2}$$

where R_i^2 is the R-squared score of the ith model

3. Perform weighted ensembling

$$\hat{y}_{ensemble} = \sum_{i=0}^{N} w_i . \hat{y}_i \tag{3}$$

where:

· N represents the number of base models,
· $\hat{y}_i$ denotes the prediction from the ith base model, and
· w_i signifies the weight assigned to the ith model.

Weighted ensembling permits the assignment of different importance to the predictions of each base model, thereby enhancing the overall performance of the ensemble. Following are the reasons of weighted ensembling being effective:

· Proportional Contribution: The weights ensure that models contributing more accurate predictions (those with higher R^2 scores) have a greater influence on the ensemble's final prediction, while models with lower accuracy contribute less.
· Reducing Model Bias: By combining the strengths of different models, weighted ensembling helps mitigate biases or weaknesses that individual models may have. For example, one model might be good at predicting certain patterns, while another is better at predicting others. The ensemble balances these differences.
· Robustness Against Overfitting: Since the ensemble relies on multiple models rather than a single one, it is less prone to overfitting. This means it generalizes better to unseen data, producing more reliable predictions.
· Application to Renewable Energy: In the context of renewable energy systems, where energy output is influenced by many fluctuating factors like weather conditions, this approach improves prediction accuracy. The ensemble can make more precise and reliable forecasts of solar or wind energy output, essential for efficient energy management and planning.

Phase 3. Optimization and Resource Allocation

The final phase involves the strategic deployment of algorithms to optimally allocate renewable energy resources based on the predictions from the weighted ensembles and demand, as illustrated in Figure 4. This phase is crucial to meet specific demand scenarios, thereby minimizing deficit between the energy produced and the energy required.

Figure 4. Proposed architecture of phase 3 (solar & wind)

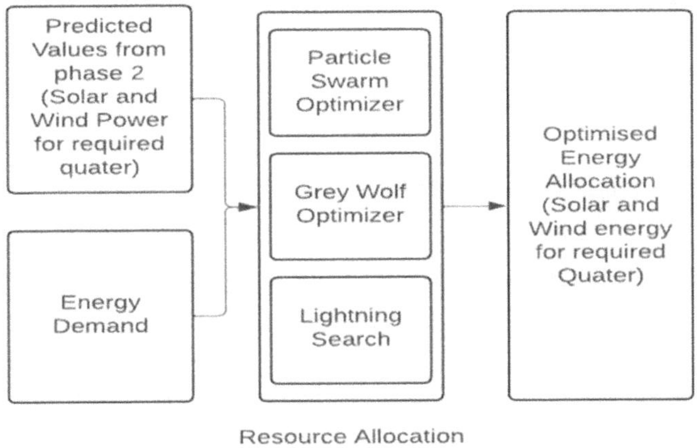

This phase employs three sophisticated optimization algorithms, each with unique mechanisms and strengths, to optimally allocate the hybrid resources:

Particle Swarm Optimization (PSO): PSO is a computational algorithm inspired by the collective social behavior of bird flocks or fish schools, which collaborate to find food or navigate toward a destination. In the context of renewable energy allocation, PSO plays a pivotal role in adjusting the distribution of solar and wind energy resources dynamically, ensuring that energy demands are met in the most efficient way possible.

In PSO, each solution to the problem is represented as a "particle" within a multi-dimensional search space. Each particle's position signifies a potential solution, indicating how much energy from solar and wind resources should be allocated to meet the energy demands at any given moment. Initially, these particles are randomly distributed throughout the search space, representing various combinations of solar and wind energy allocations. As time progresses, the particles iteratively move through the search space, updating their positions based on both their own experiences and those of other particles in the swarm.

The movement of each particle is guided by two main factors: personal best position (the best solution a particle has discovered so far) and global best position (the best solution found by any particle in the swarm). This dual guidance helps particles balance exploration (searching new areas) and exploitation (refining promising areas) of the solution space. Particles adjust their velocity and position by following the best-performing particles, thereby improving their chances of finding an optimal or near-optimal solution.

In renewable energy allocation, PSO is applied to determine how much solar and wind energy should be utilized at any given time to meet fluctuating energy demands. By dynamically adjusting the energy resource allocation, PSO ensures that the energy distribution strategy adapts to changes in generation capacity (which may fluctuate due to varying sunlight or wind conditions) and real-time demand. The ultimate goal of PSO in this context is to minimize the deficit between generated and required energy, ensuring that demand is met without over-relying on any one resource, while also maximizing efficiency.

Furthermore, PSO's ability to explore complex solution spaces makes it an excellent fit for renewable energy systems where multiple factors (such as weather forecasts, grid demand, and energy storage levels) need to be considered simultaneously. Its iterative nature means that it continually refines the allocation strategy, making it well-suited for real-time adjustments in energy distribution.

Grey Wolf Optimizer (GWO): The GWO algorithm is inspired by the social hierarchy and hunting strategies of grey wolves in nature. Grey wolves exhibit a pack structure where the group is led by the alpha wolves, followed by beta, delta, and omega wolves. This hierarchical approach to decision-making and problem-solving is replicated in GWO to solve complex optimization problems. In GWO, the wolves' positions in the solution space represent potential solutions to the problem of renewable energy allocation. The alpha wolves are considered the leaders and represent the most optimal solutions discovered so far, while the beta and delta wolves follow closely, representing the second and third best solutions. The omega wolves represent less optimal solutions but are essential for exploring the search space.

The wolves work together to "hunt" for the optimal energy distribution by following three main stages: encircling the prey, hunting, and attacking the prey. Encircling involves initializing random solutions and surrounding the search space, hunting entails moving closer to the best solutions discovered by the alpha wolves, and attacking is the process of refining and converging on the optimal solution. Each wolf's position is updated based on the positions of the alpha, beta, and delta wolves, ensuring that the pack as a whole gradually moves toward the best solution.

In the context of renewable energy allocation, GWO is particularly effective in balancing the use of solar and wind energy resources to minimize deficits between energy production and demand. By leveraging the cooperative hunting behavior of the wolves, GWO efficiently explores and exploits the solution space, identifying the most effective combination of energy resources. This adaptive algorithm ensures that the allocation strategy is flexible, allowing the system to adjust to varying conditions and demands while reducing the risk of energy shortfalls or overuse of one resource. GWO's hierarchical nature ensures that the exploration of the search space is structured and coordinated, reducing the likelihood of getting stuck in suboptimal solutions. It performs well in complex, non-linear optimization problems, making it a valuable tool in managing the allocation of renewable resources where both demand and supply can fluctuate unpredictably. The dynamic adjustment of resource allocation based on the performance of previous iterations helps ensure energy distribution is both cost-effective and efficient.

Lightning Search Algorithm (LSA): LSA takes inspiration from the natural phenomenon of lightning, specifically how lightning branches out in unpredictable, yet structured ways to find the path of least resistance. This metaphor is applied to optimization problems where the search space is vast and complex, much like the diverse factors involved in renewable energy management. The randomness and branching of lightning in LSA help the algorithm explore different regions of the solution space, while its structured crossovers and mutations ensure that the search is thorough and converges toward optimal solutions. In LSA, each potential solution is represented as a "lightning bolt," which navigates through the solution space by exploring different paths to find the optimal energy allocation. The process begins by randomly initializing a population of solutions, much like how lightning randomly strikes different locations. These solutions then undergo random mutations and structured crossover events, akin to how lightning branches out in multiple directions before converging on the final strike point.

The mutation phase in LSA introduces variability, allowing the algorithm to explore new areas of the solution space and prevent it from getting trapped in local optima. This means that even if the algorithm finds a reasonably good solution, it continues to explore other possibilities, ensuring that it doesn't miss out on potentially better solutions. The crossover phase combines elements from multiple promising solutions to create new, potentially more effective solutions, much like how lightning forks before finding the best path. LSA is particularly useful for handling complex, non-linear problems where the solution space may have multiple local optima. In renewable energy allocation, where conditions such as energy production forecasts and demand patterns can vary dramatically, LSA's ability to navigate through complex solution landscapes is invaluable. By iterating through multiple potential solutions, LSA helps ensure that the energy deficit is minimized, even when facing rapidly changing environmental conditions. Additionally, LSA's structured exploration helps to avoid common pitfalls in optimization algorithms, such as premature convergence to suboptimal solutions. Its random yet directed search strategy makes it well-suited for handling the dynamic and often unpredictable nature of renewable energy systems. The algorithm is particularly effective in identifying the most efficient energy distribution strategy, ensuring that energy production from solar and wind resources is optimized, and deficits are minimized in a constantly shifting landscape.

Together, these algorithms enhance the system's decision-making capabilities by ensuring that the allocation of renewable resources is not only optimal but also practical in real-world applications. By combining the strengths of each algorithm, the system can adapt to varying conditions, balance supply and demand, and minimize energy deficits, all while remaining cost-effective. This integration ultimately leads to more sustainable and efficient management of renewable energy resources, supporting the broader goal of reducing reliance on non-renewable energy sources and promoting environmental sustainability. Cities like Germany and Singapore have successfully implemented smart energy distribution systems. For example, Germany's 'Energiewende' policy has helped integrate renewable energy into urban grids by improving forecasting models and grid storage solutions. Singapore has developed real-time energy monitoring using IoT and AI-powered optimization techniques, providing insights into efficient hybrid renewable energy management.

With the seasonal prediction models trained and optimized, the next step involves evaluating their effectiveness across different seasonal conditions. The following section presents an analysis of how well these models perform and how optimization techniques impact energy allocation efficiency.

IV. RESULTS AND DISCUSSION

Phase 1. Experimental Results from Model Training and Validation

The evaluation of six different machine learning models across four quarters (Q1-Q4) for both the solar and wind datasets is detailed in this section, with a focus on comparing their performance based on three important metrics: Mean Squared Error (MSE), R-squared (R^2), and Mean Absolute Error (MAE). These metrics offer insight into the accuracy and reliability of each model's predictions. MSE measures the average of the squared differences between the predicted and actual values, MAE captures the average absolute error in the predictions, and R^2 represents the proportion of the variance in the dependent variable that is predictable from the independent variables.

The consolidated results for the solar dataset are presented in Table 1, allowing for a clear comparison of model performance across different quarters. This breakdown highlights the variability in model effectiveness based on seasonal factors, reflecting the complexity of renewable energy forecasting. For example, in Quarter 1, K-Nearest Neighbors (KNN) emerges as the best-performing model with an R^2 score of 0.7690, outperforming other models in accurately predicting solar energy output during this period. This suggests that KNN, with its ability to make predictions based on the closest neighbors, captures the underlying patterns in the data effectively for Q1.

In Quarter 2, the Random Forest model takes the lead with the highest R^2 score of 0.6841, indicating its superior performance in handling the solar dataset for this quarter. Random Forest, known for its robustness due to the ensemble learning approach, aggregates the output of multiple decision trees to deliver accurate and stable predictions.

In Quarter 3, Random Forest again shows its strength, achieving an R^2 score of 0.7731, the highest for that quarter, reinforcing its consistency in making precise predictions across different seasonal conditions. Finally, in Quarter 4, Lasso Regression provides the best results with an R^2 score of 0.5714, demonstrating its ability to handle the solar dataset's particular characteristics during the final quarter, possibly due to its regularization technique that helps prevent overfitting by shrinking coefficients. This quarter-based comparison showcases the varying performance of machine learning models, influenced by changes in environmental conditions throughout the year.

Table 1. Solar dataset results

Quarter	Model	Values		
		MSE	R^2	*MAE*
Q1	Decision Tree	303998.8127	0.6921	191.6211
Q1	K Neighbors	228011.9096	0.7690	170.9886
Q1	Random Forest	250531.1925	0.7462	178.5271
Q1	XGBoost	338455.8448	0.6572	181.9469
Q1	Lasso	261480.6344	0.7351	269.9899
Q1	Ridge	256873.4077	0.7398	253.9238
Q2	Decision Tree	232185.2628	0.6571	235.8093
Q2	K Neighbors	456635.7846	0.3256	388.3015
Q2	Random Forest	213882.6620	0.6841	255.5110
Q2	XGBoost	231356.4972	0.6583	249.6989
Q2	Lasso	448429.4446	0.3377	453.2844
Q2	Ridge	508933.7110	0.2483	531.2642

continued on following page

Table 1. Continued

Quarter	Model	Values		
		MSE	R^2	*MAE*
Q3	Decision Tree	480856.6672	0.5883	366.7406
Q3	K Neighbors	532165.4731	0.5444	419.6871
Q3	Random Forest	314231.7509	0.7310	317.3584
Q3	XGBoost	265370.7210	0.7728	289.2906
Q3	Lasso	445152.3100	0.6189	468.9315
Q3	Ridge	425178.3475	0.6360	430.4103
Q4	Decision Tree	234578.9763	0.4460	131.3149
Q4	K Neighbors	244224.8812	0.4232	121.1182
Q4	Random Forest	181736.7058	0.5708	122.0222
Q4	XGBoost	223616.3773	0.4719	119.4175
Q4	Lasso	181458.6815	0.5714	161.9522
Q4	Ridge	217730.1337	0.4858	147.7614

The evaluation of performance metrics across the four quarters for the wind dataset, as illustrated in Table 2, provides a detailed comparison of the predictive capabilities of various machine learning models. The models are evaluated based on key metrics, including R-squared (R^2), which serves as the primary indicator of how well the models explain the variance in wind energy output. These results highlight the seasonal variations and the effectiveness of different algorithms in handling the wind dataset. In Quarter 1, the Random Forest model outperforms all other models, achieving an impressive R^2 score of 0.9295, indicating that it provides highly accurate predictions for wind energy output during this period. Random Forest's ensemble technique, which aggregates multiple decision trees, allows it to capture complex patterns in the data, particularly when it comes to handling wind speed fluctuations and other weather-related variables that affect energy generation.

In Quarter 2, the K-Nearest Neighbors (KNN) model takes the lead with the highest R^2 score of 0.9657, reflecting its ability to effectively predict wind energy output during this quarter. KNN's method of relying on the closest data points to make predictions proves to be particularly effective during this period, likely due to the strong seasonal patterns present in the wind dataset for Quarter 2. Its ability to adapt to local data variations ensures precise forecasting of wind energy. Moving on to Quarter 3, Random Forest once again emerges as the best-performing model, with an R^2 score of 0.9748. This demonstrates the model's continued strength in accurately predicting wind energy output, further showcasing its robustness in handling seasonal shifts and complex data interactions. The high R^2 score indicates that the model is highly effective at capturing the variability in wind energy generation during this quarter.

Finally, in Quarter 4, XGBoost proves to be the top-performing model, with an R^2 score of 0.9655, outperforming the other algorithms for this period. XGBoost's ability to efficiently handle large datasets and its use of gradient boosting to minimize errors make it particularly suited for the dynamic conditions of Quarter 4. Its performance reflects the model's capability to account for seasonal fluctuations in wind energy generation, providing highly accurate predictions as compared to other algorithms.

The quarter-by-quarter comparison reveals that different models perform best in different quarters due to the changing nature of the wind dataset across seasons. The varying environmental conditions, such as wind speed patterns, air pressure, and temperature, affect each model's ability to predict energy output, and these results demonstrate how models like Random Forest, KNN, and XGBoost each excel at capturing the unique characteristics of the dataset during different times of the year.

Table 2. Wind dataset results

Quarter	**Model**	**Values**		
		MSE	R^2	*MAE*
Q1	Decision Tree	330151.8880	0.8450	203.7921
Q1	K Neighbors	351307.7596	0.8350	284.6729
Q1	Random Forest	150155.8159	0.9295	165.3163
Q1	XGBoost	164604.7276	0.9227	167.8296
Q1	Lasso	366918.9005	0.8277	390.8542
Q1	Ridge	365739.6591	0.8283	383.8782

Quarter	Model	Values		
		MSE	R^2	*MAE*
Q2	Decision Tree	60669.3567	0.9493	84.1752
Q2	K Neighbors	41038.5029	0.9657	72.9558
Q2	Random Forest	42761.6532	0.9642	68.5326
Q2	XGBoost	41500.2846	0.9653	65.5432
Q2	Lasso	44782.4875	0.9626	99.5515
Q2	Ridge	45110.6505	0.9623	95.0625
Q3	Decision Tree	55735.6853	0.9642	81.2274
Q3	K Neighbors	43621.1128	0.9720	75.4157
Q3	Random Forest	39150.3452	0.9748	64.1948
Q3	XGBoost	39510.5008	0.9746	68.7267
Q3	Lasso	53319.1017	0.9657	121.5788
Q3	Ridge	54219.0780	0.9652	120.2011
Q4	Decision Tree	120410.9119	0.9298	140.8901
Q4	K Neighbors	141352.2336	0.9176	172.3451
Q4	Random Forest	94724.8704	0.9448	136.3238
Q4	XGBoost	59075.3152	0.9655	108.7576
Q4	Lasso	140986.0055	0.9178	209.9676
Q4	Ridge	140697.0252	0.9180	210.7435

Phase 2. Experimental Results From Weighted Ensembling Techniques for all Models for Both Datasets

This section discusses the integration of outputs from six different predictive models into a weighted ensemble. This approach aims to enhance prediction accuracy by leveraging the strengths of each individual model. The results are presented to demonstrate the effectiveness of the ensemble relative to its constituent models and to explore how weight allocations influenced overall predictions. In Quarter 1, Figure 5 shows that R^2 score for weighted ensembled method i.e. 0.8896 is highest amongst that of all other algorithms, which reflects the effectiveness of the weighted ensemble approach in integrating the strengths of individual models to enhance overall predictive performance.

Figure 5. Comparison of R-squared values for different models for quarter 1 solar dataset

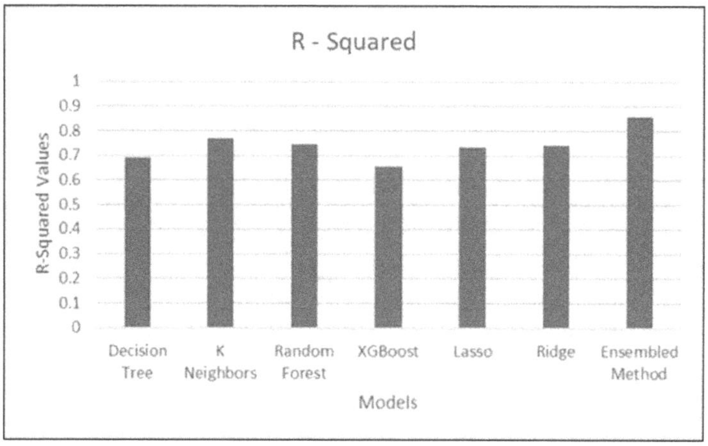

In Quarter 2, Figure 6 shows that R^2 score for weighted ensembled method i.e. 0.7938 is highest amongst that of all other algorithms, which reflects the effectiveness of the weighted ensemble approach in integrating the strengths of individual models to enhance overall predictive performance.

Figure 6. Comparison of R-squared values for different models for quarter 2 solar dataset

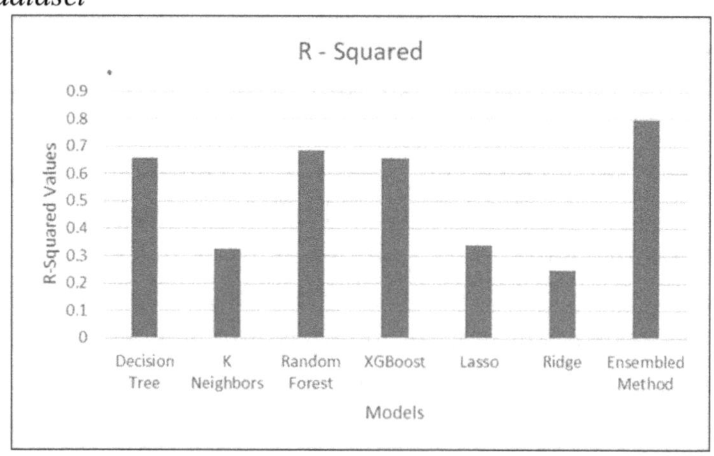

In Quarter 3, Figure 7 shows that R^2 score for weighted ensembled method i.e. 0.7751 is highest amongst that of all other algorithms, which reflects the effectiveness of the weighted ensemble approach in integrating the strengths of individual models to enhance overall predictive performance.

Figure 7. Comparison of R-squared values for different models for quarter 3 solar dataset

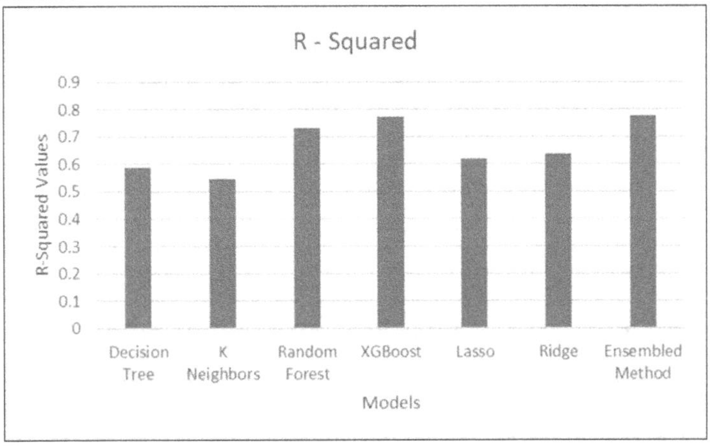

In Quarter 4, Figure 8 shows that R^2 score for weighted ensembled method i.e. 0.7126 is highest amongst that of all other algorithms, which reflects the effectiveness of the weighted ensemble approach in integrating the strengths of individual models to enhance overall predictive performance.

Figure 8. Comparison of R-squared values for different models for quarter 4 solar dataset

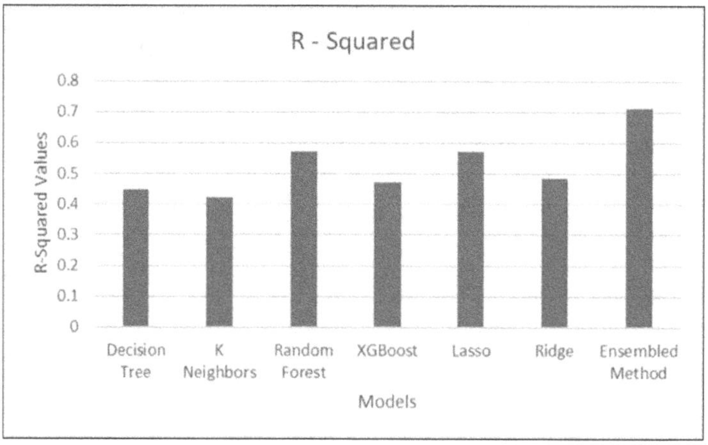

In Quarter 1, Figure 9 shows that R^2 score for weighted ensembled method i.e. 0.9463 is highest amongst that of all other algorithms, which reflects the effectiveness of the weighted ensemble approach in integrating the strengths of individual models to enhance overall predictive performance.

Figure 9. Comparison of R-squared values for different models for quarter 1 wind dataset

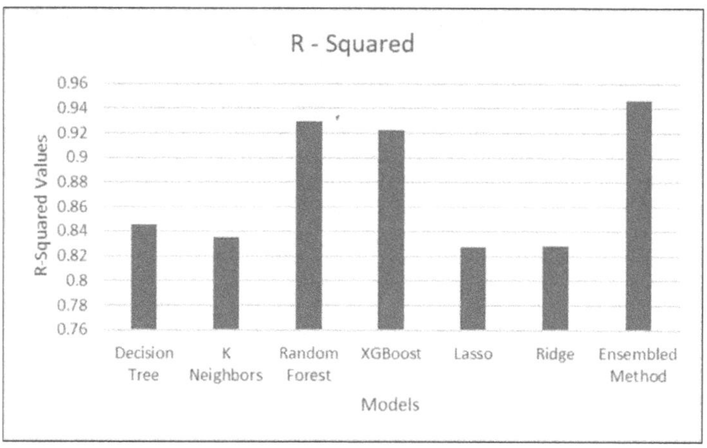

In Quarter 2, Figure 10 shows that R^2 score for weighted ensembled method i.e. 0.9763 is highest amongst that of all other algorithms, which reflects the effectiveness of the weighted ensemble approach in integrating the strengths of individual models to enhance overall predictive performance.

Figure 10. Comparison of R-squared values for different models for quarter 2 wind dataset

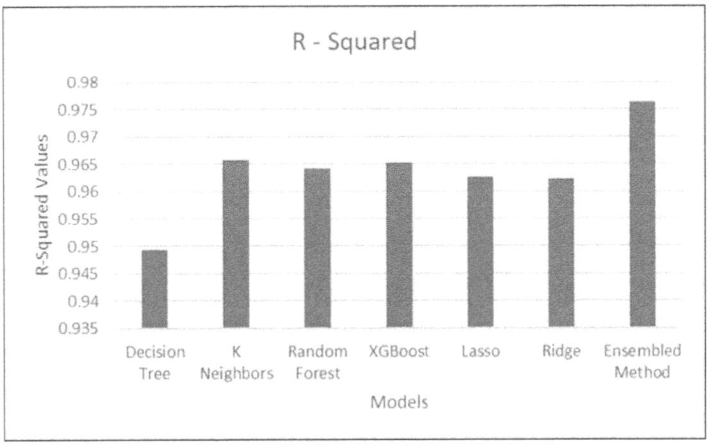

In Quarter 3, Figure 11 shows that R^2 score for weighted ensembled method i.e. 0.9804 is highest amongst that of all other algorithms, which reflects the effectiveness of the weighted ensemble approach in integrating the strengths of individual models to enhance overall predictive performance.

Figure 11. Comparison of R-squared values for different models for quarter 3 wind dataset

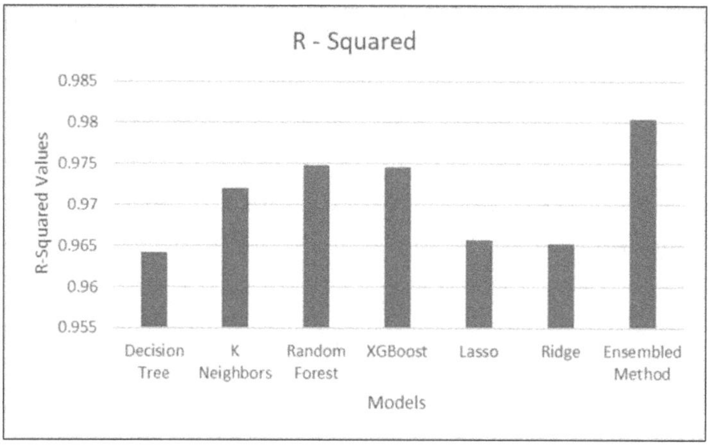

In Quarter 4, Figure 12 shows that R^2 score for weighted ensembled method i.e. 0.9724 is highest amongst that of all other algorithms, which reflects the effectiveness of the weighted ensemble approach in integrating the strengths of individual models to enhance overall predictive performance.

Figure 12. Comparison of R-squared values for different models for quarter 4 wind dataset

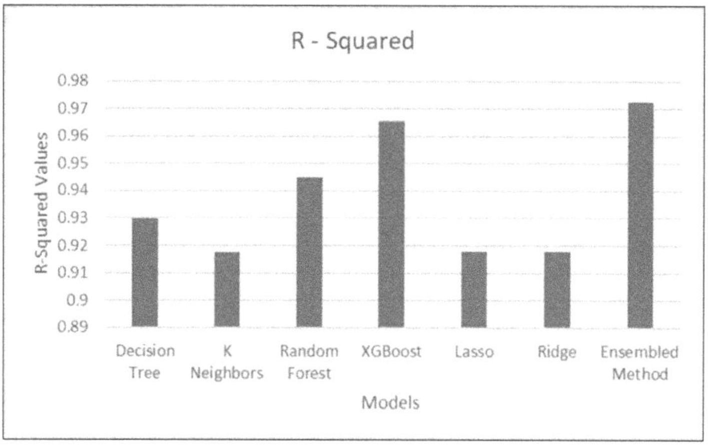

Phase 3. Experimental Results From Optimization and Resource Allocation

To thoroughly evaluate the influence of seasonality on energy distribution and optimization, our study implemented four distinct test cases, each representing different seasonal weather conditions while keeping a constant energy demand throughout all scenarios. This design ensures that the analysis can isolate and focus on the effects of varying weather patterns across the four quarters (Q1-Q4), allowing us to better understand the seasonal impact on the efficiency and effectiveness of our resource allocation strategies. By maintaining a constant energy demand across the different seasons, the test cases provide a clear view of how changes in environmental factors, such as solar radiation, wind speed, and temperature, affect the energy distribution and optimization process.

In each of these test cases, we applied three different optimized allocation strategies to assess how well they perform under the specific seasonal conditions of each quarter. These strategies involved various optimization algorithms tailored to adjust energy allocation dynamically in response to environmental variations, enabling a detailed examination of their relative strengths and weaknesses. By employing multiple optimization algorithms for each seasonal scenario, we were able to evaluate not only the overall effectiveness of these algorithms but also their adaptability to changing conditions and their ability to maintain efficient energy distribution. This comprehensive approach ensures a robust comparison between different seasons and optimization techniques, offering deeper insights into the relationship between seasonal variations and renewable energy management. The results provide a valuable understanding of how each optimization algorithm performs under specific seasonal constraints, enabling us to identify which algorithms are most effective at managing energy resources under environmental conditions. By examining the outcomes of each test case across all four quarters, we gain a clear perspective on how resource allocation strategies can be fine-tuned to maximize efficiency and minimize energy deficits throughout the year.

Test Case 1

Solar Energy Model Inputs:
Wind Speed: 3.6 m/s Sunshine: 42 hours
Air Pressure: 90 kPa Radiation: 319 W/m^2
Air Temperature: 3.8°C Relative Air Humidity: 68%
Month: March Day: 4
Hour: 13
Wind Energy Model Inputs:
Wind Speed (m/s): 3.6 Theoretical Power (KWh): 53.12
Wind Direction (°): 340 Month: March
Day: 4 Hour: 13
Energy Requirement:
Total Energy Requirement: 2000 kWh

The optimal resource allocation for Quarter 1 as seen in Figure 13(a),13(b),13(c), and Table 3 achieved through various optimization techniques. The energy demand is 2000kWh which must be satisfied using hybrid renewable energy sources. Using Particle Swarm Optimization (PSO) algorithm entire energy demand is being fulfilled using wind power without any deficit. Grey Wolf Optimizer allocates 782.62kWh using solar and 1217.38 kWh using wind power. There is no deficit hence it is a optimal solution. Lightning Search Algorithm helps us to achieve extra energy 0.52 kWh as it allocates 1655.39 kWh using wind power and 345.13 kWh using solar power. According to seasonal variations seen in Figure 1 we know that in quarter 1 Wind power is more than solar hence the allocations are optimal. Out of the three-optimization methods Lightning Search is giving a bit of extra energy along with decent amount of contributions from both energy sources, hence mitigating the imbalance cost between the renewable energy sources.

Table 3. Comparison of optimal resource allocation for quarter 1

Parameter	Values		
	With PSO	*With GWO*	*With Lightning Search Optimization*
Solar Power Generated (kWh)	2000	1219.36	1495.66
Wind Power Generated (kWh)	0.00	780.64	502.54
Total Power Generated (kWh)	2000	2000	1998.20
Energy Requirement (kWh)	2000	2000	2000
Deficit (kWh)	0.00	0.00	1.80

Figure 13. (a) Optimized allocation for quarter 1by PSO, (b) Optimized Allocation for Quarter 1 by GWO, (c) Optimized Allocation for Quarter 1 by LSO

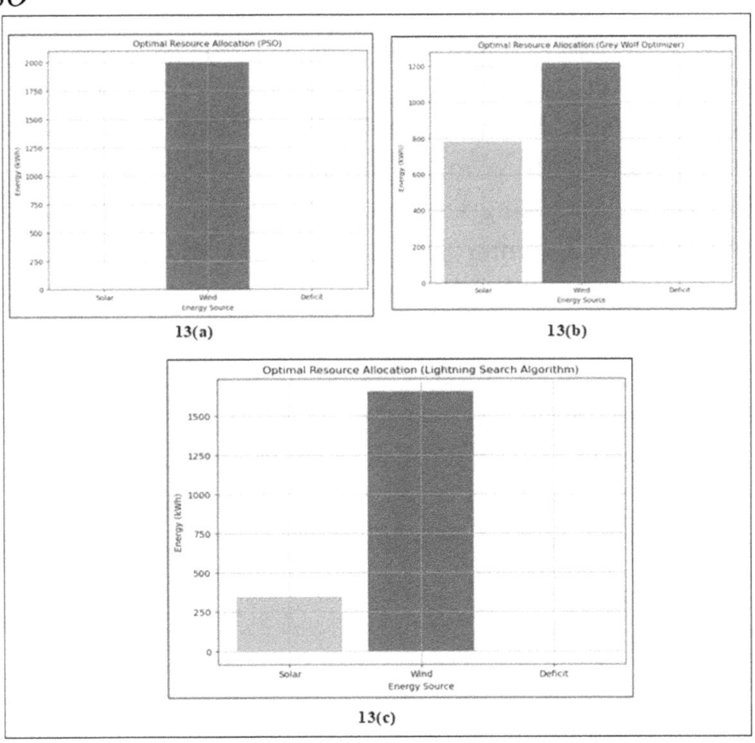

Test Case 2

Solar Energy Model Inputs:
Wind Speed: 2.6 m/s Sunshine: 55 hours
Air Pressure: 1010 hPa Radiation: 508 W/m^2
Air Temperature: 16°C Relative Air Humidity: 50%
Month: April Day: 2
Hour: 15
Wind Energy Model Inputs:
Wind Speed (m/s): 2.6 Theoretical Power (KWh): 230
Wind Direction (°): 240 Month: April
Day: 2 Hour: 15
Energy Requirement:
Total Energy Requirement: 2000 kWh

The optimal resource allocation for Quarter 2 as seen in Figure 14(a),14(b),14(c), and Table 4 achieved through various optimization techniques. The energy demand is 2000kWh which must be satisfied using hybrid renewable energy sources. Using Particle Swarm Optimization (PSO) algorithm entire energy demand is being fulfilled using solar power without any deficit. Grey Wolf Optimizer allocates 1452.86 kWh using solar and 547.14 kWh using wind power. There is no deficit hence it is a optimal solution. Lightning Search Algorithm allocates 1501.55 kWh using wind power and 497.11 kWh using solar power, along with minimum deficit of 1.34 kWh. According to seasonal variations seen in Figure 1 we know that in quarter 2 Solar power is more than Wind Power hence the allocations are optimal. Out of the three-optimization methods Grey Wolf Optimizer gives best allocation with zero deficit along with decent amount of contributions from both energy sources, hence mitigating the imbalance cost between the renewable energy sources.

Table 4. Comparison of optimal resource allocation for quarter 2

Parameter	**Values**		
	With PSO	*With GWO*	*With Lightning Search Optimization*
Solar Power Generated (kWh)	2000	1452.86	1501.55
Wind Power Generated (kWh)	0.00	547.14	497.11
Total Power Generated (kWh)	2000	2000	1998.66
Energy Requirement (kWh)	2000	2000	2000
Deficit (kWh)	0.00	0.00	1.34

Figure 14. (a) Optimized allocation for quarter 2 by PSO, (b) Optimized Allocation for Quarter 2 by GWO, (c) Optimized Allocation for Quarter 2 by LSO

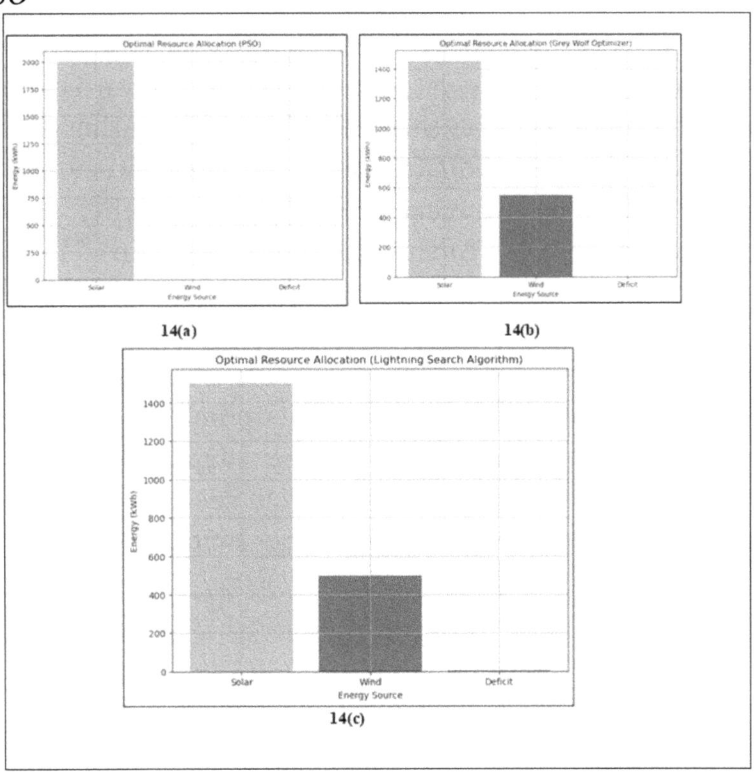

Test Case 3

Solar Energy Model Inputs:
Wind Speed: 2.6 m/s Sunshine: 1 hour
Air Pressure: 1010 hPa Radiation: 240 W/m^2
Air Temperature: 16°C Relative Air Humidity: 46%
Month: July Day: 3
Hour: 11
Wind Energy Model Inputs:
Wind Speed (m/s): 2.6 Theoretical Power (KWh): 160
Wind Direction (°): 260 Month: July
Day: 3 Hour: 11
Energy Requirement:
Total Energy Requirement: 2000 kWh

The optimal resource allocation for Quarter 3 as seen in Figure 15(a),15(b),15(c), and in Table 5 achieved through various optimization techniques. The energy demand is 2000kWh which must be satisfied using hybrid renewable energy sources. Using Particle Swarm Optimization (PSO) algorithm entire energy demand is being fulfilled using wind power without any deficit. Grey Wolf Optimizer allocates 340.69 kWh using solar and 1659.31 kWh using wind power. There is no deficit hence it is a optimal solution. Lightning Search Algorithm allocates 461.75 kWh using solar power and 1537.63 kWh using wind power, along with minimum deficit of 0.62 kWh. According to seasonal variations seen in Figure 1 we know that in quarter 3 Wind Power is more than Solar Power hence the allocations are optimal. Out of the three-optimization methods Grey Wolf Optimizer gives best allocation with zero deficit along with decent amount of contributions from both energy sources, hence mitigating the imbalance cost between the renewable energy sources.

Table 5. Comparison of optimal resource allocation for quarter 3

Parameter	Values		
	With PSO	*With GWO*	*With Lightning Search Optimization*
Solar Power Generated (kWh)	2000	340.69	461.75
Wind Power Generated (kWh)	0.00	1659.31	1537.63
Total Power Generated (kWh)	2000	2000	1999.38
Energy Requirement (kWh)	2000	2000	2000
Deficit (kWh)	0.00	0.00	0.62

Figure 15. (a) Optimized allocation for quarter 3 by PSO, (b) Optimized Allocation for Quarter 3 by GWO, (c) Optimized Allocation for Quarter 3 by LSO

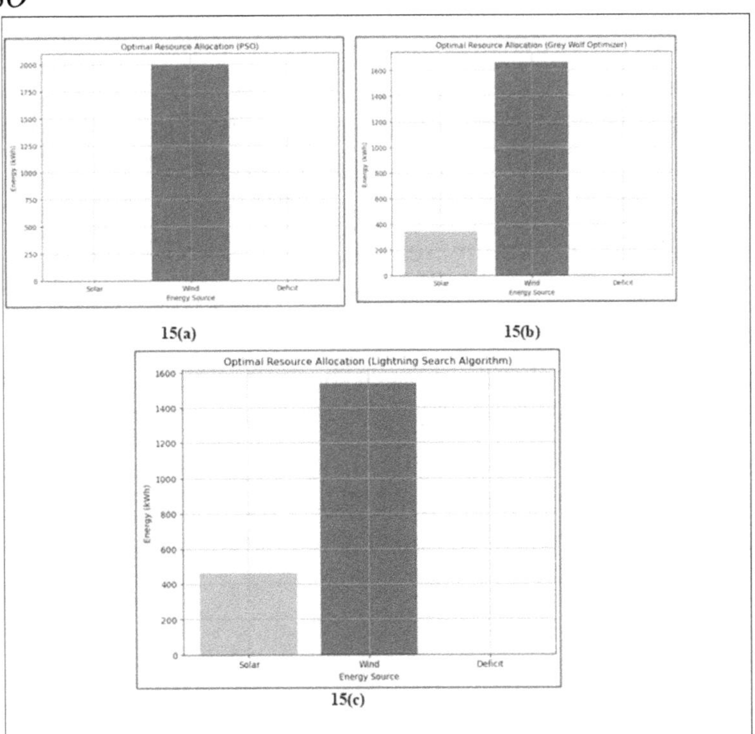

Test Case 4

Solar Energy Model Inputs:
Wind Speed: 1.5 m/s Sunshine: 1 hour
Air Pressure: 1000 hPa Radiation: 90 W/m^2
Air Temperature: 5°C Relative Air Humidity: 94%
Month: October Day: 11
Hour: 12
Wind Energy Model Inputs:
Wind Speed (m/s): 1.5 Theoretical Power (KWh): 2000
Wind Direction (°): 28 Month: October
Day: 11 Hour: 12
Energy Requirement:
Total Energy Requirement: 2000 kWh

The optimal resource allocation for Quarter 4 as seen in Figure 16(a),16(b),16(c), and in Table 6 achieved through various optimization techniques. The energy demand is 2000kWh which must be satisfied using hybrid renewable energy sources. Using Particle Swarm Optimization (PSO) algorithm entire energy demand is being fulfilled using wind power without any deficit. Grey Wolf Optimizer allocates 212.04 kWh using solar and 1787.96 kWh using wind power. There is no deficit hence it is an optimal solution. Lightning Search Algorithm allocates 765.66 kWh using solar power and 1242.87 kWh using wind power, along with extra energy of 8.34 kWh. According to seasonal variations seen in Figure 1 we know that in quarter 4 Wind Power is more than Solar Power hence the allocations are optimal. Out of the three-optimization methods Lightning Search Algorithm shows best result as it leaves extra energy along with decent amount of contributions from both energy sources, hence mitigating the imbalance cost between the renewable energy sources.

Table 6. Comparison of optimal resource allocation for quarter 4

Parameter	**Values**		
	With PSO	*With GWO*	*With Lightning Search Optimization*
Solar Power Generated (kWh)	2000	212.04	765.66
Wind Power Generated (kWh)	0.00	1787.96	1242.87
Total Power Generated (kWh)	2000	2000	2008.54
Energy Requirement (kWh)	2000	2000	2000
Deficit (kWh)	0.00	0.00	-8.54

Figure 16. (a) Optimized allocation for quarter 4 by PSO, (b) Optimized Allocation for Quarter 4 by GWO, (c) Optimized Allocation for Quarter 4 by LSO

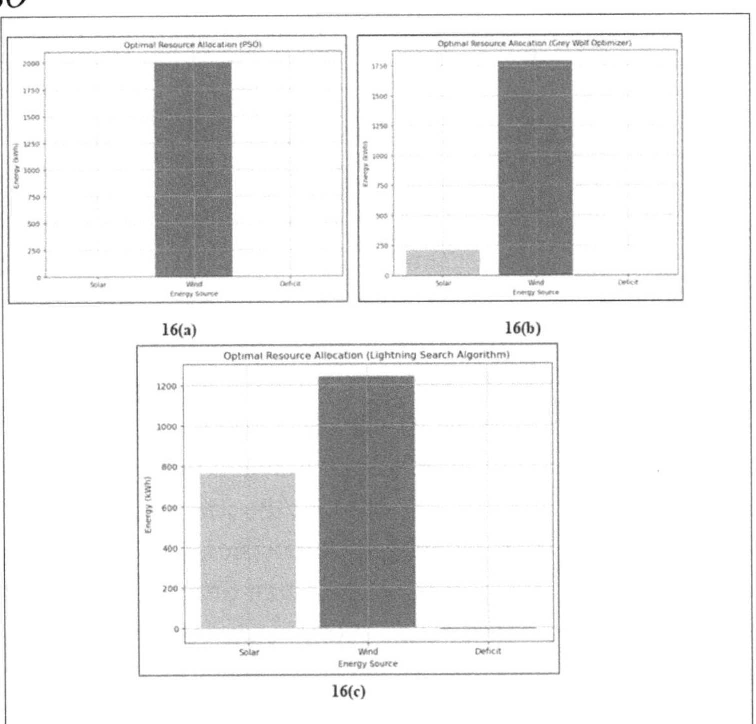

Hybrid renewable energy systems provide environmental and economic benefits but require high initial investment. While installation costs are significant, long-term savings from lower maintenance and stable energy prices make them financially viable. Incentives like subsidies, tax credits, and PPPs can ease the financial burden, while smart energy management optimizes cost efficiency. Future research should assess real-world case studies, while policies must lower capital costs through green bonds and carbon credits. User adoption remains a challenge, requiring coordinated efforts to address policy barriers, public awareness, and integration issues through financial incentives and simplified grid access.

The experimental results demonstrate the effectiveness of the proposed hybrid energy allocation model across different seasonal conditions. Based on these findings, the concluding section summarizes key takeaways, discusses practical implications, and highlights potential areas for future research.

V. CONCLUSION

The Seasonal Optimal Renewable Energy Allocation Model (SOREAM) has effectively tackled the variability challenges of renewable energy sources such as solar and wind. Throughout its development and application phases, SOREAM utilized weighted ensembled machine learning algorithms and optimization techniques to adjust to environmental changes and optimize hybrid renewable energy resource allocation. The high accuracies achieved in both solar and wind energy predictions across all quarters demonstrate the robustness and reliability of SOREAM's modelling techniques, significantly enhancing renewable resource management, and contributing to global sustainability efforts. Throughout the four quarters of the year, SOREAM has shown its robustness by consistently optimizing energy allocation. However, it is important to note that different algorithms have proven to be more effective depending on the specific quarter and its associated conditions. In the case of Quarter 1, for example, the Lightning Search Algorithm emerged as the most efficient in handling the energy distribution. This algorithm not only optimally allocated energy between solar and wind sources but also managed to generate some extra energy, providing an important buffer for times when energy demand spikes unexpectedly.

Moving into Quarter 2, SOREAM's optimization techniques shifted slightly, with the Grey Wolf Optimizer taking the lead as the most effective algorithm. The Grey Wolf Optimizer, inspired by the social dynamics of wolf packs during hunting, was able to balance the energy load between solar and wind sources more effectively. The result was a more balanced energy distribution that left no deficits, which is critical in mitigating potential high-cost scenarios that could arise from energy shortages or imbalanced supply.

The Grey Wolf Optimizer continued to shine in Quarter 3 as well. Once again, the algorithm managed to distribute energy between solar and wind sources in a way that ensured no deficits were left unaddressed. By balancing the energy load, the algorithm minimized the possibility of cost spikes due to sudden shortages in energy production, which could otherwise force reliance on more expensive, non-renewable energy sources. This performance highlights the versatility and effectiveness of the Grey Wolf Optimizer, especially during quarters where environmental conditions make energy production particularly unpredictable.

By the time Quarter 4 arrived, SOREAM once again adapted its approach, and the Lightning Search Algorithm reclaimed its position as the most effective optimization technique. In this period, the algorithm demonstrated its ability to allocate energy efficiently between solar and wind sources, ensuring an optimal distribution that not only met the energy demand but also generated extra energy. This surplus energy is particularly useful in managing unexpected energy consumption spikes that often occur during colder months when heating demand increases, or during periods of adverse weather conditions that affect both solar and wind energy production.

While this study has successfully optimized renewable energy allocation through machine learning and optimization techniques, there remain several avenues for further exploration. The next section outlines future research directions, focusing on expanding the model's applicability and enhancing real-time decision-making in hybrid energy systems.

VI. FUTURE WORK

While SOREAM's achievements in optimizing solar and wind energy allocation are impressive, the future of the model looks even more promising. Plans for future enhancements aim to expand SOREAM's scope by integrating additional renewable energy sources into its framework. Currently focused on solar and wind, the model will soon incorporate other forms of renewable energy, such as hydroelectric power, geothermal energy, and biomass. This expansion will transform SOREAM into a more comprehensive energy management system, capable of handling a broader array of resources, each with its own unique production characteristics and challenges. The integration of hydroelectric energy, for example, could provide a more stable and consistent source of power to complement the intermittent nature of solar and wind, while geothermal and biomass energy could further diversify the system's energy portfolio. Another critical area of development for SOREAM is the enhancement of its real-time data processing capabilities. As the renewable energy sector continues to evolve, there is an increasing need for systems that can quickly adjust energy distribution in response to immediate environmental changes. By improving its ability to process real-time data, SOREAM will become even more responsive, allowing energy managers to make more informed decisions on energy allocation in real time. This capability will be especially useful during extreme weather events or other situations that cause sudden fluctuations in energy availability or demand.

SOREAM will be able to tailor its energy allocation strategies to the specific climatic conditions and renewable energy availability of different areas. For instance, regions with higher solar exposure might benefit more from solar energy optimization, while wind-rich areas could see a greater focus on wind energy. In addition to expanding its energy sources and geographic reach, future enhancements to SOREAM will also include the development of an advanced user interface and decision-support tools. By fostering informed decision-making, these enhancements will promote the broader adoption of renewable energy systems and ensure that stakeholders can make the most of SOREAM's powerful capabilities.

Ultimately, SOREAM's ongoing development and future enhancements underscore its mission to support sustainable energy use on a global scale SOREAM is poised to play an increasingly important role in global sustainability efforts. Its contributions to reducing reliance on non-renewable energy, minimizing energy costs, and ensuring a stable energy supply will help advance the transition to a cleaner, more sustainable energy future. Integrating hybrid energy systems into urban infrastructure presents several challenges despite advancements in renewable energy optimization. Compatibility issues with aging power grids, regulatory constraints, and the substantial costs associated with upgrading infrastructure for real-time energy distribution remain major obstacles.

REFERENCES

Abdolrasol, M. G., Mohamed, R., Hannan, M. A., Al-Shetwi, A. Q., Mansor, M., & Blaabjerg, F. (2021). Artificial neural networkbased particle swarm optimization for microgrid optimal energy scheduling. *IEEE Transactions on Power Electronics*, *36*(11), 12151–12157. DOI: 10.1109/TPEL.2021.3074964

Ammari, C., Belatrache, D., Touhami, B., & Makhloufi, S. (2022). Sizing, optimization, control and energy management of hybrid renewable energy system—A review. *Energy and Built Environment*, *3*(4), 399–411. DOI: 10.1016/j.enbenv.2021.04.002

Barakat, S., Ibrahim, H., & Elbaset, A. A. (2020). Multi-objective optimization of grid-connected PV-wind hybrid system considering reliability, cost, and environmental aspects. *Sustainable Cities and Society*, *60*, 102178. DOI: 10.1016/j.scs.2020.102178

Federal Ministry for the Environment, Nature Conservation, and Nuclear Safety. (2020). The German Government's Climate Action Programme 2030.

Gabbar, H. A., Abdussami, M. R., & Adham, M. I. (2020). Optimal planning of nuclear-renewable micro-hybrid energy system by particle swarm optimization. *IEEE Access : Practical Innovations, Open Solutions*, *8*, 181049–181073. DOI: 10.1109/ACCESS.2020.3027524

Ha, M. P., Nazari-Heris, M., Mohammadi-Ivatloo, B., & Seyedi, H. (2020). A hybrid genetic particle swarm optimization for distributed generation allocation in power distribution networks. *Energy*, *209*, 118218. DOI: 10.1016/j.energy.2020.118218

Jia, K., Liu, C., Li, S., & Jiang, D. (2023). Modeling and optimization of a hybrid renewable energy system integrated with gas turbine and energy storage. *Energy Conversion and Management*, *279*, 116763. DOI: 10.1016/j.enconman.2023.116763

Mahesh, A., & Sandhu, K. S. (2020). A genetic algorithm based improved optimal sizing strategy for solar-wind-battery hybrid system using energy filter algorithm. *Frontiers in Energy*, *14*(1), 139–151. DOI: 10.1007/s11708-017-0484-4

National Development and Reform Commission. (2021). The 14th Five-Year Plan for Economic and Social Development of the People's Republic of China and the Long-Range Objectives Through the Year 2035.

Roy, P., He, J., Zhao, T., & Singh, Y. V. (2022). Recent advances of wind-solar hybrid renewable energy systems for power generation: A review. *IEEE Open Journal of the Industrial Electronics Society*, *3*, 81–104. DOI: 10.1109/OJIES.2022.3144093

Suresh, V., Muralidhar, M., & Kiranmayi, R. (2020). Modelling and optimization of an off-grid hybrid renewable energy system for electrification in a rural area. *Energy Reports*, *6*, 594–604. DOI: 10.1016/j.egyr.2020.01.013

U.S. Energy Information Administration. (2022). Monthly Energy Review. https://www.eia.gov/totalenergy/data/monthly/

Zhang, Z., Hong, W. C., & Li, J. (2020). Electric load forecasting by hybrid self-recurrent support vector regression model with variational mode decomposition and improved cuckoo search algorithm. *IEEE Access : Practical Innovations, Open Solutions*, *8*, 14642–14658. DOI: 10.1109/ACCESS.2020.2966712

Chapter 5
Air Sense:
An Integrated Air Quality Monitoring System

Syed Ali Haider Shirazi
https://orcid.org/0009-0003-9796-979X
SEECS, National University of Sciences and Technology, Pakistan

Rafia Mumtaz
SEECS, National University of Sciences and Technology, Pakistan

Khizar Imran
https://orcid.org/0009-0003-2016-6825
SEECS, National University of Sciences and Technology, Pakistan

Umer Amer Khan
https://orcid.org/0009-0008-2424-0304
SEECS, National University of Sciences and Technology, Pakistan

ABSTRACT

Air pollution is a significant public health concern in developing countries like Pakistan due to inadequate monitoring systems, poor enforcement of environmental regulations, and major pollution sources like vehicular emissions and industrial activities. This research project introduces innovative techniques tailored to Pakistani conditions. The project focuses

DOI: 10.4018/979-8-3693-9030-6.ch005

on developing IoT devices with air quality sensors and GPS tracking, deployed on vehicles to monitor areas like markets and highways. Data collected is analyzed using machine learning for real-time air quality forecasting. The results will be displayed on a public website featuring heat maps, pollution level forecasts, and trends over time, aiming to provide accessible and actionable insights.

INTRODUCTION

Air pollution is a worldwide problem, especially in developing countries like Pakistan. Pakistan does not have sufficient resources or structures in place to cope with the dangerous results of air pollutants on the health and fitness of its citizens. Even though the government has made multiple attempts to tackle this problem, there is not a very good air quality monitoring system in place that can help the masses.

In Pakistan, urbanization is taking place at a rapid pace and more factories and industries are popping up. This makes the threat of air pollution even worse, urban citizens are more exposed to this threat than others. Also, many corporations do not follow the regulations intended to keep the air clean, which makes matters even worse. So, we must find simple and realistic approaches to monitor air quality. Our venture, "AirSense" is a step in that course.

Pakistan's environmental challenges highlight the pressing need for creative solutions that fit its unique circumstances. Air pollution in Pakistan comes from many sources like vehicles, factories, farms, and even natural events. Because of this mix, air quality varies a lot from one place to another. To really understand and fix the problem, we need to monitor air quality closely in each area and come up with plans that work for each one. Area-wise monitoring of Air Quality is essential to come up with a solution to this fatal challenge.

Considering these challenges, "AirSense," shines as a ray of hope, presenting a fresh perspective on air quality monitoring in Pakistan. At its heart, "AirSense" seeks to introduce a groundbreaking method: monitoring air quality field by field. This innovative approach goes beyond the usual methods, giving us a deeper insight into how air quality changes across the country. This approach emphasizes high-density Air Quality data collection.

At the heart of our project lies the creation of sophisticated Internet of Things (IoT) devices tailored for monitoring air quality in real-world settings. These devices boast cutting-edge air quality sensors and GPS trackers, carefully integrated to ensure precise data collection. Strategically positioned on vehicles, they traverse through bustling markets, industrial zones, and major highways, providing a comprehensive snapshot of air quality dynamics. This approach allows us to capture pollution in real time, painting a detailed picture of its distribution across different times and locations. Through these mobile devices, we aim to gather a rich dataset, empowering us to unravel the complexities of air pollution patterns and inform effective interventions for a cleaner, healthier environment.

Moreover, "AirSense" strives to employ advanced data analytics methods, including machine learning algorithms, to manage the extensive datasets gathered and generate actionable insights. By forecasting trends in air quality and identifying regions with elevated pollution levels, our project equips stakeholders with valuable knowledge to inform decision-making processes. This empowers them to enact targeted interventions aimed at improving air quality and safeguarding public health.

The upcoming sections focus on the design and setup of the smart devices, how all the data was gathered and analyzed, and the creation of a website that anyone can use to check air quality. The focus of this research work is to make a difference and help make Pakistan a cleaner, healthier place for everyone.

LITERATURE REVIEW

This section includes the research work that has been carried out in the past years to determine air quality using state-of-the-art technology and IoT devices. Air quality prediction and analysis have been addressed by researchers using advanced machine learning algorithms and various other techniques.

Open Sense

In 2014, the Open Sense project was deployed in the cities of Switzerland and Zurich by deploying mobile sensing nodes consisting of low-cost sensors on trams and buses. The mobile sensing nodes collected data for ultrafine particles (UFPs) for more than two years and based on the data land-use regression models were trained to make maps with a high spatial resolution of 100 m × 100 m (Hasenfratz et al., 2014). To improve the model, past data was incorporated as well, reducing the RMS by 26%. This project helped epidemiologists to get useful insights into the effects of UFPs on human health.

City-Sense-MOB

In 2015, the City-Sense-Mob project in Oslo used buses and electrical bicycles to monitor air quality on a road level (Castell et al., 2015). In Oslo there is a wide range of stationary nodes, however, these nodes do not provide personalized and real-time data to the citizens. The data collected from this project was accessible to the authorities as well in the form of detailed air quality maps. The City-Sense-Mob project also emphasized the use of low-cost sensors to collect mobile air quality data. Additionally, this project aims to develop various social media platforms to promote communication between users, stakeholders, and government authorities.

City Scanner

In 2018, a general-purpose portable sensing platform called City Scanner was deployed in Cambridge (Anjomshoaa et al., 2018). This portable sensing platform was attached to garbage trucks, in a way the vehicle is not affected by this device. This approach was used as proof of concept and data for over 8 months was collected. Government-owned vehicles like the Garbage truck are selected for mobile data collection because they have a predefined route and fixed timetable. Apart from measuring gases, this project is also capable of determining other environmental indicators as well such as thermal flux. The acquired data empowers municipal and law-making authorities to introduce valid policies to tackle the problem of air quality. The following table compares different environmental monitoring platforms (Fekih et al., 2020, p. 4):

Table 1. Comparisons of different environmental monitoring platforms

Projects	Fixed/ mobile	Measured parameters	Sampling Frequency	Local Storage	Communication Technology	Energy consumption
Castell et al.	Mobile	NO2, NO, CO, SO2, O3, CO2, temperature and relative humidity	30 sec	No	Bluetooth	104 to 270 mA
Airsense	Mobile	PM2.5, temperature and relative humidity	3 sec	Yes	Bluetooth	104 to 270 mA
City Scanner	Mobile	Temperature, humidity, and particulate matter	3 sec	Yes	WIFI	104 to 270 mA
UrPolSens	Fixed	Temperature, humidity and NO2	1 sec	Yes	LoRa / Cellular	18 mA
OpenSense	Mobile	Temperature, humidity, O3, CO, NO2 and particulate matter	1 sec	Yes	WIFI / Cellular	Permanently plugged
Lombardo et al	Fixed	Temperature and relative humidity	15 min	Yes	BLE	20 mA
Ferdoush and Li	Fixed	Temperature and relative humidity	35 min	No	Zigbee	20 mA

Volunteer Work for air Quality Data Collection

Across the world, various methods have been deployed to collect Air Quality data. While the above air monitoring systems use VSN (vehicular sensor networks) to collect data, the use of public or volunteers to collect data is quite effective as well. In Malaysia (2020), IoT devices to monitor AQI were distributed among the general public, each of them acting as a mobile monitoring node (Fekih et al., 2020). The device collected data with the help of air quality sensors and transferred it to a web server via WIFI for collection. This resulted in high-density and resolution data for the specific data. Similarly, in Ho Chi Minh City (2020), a dataset was collected using a volunteer as well because the global AQI from remote stations had a very low resolution (Fekih et al., 2020).

AQI Prediction by Machine Learning Techniques in Different Countries

In 2011, Anikender Kumar, and Pramila Goyal in Delhi forecasted the daily AQI using Principle Component Regression (PCR) and Multiple Linear Regression techniques (Patil et al., 2020). The data record for 2000-2005, along with the meteorological parameters were used to predict the daily AQI for 2006 and then the predicted values were compared with the actual ones using multiple linear regression. The PCR gave the most accurate results for predicting AQI during winters, compared with other seasons of the year.

In 2019, Huixiang Liu predicted AQI for two Beijing and Italian cities using Support Vector Regression (SVR) and Random Forest Regression (RFR) (Patil et al., 2020). For the Beijing city, the dataset for the period of December 2013 to August 2018 collected by the Beijing Municipal Environmental Centre was used to forecast the AQI.

The Italian compromised of 9358 instances, collected between March 2004 to February 2005, containing hourly concentrations of CO, Non-methane Hydrocarbons, Benzene, NOx, and NO2. In Italy, more, work was done on predicting the oxides of nitrogen.

In 2019, Heidar Malki in Iran forecasted the predicted values of common air pollutants such as NO2, SO2, PM10, PM2.5, CO, and O3 (Patil et al., 2020). Four air quality monitoring stations: Naderi, Havashenasi, MohiteZist, and Behdasht in Ahvaz, the most polluted city in Iran were targeted. Artificial neural networks (ANN) machine learning algorithm was implemented to predict hourly air pollutant concentrations and AQI for 1 year between August 2009 and 2010.

In 2018, Nidhi Sharma and her team conducted an extensive analysis of air pollutant data spanning from 2009 to 2017 in Delhi, India (Patil et al., 2020). Using data analytics and time series regression forecasting techniques, they made predictions of levels of various pollutants including Sulfur Dioxide (SO2), Nitrogen Dioxide (NO2), Suspended Particulate

Matter (PM), Ozone (O3), Carbon Monoxide (CO), and Benzene based on historical records. This study revolved around the monitoring stations in AnandVihar and Shadipur in Delhi. The following table shows comparison among different models for estimating AQI values (Duong et al., 2021, p. 12):

Table 2. The comparison among different models for estimating AQI values on the "MNR-HCM II" data set

	SENSOR RAW			SENSOR + TL			SENSOR + TLPW		
Model	**RMSE**	**MAE**	**RÂ^{2}**	**RMSE**	**MAE**	**RÂ^{2}**	**RMSE**	**MAE**	**RÂ^{2}**
CatBoost	46.67	34.3	0.66	36.47	25.2	0.79	18.59	12.18	0.95
Extra Trees	45.03	32.98	0.69	38.89	27.19	0.77	18.51	12.6	0.95
Linear Regression	70.67	53.3	0.23	68.36	51.71	0.28	56.61	43.32	0.5
Random Forest	45.14	31.18	0.68	37.33	25.45	0.78	17.59	11.97	0.95
SVM	53.22	37.32	0.56	45.49	31.73	0.68	24.5	15.74	0.91
XGBoost	50.05	30.74	0.61	38.8	22.39	0.77	18.82	10.21	0.95
Stacking	45.28	32.75	0.68	36.93	24.76	0.79	17.24	11.23	0.95

RESEARCH GAP

Air quality monitoring systems are essential tools for evaluating and addressing environmental pollution, offering critical insights into the state of our atmosphere and enabling effective mitigation strategies. However, these systems face several limitations that reduce their overall effectiveness, underscoring the need for innovation and refinement. Addressing these shortcomings is vital to advance the development of more comprehensive, accurate, and sustainable monitoring methodologies. Several challenges associated with current air quality monitoring systems merit detailed examination, particularly in the areas of geographic coverage, data accuracy, long-term sustainability, and mobility.

Limited Geographic Coverage

One of the most significant challenges facing IoT-based air quality monitoring systems is their limited geographic coverage. These systems are typically deployed in specific locations, where they provide localized data within a restricted radius. While this data is valuable for understanding air quality in particular areas, it is insufficient for achieving a comprehensive understanding of air quality over larger regions. This limitation often results in these systems being used primarily as proof-of-concept installations, rather than being scaled up to monitor vast areas comprehensively. For larger-scale monitoring, satellite imaging is frequently considered a viable alternative. Satellite systems excel in providing extensive spatial data, allowing them to capture a broader picture of air quality across large geographical areas. However, satellite-based monitoring is not without its flaws. These systems often suffer from lower temporal resolution, which reduces their ability to provide frequent updates. Additionally, satellites struggle to accurately measure ground-level pollutant concentrations, which are critical for assessing the air quality that people directly experience. This underscores a crucial research gap: the need to integrate localized IoT-based monitoring systems with satellite data. Such integration could offer a powerful solution by combining the granularity and precision of ground-based sensors with the extensive spatial coverage provided by satellites, striking a balance between detail and scope.

Data Accuracy and Sensor Calibration

Data accuracy is another critical issue that hinders the effectiveness of air quality monitoring systems. Most current systems rely on low-cost sensors for data collection, which makes them accessible and economically viable. However, these sensors frequently encounter significant challenges related to accuracy. One major issue is that many of these low-cost sensors lack proper calibration. Without calibration to align with established pollutant concentration standards, the data produced by these sensors is often biased and unreliable. This lack of accuracy makes it difficult to derive meaningful insights from the data or to use it for informed decision-making and policy formulation. Furthermore, environmental factors such as temperature, humidity, and the presence of other pollutants can further compromise the accuracy of sensor readings. This is particularly problematic in regions with highly variable environmental conditions, where such interference can lead to inconsistent or erroneous data. Addressing these data accuracy challenges requires the development of cost-effective yet highly accurate sensors, alongside robust calibration methodologies. Emerging technologies such as machine learning could play a pivotal role in this context. By using advanced algorithms, machine learning systems can identify and correct biases in sensor data in real time, significantly improving the reliability of air quality measurements.

Long-Term Sustainability

Long-term sustainability is another pressing concern for air quality monitoring systems. These systems consist of various components, including sensors, power sources, device bodies, and communication and processing equipment. Over time, these components are subject to wear and tear, technical failures, and environmental stressors, all of which can compromise the longevity and reliability of the systems. One of the primary challenges in this regard is the need for regular maintenance. Ensuring accurate and reliable readings requires routine upkeep, but frequent maintenance can significantly increase operational costs. This poses a barrier to scaling up these systems for widespread deployment. Another challenge lies in maintaining a consistent power supply. Many monitoring systems rely on batteries or solar panels, which can degrade over time, particularly in harsh environmental conditions. Without a reliable power source, the systems cannot function continuously, reducing their effectiveness. Additionally, the physical durability of the systems is a critical factor. The device bodies and sensors must be designed to withstand extreme weather conditions, physical damage, and even vandalism. Achieving long-term sustainability for these systems will require innovative approaches, including the development of self-healing materials, energy-efficient designs, and automated maintenance protocols. Such advancements could significantly enhance the durability and cost-effectiveness of air quality monitoring systems, making them more feasible for widespread use.

Mobility and Connectivity

Mobility presents both an opportunity and a challenge for air quality monitoring systems. Integrating these systems with mobile platforms, such as vehicles, offers the potential to collect data over much larger areas. This capability is particularly valuable for monitoring air quality in regions that are not easily accessible by stationary systems. However, the mobility of these systems introduces several technical and logistical challenges. One significant issue is maintaining stable connectivity between the mobile monitoring system and the central server. In densely populated urban areas, network congestion can disrupt communication, while in rural areas, limited infrastructure can make connectivity unreliable. Such disruptions can lead to data loss or inconsistencies, undermining the reliability of the monitoring efforts. Another challenge is the integration of large volumes of data generated by mobile systems. Data collected from multiple locations must be combined into a cohesive framework for analysis and visualization, which requires advanced algorithms and substantial computational resources. Additionally, environmental factors associated with mobility, such as noise and vibrations caused by vehicle motion, can affect sensor readings. Variations in vehicle speed and route can also result in uneven data coverage, making it difficult to obtain a consistent and representative picture of air quality. Overcoming these challenges will require further research and development, particularly in areas such as data integration techniques and sensor technologies that are resilient to motion-related interference.

PROBLEM DEFINITION

Pakistan, the world's fifth most populous nation, grapples with significant environmental challenges that give rise to potential health hazards. As a developing country with limited infrastructure for comprehensive air quality monitoring and management, Pakistan faces obstacles in addressing these issues effectively. While ongoing efforts are in place to monitor air quality, the available data lacks regional specificity. Moreover, the absence of a user-friendly interface impedes the analysis and interpretation of air quality data, making it difficult to identify patterns and correlations across different geographical areas.

In response to these challenges, existing efforts to monitor air quality are underway, albeit with limitations. One notable drawback is the lack of regional specificity in the available data, which hampers our ability to accurately assess the extent of air pollution across different geographical areas. This deficiency not only impedes targeted interventions but also undermines the formulation of evidence-based policies aimed at addressing specific pollution hotspots and safeguarding vulnerable communities.

Moreover, the absence of a user-friendly interface compounds the problem by hindering the analysis and interpretation of air quality data. Without intuitive tools for data visualization and analysis, stakeholders struggle to identify emerging patterns and correlations, thereby limiting the effectiveness of decision-making processes and interventions.

To overcome these challenges, this project endeavors to pioneer innovative solutions tailored to Pakistan's unique context. By deploying a network of advanced IoT devices equipped with state-of-the-art sensors, this research work aims to enhance data resolution and coverage, thereby filling critical gaps in regional air quality monitoring. Additionally, this project places a strong emphasis on developing a user-friendly interface for data visualization and analysis, empowering stakeholders to make informed decisions and implement targeted interventions to improve air quality and protect public health. Through collaboration, innovation, and a steadfast commitment to our mission, this project strives to catalyze positive change and pave the way for a cleaner, healthier future for Pakistan.

PROPOSED SOLUTION

This research project has developed a comprehensive solution, organized into four key steps.

Device Creation

The first step involves designing and fabricating a cutting-edge device equipped with air-quality sensors capable of accurately collecting data while concurrently retrieving GPS coordinates for location tracking.

Data Validation

After the creation of the device, the next crucial step involves subjecting the gathered air quality data to rigorous testing and validation procedures. This meticulous process ensures that the collected data meets the most stringent standards of accuracy and reliability, laying a solid foundation for the subsequent phases of our analysis. Through exhaustive testing protocols and validation techniques, the integrity of the data is verified, identifying any potential discrepancies or anomalies that may arise. By adhering to these rigorous standards, the study aims to instill confidence in the accuracy and credibility of the findings, ultimately bolstering the effectiveness of our project in addressing air quality challenges in Pakistan.

Field Deployment

In the third phase, the devices will be strategically deployed in specific areas, such as high-traffic highways, to continuously monitor air quality. This extensive dataset, collected from multiple locations, will serve as the basis for implementing advanced deep-learning techniques.

Data Visualization and Prediction

The final step involves presenting the collected data to the public through an accessible website (Kok et al., 2020). This is to generate insightful heatmaps that provide a visual representation of air quality trends. Additionally, machine-learning algorithms are employed to 'nowcast' pollution levels, offering real-time predictions of air quality conditions.

By implementing these four steps, the research study aims to provide valuable insights into air quality, enabling both informed decision-making and public awareness of environmental conditions.

METHODOLOGY

Air Quality IoT Device

In the initial phase of the project methodology, the focus was on developing a portable IoT Air Quality Device tailored for efficient data collection.

Grove - Laser PM Sensor (HM3301)

The Grove - Laser PM2.5 Sensor (HM3301) is a laser dust detection sensor, which is used for real-time detection of particulate matter (PM) in the air. The HM-3301 utilizes fan blades to drive air through the detection chamber which is used as a sample to monitor the dust particles in the air.

The specifications for this device include operating voltage, operating temperature, operating humidity, particle size, range, resolution, stability time, interface, and I2C address. The operating voltage is 3.3V or 5V. The operating temperature ranges from -10 to 60 degrees Celsius. The operating humidity ranges from 10% to 90% RH (non-condensing). The particle size can be 2.5 micrometers, 5 micrometers, or 10 micrometers. The range is 1 to 500 micrograms per cubic meter (effective range) and 1000 micrograms per cubic meter (maximum range). The resolution is 1 microgram per cubic meter for concentration and 1 second per 0.1 liters for counting concentration. The stability time is 30 seconds after power-on. The interface is I2C, and the I2C address is 0x40.

The Laser PM sensor is interfaced with the ESP32 microcontroller using the I2C protocol. This allows the sensor to continuously monitor real-time values of PM2.5, PM5, and PM10. Although the measurements were initially in micrograms per cubic meter (ug/m3), they were converted to parts per million (ppm) by dividing by 1000. To ensure stability, the sampling frequency to 1/30 Hz, allowing the sensor to stabilize effectively.

Grove - Multichannel Gas Sensor V2

Grove - Multichannel Gas Sensor V2 is based on MEMS technology and has 4 measuring units, each of them is sensitive to different gases ((CO), Nitrogen dioxide (NO2), Ethyl alcohol(C2H5CH), Volatile Organic Compounds (VOC)). The sensor has a compact form factor and is suitable for qualitative rather than quantitative measurement.

The multichannel gas sensor module is designed for air quality monitoring. It operates with 3.3V to 5V and can handle temperatures from -10 to 60 degrees Celsius. It works in humidity levels from 10% to 90% RH. It can detect particles of 2.5, 5, or 10 micrometers in size. The range for measuring air quality is from 1 to 500 micrograms per cubic meter, with a maximum of 1000 micrograms per cubic meter. It provides high-resolution measurements and stabilizes within 30 seconds of turning on. It uses the Grove I2C interface and has an address of 0x40. It works with various gas sensors like GM-102B, GM-302B, GM-502B, and GM-702B for comprehensive air quality monitoring.

The Grove - Multichannel Gas Sensor V2 was connected to the ESP32 microcontroller via the I2C protocol, enabling continuous monitoring of CO and NO2 levels. Initially, the sensor provided voltage values, but they were transformed into concentrations in mol/m2 with assistance from the Sentinel 5P satellite.

UBLOX NEO-6M V2 GPS Module

The GPS module is based on the latest Ublox technology to give accurate longitude and latitude values. It includes a built-in 25 x 25mm active GPS antenna with a UART TTL socket.

It is interfaced with the ESP32 using its UART (Universal Asynchronous Receiver-Transmitter) interface, utilizing the TTL RX and TX pins. It is used to capture accurate longitude and latitude values, crucial for pinpointing the location of recorded data on heatmaps.

ESP32 Microcontroller

Esp32 are low-cost system-on-chip microcontrollers with integrated WIFI and Bluetooth module. The ESP32 is the brain of the air quality monitoring device and acts as the central processing unit, integrating all connected sensors. This economical system-on-chip solution enables real-time data collection and transmission.

5000 mAh 3.7V Lipo Battery and Power Bank Module

The Lipo Battery is a rechargeable lithium-ion battery that uses polymer electrolyte technology. The power bank module allows easy recharging of the device on the go. The 5000mAh 3.7V LiPo battery and power bank module provide a portable power solution for the Air Quality IoT device (Zhang & Liu, 2019). With a high capacity of 5000mAh, this lithium polymer battery ensures extended operation of more than 8 hours without frequent recharging, suitable for in-field deployments. This power circuitry allows the device to be portable, enabling it to function effectively in various environments without any fixed connection to a power source.

DS3231 Real Time Clock (RTC)

The DS3231 is a low-cost, highly accurate Real Time Clock that can maintain hours, minutes, and seconds, as well as, day, month, and year information. Also, it has automatic compensation for leap years and months with fewer than 31 days.

In this project, DS3231 Real-Time Clock (RTC) is integrated to accurately timestamp the data collected by the sensors. The DS3231 provides accurate measurements of hours, minutes, and seconds as well as the dates of the collected data.

SD Card Module Reader and 16 GB Memory Card

The microSD card module communicates using the SPI protocol and stores data in the 16GB memory card. When the device is deployed in the field, the values of air quality are stored in the Memory card in text format. The values are analyzed after the collection is done and transmitted to our website for visualization and processing. The robust storage ensures secure retention of data.

Design of the Device

The body of the device is designed using Blender software. Through innovative design techniques, we've ensured that the design is aerodynamic and optimizes the airflow through its sleek appearance. Once the design is finalized, we utilize 3D printing technology to print the body. The following figures show the design of the device and the actual device in hand:

Figure 1. Design of the device

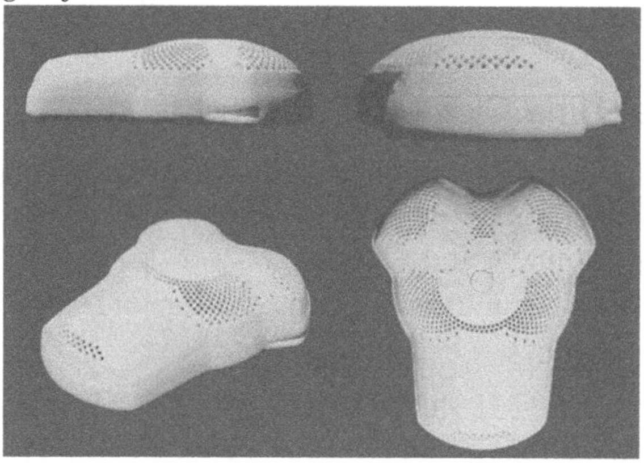

Data Collection

In the second stage of the project outdoor air quality data was collected.

Vehicular Sensing Network (VSN)

For data collection, the Vehicle Sensing Network (VSN) approach is adopted, deploying the device on a vehicle to create a moving node for point-to-point data collection. This decision was motivated by the need for higher-density data compared to stationary nodes.

Imagine this: if we were to rely solely on stationary nodes, we'd gather data only from specific fixed locations, potentially missing out on crucial insights from areas in between. By incorporating a VSN, the device becomes mobile, allowing it to cover a broader geographical area and collect data from various points along the vehicle's route. This approach enhances the density of the data collection, providing a more comprehensive understanding of air quality variations across different regions. The project's target area was the National University of Sciences and Technology (NUST).

Due to limitations, data collection spanned a period of 20 days. At this stage, our primary aim is to present a proof of concept. The data was collected during both daytime and night periods on each day. This protocol allowed to gather information from two distinct timeframes to analyze the trends.

Suction Cups

The device was attached to the roof of the car using suction cups. The device remained fixed at high speeds and abrupt stops, proving this method to be very realistic and practical. The following figure shows the device attached to the vehicle:

Figure 2. Vehicular deployment of device

Data Processing and Visualization

In the third stage of the project, the collected data was processed to extract valuable insights. This involved cleaning the data and setting the ranges to prepare it for visualization. Once processed, the data was transmitted for visualization, allowing users to the information conveniently.

Sentinel 5P

Sentinel 5P satellite, part of the European Union's Copernicus program, was successfully launched on 13 October 2017 from Russia with an objective to perform atmospheric measurements for air quality. Equipped with the state-of-the-art Tropomi (TROPOspheric Monitoring Instrument) sensor, Sentinel 5P is designed to perform high-resolution atmospheric measurements of air quality.

In this project, data from the Sentinel 5P satellite helped to calibrate the readings from the NO2 and CO sensors (Veefkind et al., 2012). The voltage values obtained from the sensors were mapped to the corresponding concentrations in units of mol/m2 with the help of the satellite data. In essence, the satellite data acted as a reference point to validate the readings.

Website for Data Visualization

JavaScript and Node.js are foundational technologies in modern web development. JavaScript, a versatile programming language, is primarily used for creating interactive and dynamic content on websites. It runs directly in the web browser and enables developers to manipulate webpage elements, handle user interactions, and dynamically update content without reloading the page. Its versatility extends beyond the client side, as JavaScript can also be used for server-side programming through platforms like Node.js. Node.js, built on Chrome's V8 JavaScript engine, is a server-side JavaScript runtime environment. It allows developers to write server-side applications using JavaScript, leveraging its event-driven, non-blocking I/O model to handle concurrent connections efficiently. Node.js is well-suited for building scalable, real-time web applications and APIs.

JavaScript and Node.js were utilized to develop the website, leveraging their capabilities to create an interactive and efficient platform for data visualization. Once the data has been processed, it is transmitted to the website for visualization. Air quality heat maps are generated for each gas, providing a high-density point-to-point representation of pollutant concentrations in the monitored area. Additionally, line graphs are utilized to represent daily trends in air quality over time. Offers users a user-friendly interface for visualizing the collected data.

Deploying Machine Learning for Air Quality forecasting

Long Short-Term Memory (LSTM) is a type of recurrent neural network (RNN) architecture specifically designed to capture long-term dependencies in sequential data (Hochreiter & Schmidhuber, 1997). Unlike traditional feedforward neural networks, LSTM networks have feedback connections that enable them to maintain information over long periods, making them well-suited for time series prediction tasks. LSTM units contain a cell state that can preserve information over time steps, allowing them to learn and remember patterns in sequential data. This ability to capture temporal dependencies makes LSTMs particularly effective for forecasting tasks where historical data is crucial for making accurate predictions.

In this project, LSTM neural networks were deployed to forecast air quality values. The input to the LSTM model consists of timestamps, longitude, and latitude data obtained from the GPS module. These features serve as predictors for air quality, capturing both temporal and spatial information. The LSTM model learns from historical air quality data collected by our IoT device and uses this information to predict future air quality values. By incorporating both temporal and spatial features, the LSTM model provides a comprehensive approach to air quality forecasting, enabling to anticipate changes in air quality levels with high accuracy.

DETAILED DESIGN AND ARCHITECTURE

Air Quality Device Design and Architecture

In this section, the details of the of the design and architecture of the air quality monitoring device are discussed. The device incorporates different components interfaced with the ESP32 microcontroller via different communication protocols.

Sensor Interfacing

The system incorporates various sensors that rely on distinct communication protocols to interact with the ESP32 microcontroller. These protocols are selected based on the functionality and data transmission requirements of each sensor. Among the sensors, the Grove-Laser PM Sensor HM3301 and the Grove-Multichannel Gas Sensor V2 both utilize the Inter-Integrated Circuit (I2C) protocol. This protocol is particularly advantageous for devices with relatively low-speed data transfer requirements, allowing multiple components to communicate with the microcontroller using a shared data line and clock line.

The Grove-Laser PM Sensor HM3301 is specifically designed to monitor particulate matter concentrations, such as PM2.5, PM5, and PM10, in real time. These parameters are critical for assessing air quality, as particulate matter can significantly impact respiratory health (Wang et al., 2019). The HM3301 collects continuous measurements and transmits this data to the ESP32 using the I2C protocol. This ensures that the ESP32 receives accurate and timely data for further processing or display.

Similarly, the Grove-Multichannel Gas Sensor V2 is equipped to detect and measure levels of gaseous pollutants, including carbon monoxide (CO) and nitrogen dioxide (NO2). These gases are common air pollutants that pose risks to human health and the environment. Like the HM3301, this sensor employs the I2C protocol to communicate with the ESP32 (Wang & Chen, 2021). By sharing the same protocol, these two sensors simplify the wiring and setup process, enabling the microcontroller to handle data from multiple sources efficiently.

On the other hand, the system also includes an SD Card Module Reader paired with a 16 GB memory card, which uses the Serial Peripheral Interface (SPI) protocol for communication. Unlike I2C, the SPI protocol is designed for faster data transfer rates, making it ideal for storage applications. The SD card module plays a crucial role in the system by providing a reliable and secure means of storing the data collected from the sensors. This is particularly useful for applications that require data logging or long-term environmental monitoring.

The stored data can later be accessed and analyzed to identify patterns, trends, or anomalies in the monitored environment. For instance, by reviewing historical data on particulate matter and gas concentrations, researchers can study the impact of urban development or industrial activity on air quality. Additionally, secure storage ensures that no critical information is lost, even in the event of power failures or communication interruptions between the sensors and the microcontroller.

Veroboard Soldering

To ensure stable and reliable electrical connections, all the connections between the sensors, ESP32 microcontroller, and other components are meticulously soldered onto a Veroboard. This Veroboard serves as the central hub where all the electronic components are interconnected, providing a robust foundation for the functionality of our air quality monitoring device. By soldering the connections onto the Veroboard, the risk of loose connections or signal interference is minimized, which could potentially compromise the accuracy and reliability of the data collection process. Additionally, the Veroboard facilitates ease of maintenance and troubleshooting. The following figures show the connections on the Veroboard:

Figure 3. Device internal circuitry

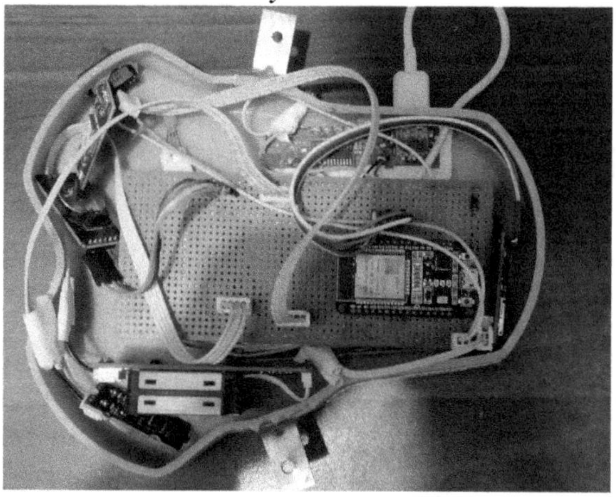

Power Supply

The device is powered by a 5000 mAh 3.7V LiPo battery and TP4056 charging module. This allows the device to operate in the field without a fixed power source. The following figure shows the power circuitry of the device:

Figure 4. Power supply circuitry

Design Considerations

The design of the air quality monitoring device prioritizes both compactness and robustness to meet the demands of real-world deployment scenarios. The device boasts a sleek and ergonomic design, optimizing space efficiency without compromising functionality. Its compact form factor allows for easy transportation and deployment in various environments, whether mounted on vehicles for mobile data collection or installed in stationary monitoring stations.

Furthermore, the device is constructed with robust materials and components, ensuring durability and resilience against harsh environmental conditions. Each component is securely fastened to withstand the rigors of high-speed vehicular movement and abrupt stops. By combining compactness with robustness, our air quality monitoring device offers a versatile solution for accurate and dependable data collection in diverse field conditions.

Design of Data Collection and Processing

Device Deployment on Vehicle (VSN)

The device is deployed on a vehicle to create a Vehicular Sensing Network (VSN) for data collection. The sampling frequency is set to 1/30 seconds. Our target area for data collection is the National University of Sciences and Technology (NUST) campus.

The vehicle follows a predetermined route within the NUST campus:

- Boys Hostel
- C1 Cafeteria
- Main Gymnasium
- SINES/NSTEP Building
- Sports Complex
- Boys Hostel (return point)

Data collection occurs twice a day:

- Evening (4-5 PM)
- Night (10-11 PM)

Data Processing

PM2.5, PM5, and PM10 values, initially measured in micrograms per cubic meter (ug/m3), are converted to parts per million (ppm) by dividing by 1000. The air quality is then categorized with the help of the following table (Kalajdjieski et al., 2020)

Figure 5. PM value chart

AQI Value Of Index	Levels of Health Concern	$PM_{2.5}$ Conc. (μg/m³)	PM_{10} Conc. (μg/m³)	Daily AQI Color	Air Pollution Level
0–50	Good	0–12	0–54	green	Level 1
51–100	Moderate	12.1–35.4	55–154	yellow	Level 2
101–150	Unhealthy for sensitive groups	35.5–55.4	155–254	orange	Level 3
151–200	unhealthy	55.5–150.4	255–354	Red	Level 4
201–300	Very unhealthy	150.5–250.4	355–424	Purple	Level 5
301 and Higher	Hazardous	250.5–Higher	425–Higher	Maroon	Level 6

Air quality index (AQI) values, PM2.5 and PM10 conc. color codes, air pollutant level of health concern.

For CO and NO2 measurements, we leverage data from the Sentinel 5P satellite for mapping voltage values obtained from sensors to concentrations in units of mol/m2. In the target area, we utilize data from the Sentinel 5P satellite, which provides satellite imagery alongside a conversion chart. The following figure shows the CO air quality according to the state-of-the-art Tropomi (TROPOspheric Monitoring Instrument) sensor:

Figure 6. Satellite imagery for CO

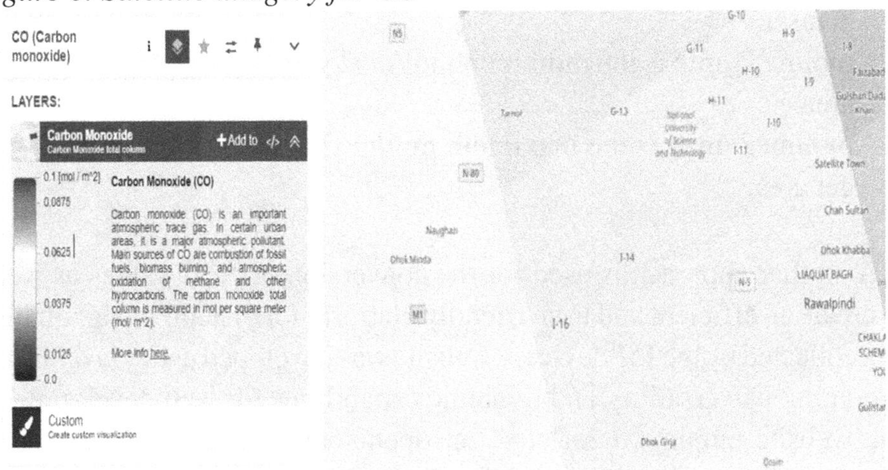

Based on the figure, it's evident that NUST falls within the light blue region, where the mol/m^2 values range between 0.02 and 0.0375. To align our CO voltage levels calculated by the V2 gas sensor with this range, a mapping formula was employed. This formula allows us to convert the voltage readings obtained from the sensor into the corresponding mol/m^2 values observed by the Sentinel 5P satellite.

In the collected dataset, we've determined that the maximum global CO voltage recorded is 0.880 V, while the minimum is 0.258 V. Using this information, along with the mapping formula, we can accurately map our sensor data to the mol/m^2 range depicted in the satellite imagery. The following formula can be utilized:

CO_mol/m^2 = (CO_voltage - CO_min) * (mol/m^2_max - mol/m^2_min) / (CO_max - CO_min) + mol/m^2_min

Where:

- CO_voltage is the measured voltage level of CO.
- CO_mol/m^2 is the corresponding concentration of CO in mol/m^2.
- CO_min is the minimum voltage level of CO observed in the dataset.

- CO_max is the maximum voltage level of CO observed in the dataset.
- mol/m^2_min is the minimum mol/m^2 value observed in the target area.
- mol/m^2_max is the maximum mol/m^2 value observed in the target area.

A similar approach is used for the conversion of NO2 values as well. To create an efficient and user-friendly platform for visualizing air quality data collected by the IoT device, a website was developed using JavaScript, leveraging its versatility and dynamic capabilities for web development. The website employs Leaflet.js, an open-source JavaScript library, to generate interactive heat maps for displaying pollutant concentrations across the NUST campus area. Additionally, APIs were utilized to fetch real-time air quality data and populate the heat maps and line graphs with up-to-date information.

The central feature of the website is the interactive heat maps, which visualize pollutant concentrations across the NUST campus area. Using Leaflet.js, we plot color-coded markers on the map to represent air quality levels, with different colors indicating varying degrees of pollution. Areas with good air quality are depicted in green, moderate levels in yellow, and poor air quality in red. Users can zoom in and out of the map to explore specific regions and view detailed pollutant concentration data for each location.

In addition to heat maps, the website also features line graphs illustrating daily trends of air quality over time. These line graphs provide users with insights into how pollutant concentrations fluctuate throughout the day, allowing them to identify patterns and trends. The line graphs cover the entire day, with data points plotted at regular intervals to capture changes in air quality levels.

To enhance the user experience further, predictive modeling was incorporated into the website, forecasting future air quality values based on historical data. Using machine learning algorithms such as LSTM, the concentrations of gases like CO and NO2 for the upcoming days were predicted.

Overall, the website offers a comprehensive platform for visualizing air quality data, combining interactive heat maps, informative line graphs, and predictive modeling to empower users with actionable insights for better understanding and monitoring of air pollution in the NUST campus area.

Design of Machine Learning Model for Air Quality Forecasting

In the machine learning approach for air quality forecasting, Long Short-Term Memory (LSTM) neural network architecture was utilized, a type of recurrent neural network (RNN) designed specifically for handling sequential data. The LSTM model was implemented using Python libraries such as pandas, NumPy, matplotlib, seaborn, and keras.

Firstly, the dataset was loaded from an Excel file containing air quality data collected by the IoT device. The dataset was preprocessed by converting the datetime columns into the appropriate format and normalizing the input features using MinMaxScaler to ensure consistency and facilitate model training.

Next, the dataset was split into training, validation, and test sets to train and evaluate the model effectively. The input features comprised temporal information such as year, month, day, hour, minute, second, as well as geographical coordinates (longitude and latitude). The output consisted of various air quality parameters, including CO (carbon monoxide), NO2 (nitrogen dioxide), and particulate matter (PM2.5, PM5, PM10), both in mol/m2 and raw sensor readings.

The LSTM model architecture consisted of a single LSTM layer with a relu activation function, followed by a dropout layer to prevent overfitting, and a dense output layer with 7 units corresponding to the 7 output columns. The model was compiled using the Adam optimizer with a lower learning rate to optimize training. Early stopping with patience of 10 epochs was implemented to prevent overfitting and restore the best weights based on validation loss. The input data was reshaped to fit the LSTM input shape requirement.

The model was trained on the training data for 100 epochs with a batch size of 32, while validation data were used to monitor model performance during training. After training, the model was evaluated on the test set to assess its performance. Mean Squared Error (MSE) and Mean Absolute Error (MAE) metrics were calculated to quantify the model's accuracy in predicting air quality values.

In the machine learning approach for air quality forecasting, we achieved an accuracy of **0.9036** using a Long Short-Term Memory (LSTM) neural network architecture. This accuracy score reflects the model's ability to predict air quality values with high precision, demonstrating its effectiveness in leveraging temporal and spatial features for accurate forecasting.

In summary, our LSTM-based machine learning approach offers a robust framework for forecasting air quality values, leveraging temporal and spatial features to provide accurate predictions for better understanding and management of air pollution.

IMPLEMENTATION AND TESTING

Creating the Device

After finalizing the selection of components and procuring them, the next step was to design a circuit that would seamlessly integrate all the chosen components with a Microcontroller Unit (MCU). This circuit was crucial as it served as the backbone of our device, facilitating the interaction and coordination among the various hardware elements. We carefully planned the layout and connections, ensuring optimal functionality and efficient power management in our design.

A simulation was conducted to assess the functionality of the circuit design. Below is the schematic representation of our circuit:

Figure 7. Schematic diagram of the circuit

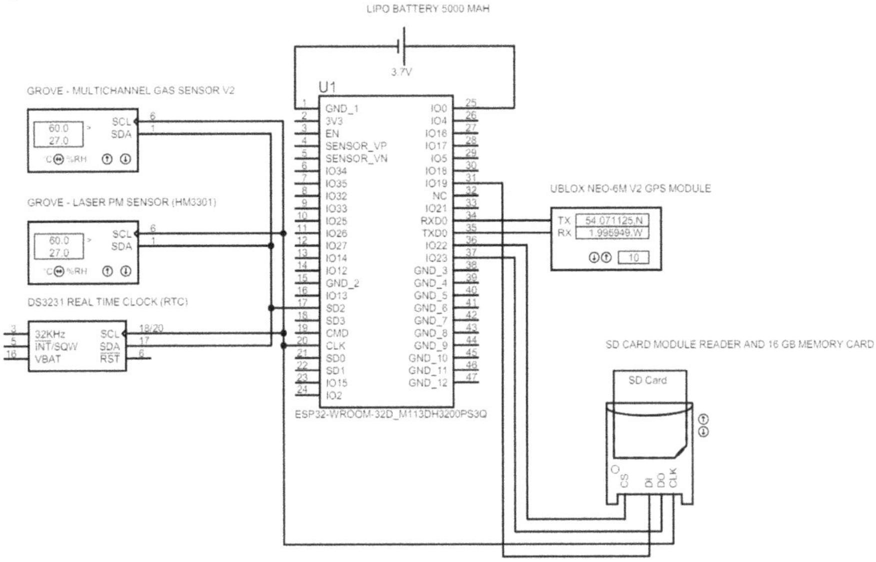

Satisfied with the simulation results aligning with our expectations, we proceeded to implement the circuit design on the hardware. This involved meticulously assembling the components according to the schematic.

Utilizing a veroboard and soldering iron, we carefully soldered the components as per the planned circuit layout. This manual process posed challenges, notably weak solder connections leading to failed short tests, so inspection and correction of each connection using a multimeter was done. Once the circuit was fully patched, we plugged in all components, monitoring ESP32 readings to ensure sensors, GPS module, and RTC module provided the desired data, ensuring the circuit's functionality.

Using the Device

After completing the soldering of the circuit, it was carefully placed inside the 3D-printed CAD model of the device and powered on. To initiate the data collection process, specific protocols were followed to ensure accurate and reliable data acquisition. These protocols were crucial for maintaining consistency and integrity in the collected data, laying the foundation for effective analysis and interpretation.

During our testing phase, we observed that the Grove – Multichannel Gas Sensor V2 requires approximately 30-35 minutes to reach optimal operating temperature and produce stable gas readings, especially if the device has been powered off for an extended period. To account for this delay, we carefully managed the timing before initiating data collection. The graph below illustrates this aspect:

Figure 8. Sensor pre-heat time

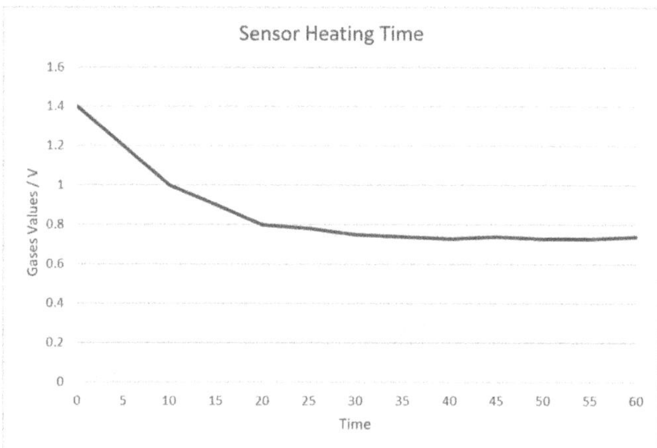

Setting up an error check mechanism to ensure the correct functioning of each module/component is paramount for successful data collection. Avoiding incomplete datasets is crucial, necessitating the implementation of protocols to facilitate smooth data collection without overlooking any malfunctions in the modules. This proactive approach guarantees the reliability and integrity of the collected data, enhancing the overall effectiveness of the project.

Instructions are coded within the ESP32 to trigger a flag if any of the module readings deviate from the normal or if they are completely missing. Initially, all flags are set to high as a standard, and as the device powers up, each flag starts to be set to low, indicating that the modules are functioning correctly. All the flags are OR gated, ensuring that even if a single flag is set to high, the error LED would illuminate, indicating that the device is not operating properly and requires attention.

One of the flags is associated with the GPS module's lock with satellites, indicating that data collection should only commence when this flag is set to low. During our testing phase, we observed that once the device was powered on and placed outside in an open area, it took approximately 2 minutes for the error check LED to turn off.

There were instances where the error LED remained illuminated, indicating a problem with a module other than the GPS module.

Figure 9. Modules error checks

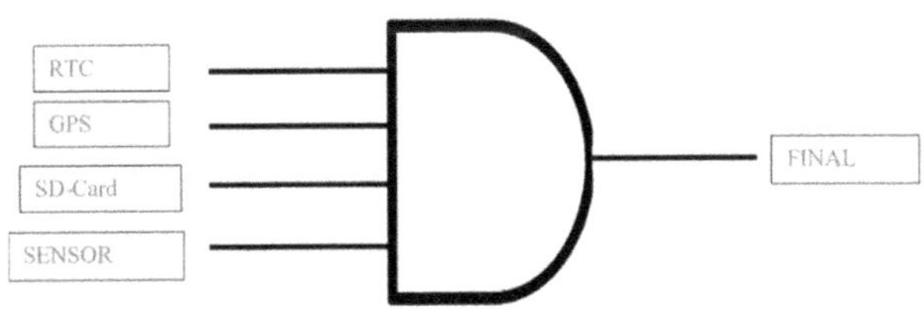

Mode of Data Collection

We employed two primary approaches for collecting air quality data, each tailored to specific scenarios and conditions. The first approach involved affixing suction cups to the flat bottom part of the device and securing it onto the roof of a car. Through this method, we conducted tests by varying the speed of the car to assess the stability and durability of the suction cups. This allowed us to evaluate their reliability, ensuring they could withstand emergency situations without compromising data collection integrity.

In our second approach, we utilized a motorbike for data collection, which proved to be the most frequently employed method. This approach necessitated the presence of two individuals: a driver and another person responsible for holding the device securely. Given the dynamic nature of this setup, meticulous care was exercised throughout the data collection process to prevent any damage to the device. Such precautions were essential, as any potential damage would not only incur significant time and effort but also impose financial constraints on our project.

RESULTS AND DISCUSSION

Following extensive data collection efforts, the gathered data was processed and analyzed using a spreadsheet software. It was imperative to ensure the accuracy and reliability of our analysis, and thus, only data collected during the designated data collection period was considered for analysis. This involved filtering out data points that fell outside the timeframe of the actual data collection process. As the device had been powered up well in advance of data collection, this filtering ensured that our analysis was based solely on relevant and valid data points.

Heatmaps

Utilizing React and Node.js, we imported the data from an Excel file and processed it to generate visualizations plotted over a map. To enhance the clarity of the visual representation, we implemented a color-coding scheme, which effectively illustrated the concentration of values and the range in which they fell. Below is a heatmap generated from a dataset acquired from NUST and its surrounding areas:

Figure 10. Air quality heatmaps of NUST

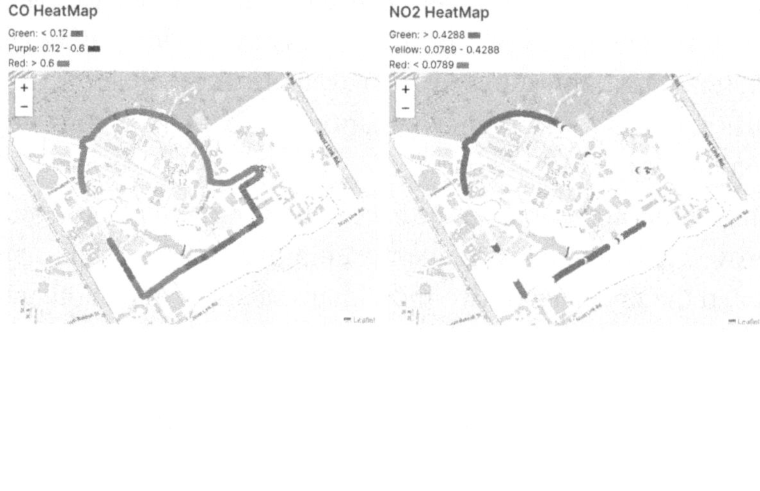

Presented below are two heatmaps illustrating the concentration levels of two gases: NO2 and CO. These values are derived directly from the sensors in volts. Despite being in volts, we opted to utilize these values as they effectively capture the trend of gas concentration.

It's worth noting that these volt values can be readily converted into their appropriate units, such as parts per million or micrograms per cubic meter. Additionally, the concentration ranges can be adjusted accordingly, ensuring that the heat maps accurately depict the distribution of gas concentration levels across the region. This adaptability ensures the consistency and reliability of the heatmaps, facilitating informed decision-making in environmental management initiatives.

The heatmaps are generated based on daily data collection, providing a comprehensive overview of gas concentration levels over time. This data-driven approach enables the identification of areas consistently exhibiting poor concentration values. Visiting such sites can help uncover the underlying reasons behind the elevated pollution levels, facilitating targeted interventions for environmental improvement.

It's important to note that the effectiveness of this technique relies on the size of the dataset and the frequency of data collection. A robust dataset with numerous instances allows for more accurate flagging of areas with problematic concentration levels, enhancing the reliability of the analysis and subsequent decision-making processes.

In the provided diagram, the color-coded representation of CO values is based on predefined thresholds. CO values below 0.12 are categorized as "very good" and are visually represented by the color green. Values ranging between 0.12 and 0.6 are considered "moderate" and are depicted in purple. The red region indicates concentrations exceeding the threshold, which may result from direct exposure to the gas or errors in measurement. This color scheme enables quick and intuitive interpretation of the data, facilitating the identification of areas with varying levels of air quality and potential concerns in Pakistan.

Gases Concentration Graphs

To complement our analysis, we have plotted the concentration of gases against the actual time of data collection. Utilizing a predetermined route, users can track the variation in concentration levels at different times, providing valuable insights into temporal trends.

Below are graphs from a specific dataset depicting the values of CO and NO2 over a period of 20 minutes.

Figure 11. Line graphs depicting values of CO and NO2

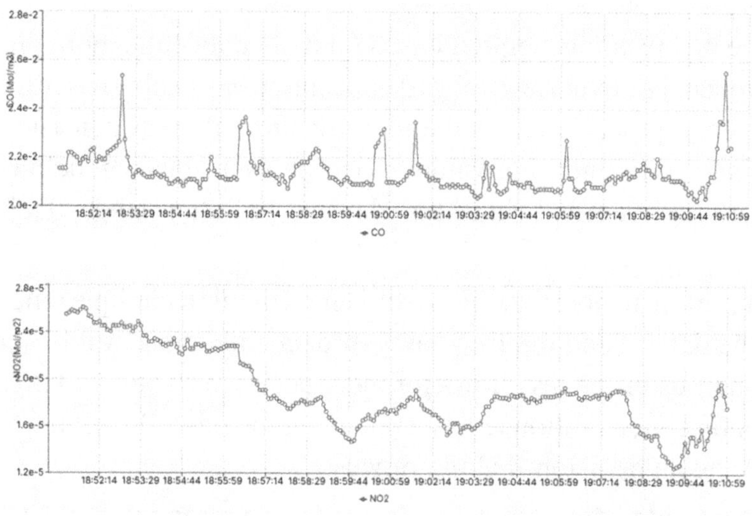

The graph clearly illustrates variations in gas concentration along the routes, reflecting fluctuations that can be attributed to several factors. Gas concentrations may vary depending on the time of day due to factors such as traffic patterns, weather conditions, and human activity levels, all of which can influence emissions and atmospheric dispersion.

Number of Surrounding Vehicles

The density of vehicles in the vicinity can significantly impact gas concentrations, as higher traffic volumes typically lead to increased emissions and pollutant levels in the air.

Exact Location

Gas concentrations may differ based on the specific location along the route, influenced by factors such as proximity to industrial areas, urban centers, or green spaces, each of which can have distinct effects on air quality.

Direct Source of The Gas Nearby

Elevated gas concentrations may result from direct sources of pollution in the vicinity, such as industrial facilities, construction sites, or vehicular emissions, contributing to localized spikes in pollutant levels.

By considering these factors, we can gain a more comprehensive understanding of the dynamics driving variations in gas concentrations along the routes, enabling more informed assessments of air quality and potential sources of pollution.

Another graph was generated to visualize the concentrations of PM2.5, PM5, and PM10, measured in parts per million (ppm), representing the levels of particulate matter in the air. The data collected from NUST indicated that these concentrations fell within the safe range, underscoring the accuracy of our results.

NUST's low pollution levels and the presence of abundant trees and clean environments contribute to maintaining air quality within safe limits. The graph provides visual confirmation of this, reinforcing the notion that NUST offers a healthy and environmentally friendly atmosphere.

Figure 12. Line graphs of different dust concentrations

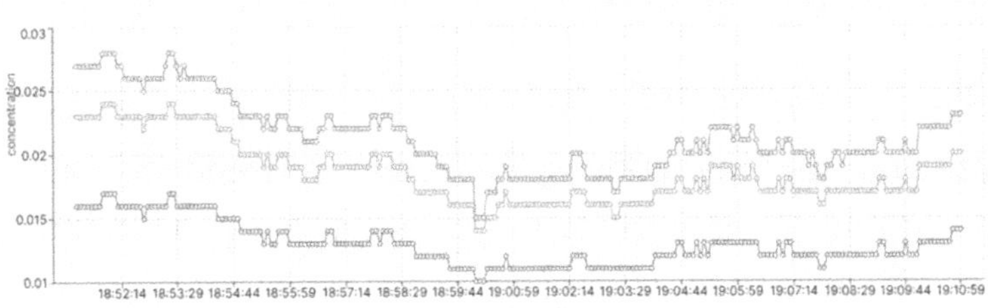

Machine Learning and Prediction

We applied the LSTM neural network to the entirety of our collected data, aiming to predict various air quality parameters, such as CO (carbon monoxide), NO2 (nitrogen dioxide), and particulate matter (PM2.5, PM5, PM10), both in mol/m2 and raw sensor readings.

The ML model underwent training on our dataset, and subsequently, we generated training loss and validation loss graphs to evaluate its performance. These visualizations provide insights into the model's learning process and its ability to generalize unseen data.

Figure 13. Training loss and validation loss

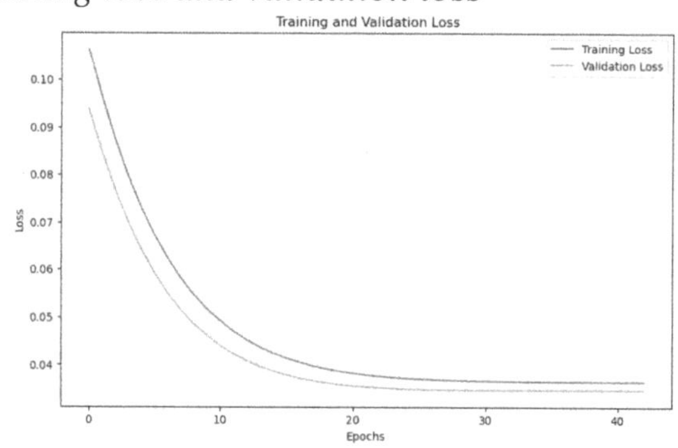

The graph illustrates the training and validation loss curves over epochs during the training of a machine learning model, specifically an LSTM neural network. The x-axis represents the number of epochs, while the y-axis denotes the loss values.

Training Loss (Blue curve)

This curve depicts the loss incurred on the training data as the model iterates through multiple epochs. A decreasing trend indicates that the model is learning and improving its performance on the training dataset.

Validation Loss (orange curve)

This curve illustrates the loss calculated on a separate validation dataset, which is unseen by the model during training. Similar to the training loss, a decreasing trend signifies that the model is generalizing well to new data and is not overfitting.

Overall, this graph serves as a visual indicator of the training progress and the model's performance in terms of minimizing loss.

Below is the table that provides a summary of the model's performance metrics, specifically the Mean Squared Error (MSE) and Mean Absolute Error (MAE), for predicting various air quality parameters. Each row corresponds to a different pollutant, and the columns represent the MSE and MAE values, respectively.

Table 3. Mean Squared Error (MSE) and Mean Absolute Error (MAE) in the prediction of different pollutants

Pollutant	MSE	MAE
CO(mol/m2))	0.022	0.12
NO2(mol/m2)	0.063	0.186
PM 2.5 (ppm)	0.050	0.185
PM 5 (ppm)	0.044	0.173
PM 10 (ppm)	0.041	0.167

MSE (Mean Squared Error) quantifies the average squared difference between predicted and actual values. A lower MSE indicates better accuracy, as it signifies closer alignment between predictions and observed data.

MAE (Mean Absolute Error) measures the average absolute difference between predicted and actual values. Similarly, a lower MAE indicates better accuracy, reflecting closer proximity of predictions to actual values. Both MSE and MAE serve as essential metrics for evaluating model performance in predictive modeling tasks.

Upon interpreting the values in the table, several insights emerge regarding the model's performance in predicting air quality parameters. Notably, the model demonstrates particularly accurate predictions for carbon monoxide (CO) and particulate matter with a diameter of 10 micrometers (PM10). Both pollutants exhibit relatively low Mean Squared Error (MSE) and Mean Absolute Error (MAE) values, signifying that the model's predictions closely align with the actual measurements.

Conversely, nitrogen dioxide (NO2) and particulate matter with a diameter of 2.5 micrometers (PM2.5) display slightly higher MSE and MAE values when compared to CO and PM10. While these values indicate slightly less accuracy in predicting NO2 and PM2.5 concentrations, they still suggest reasonably accurate performance by the model.

Overall, the model demonstrates an acceptable level of accuracy across all pollutants considered, as evidenced by the relatively low MSE and MAE values. Despite minor discrepancies observed in predicting NO2 and PM2.5, the model's overall performance remains desirable.

These histograms visualize the distribution of air quality parameters, including CO, NO2, and particulate matter, along with their raw sensor readings. Each graph illustrates the frequency distribution of values for a specific parameter.

Figure 14. Actual vs predicted values of pollutant concentrations

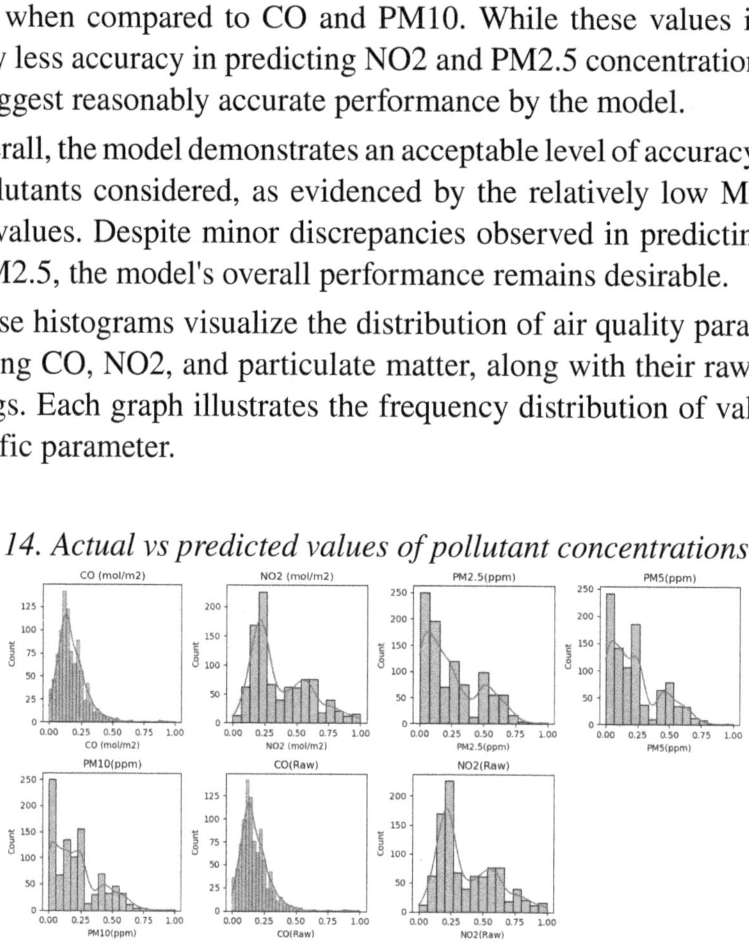

These histograms provide a visual representation of both actual and predicted values for various air quality parameters. The bar graphs illustrate the frequency distribution of observed values, while the line graphs depict the model's predicted values. Comparing these distributions allows us to evaluate the model's performance, with a close alignment suggesting accurate predictions and discrepancies indicating areas for improvement.

Analyzing the distributions' shape and spread provides valuable insights into the data. Skewed distributions may signal non-normality, while differences between actual and predicted values highlight areas for potential model refinement. Despite challenges in data collection, these histograms offer essential guidance for optimizing model performance and understanding air quality parameters.

CONCLUSION AND FUTURE WORK

Conclusion

This project emerged from a visionary concept aimed at revolutionizing air quality monitoring across various urban and intercity environments. The primary focus was the development of a robust system capable of consistently and accurately assessing air quality levels. The device we engineered for this purpose proved reliable throughout the rigorous data collection phase, which presented numerous challenges. Ensuring the integrity of our data was important, and we dedicated ourselves to maintaining rigorous standards throughout the collection and processing stages.

The visualization of the collected data provided compelling insights, with heatmaps revealing consistent trends that aligned with our expectations and reflected the air quality of specific locales. This valuable information is readily accessible through the Airsense website, offering users the opportunity to see historical data and leverage machine learning models for predicting future air quality levels. Such forecasts hold practical significance, aiding users in making informed decisions about their routes and potentially informing governmental policymaking efforts. Looking ahead, in a world where pollution levels continue to escalate annually, our project serves as a beacon of innovative solutions. Although currently operating on a smaller scale, it presents a proof of concept with far-reaching implications for addressing environmental challenges in the decades to come.

Future Work

During our project, we encountered several challenges in our device, data collection process, and overall approach. These experiences provide valuable insights that will inform our future efforts and serve as the foundation for further development in this project. Enhancing our device with an OLED display to showcase concentration values and provide real-time data collection readiness indications will streamline the process, saving time and reducing preparation hassles. The display will make the device easier to use.

Integrating electric vehicles promises more accurate data readings without exhaust emissions. Their mobility will expand our monitoring system's reach, enhancing data collection in various environments for a comprehensive understanding of air quality dynamics.

Scaling up production to manufacture multiple devices will increase accessibility and adoption rates, allowing for broader implementation and more comprehensive data collection. Connecting multiple devices to different cars will increase the area span for data collection, making the research work more effective.

Expanding our dataset by incorporating additional parameters or monitoring locations will provide deeper insights into air quality trends and facilitate more robust analysis for informed decision-making.

REFERENCES

Anjomshoaa, F., Duarte, D., Rennings, T. J., Matarazzo, P., deSouza, P., & Ratti, C. (2018). City scanner: Building and scheduling a mobile sensing platform for smart city services. *IEEE Internet of Things Journal*, *5*(6), 4567–4579. DOI: 10.1109/JIOT.2018.2839058

Castell, N., Kobernus, M., Liu, H.-Y., Schneider, P., Lahoz, W., Berre, A. J., & Noll, J. (2015). Mobile technologies and services for environmental monitoring: The citi-sense-mob approach. *Urban Climate*, *14*, 370–382. DOI: 10.1016/j.uclim.2014.08.002

Duong, D., Le, Q. M., Nguyen-Tai, T. L., & Nguyen, H. D. (2021). An effective AQI estimation using sensor data and stacking mechanism. In *New Trends in Intelligent Software Methodologies, Tools and Techniques* (pp. 123–134). IOS Press. DOI: 10.3233/FAIA210040

Fekih, M. A., Bechkit, W., Rivano, H., Dahan, M., & Rena, F. (2020). Participatory air quality and urban heat islands monitoring system. *IEEE Sensors Journal*, *20*(12), 6789–6800.

Hasenfratz, D., Saukh, O., Walser, C., Hueglin, C., Fierz, M., & Thiele, L. (2014). Pushing the spatio-temporal resolution limit of urban air pollution maps. In *2014 IEEE International Conference on Pervasive Computing and Communications (PerCom)* (pp. 69–77). IEEE. DOI: 10.1109/PerCom.2014.6813946

Hochreiter, S., & Schmidhuber, J. (1997). Long short-term memory. *Neural Computation*, *9*(8), 1735–1780. DOI: 10.1162/neco.1997.9.8.1735 PMID: 9377276

Kalajdjieski, J., Zdravevski, E., Kalajdziski, S., Corizzo, R., Pires, I. M., Lameski, P., Garcia, N. M., & Trajkovik, V. (2020). Air pollution prediction with multi-modal data and deep neural networks. *Sensors (Basel)*, *20*(24), 1–20.

Kok, C. H., Azlan, M. A. M., & Ong, S. E. (2020). IoT-based low-cost distributed air quality monitoring system for big data collection. In *2020 10th IEEE International Conference on Control System, Computing and Engineering (ICCSCE)* (pp. 123–130). IEEE. DOI: 10.1109/ICCSCE50387.2020.9204954

Patil, R. M., Dinde, H. T., & Powar, S. (2020). A literature review on prediction of air quality index and forecasting ambient air pollutants using machine learning algorithms. *International Journal of Innovative Science and Research Technology*, *5*(8), 1234–1240. DOI: 10.38124/IJISRT20AUG683

Veefkind, J. P., Aben, I., McMullan, K., Förster, H., de Vries, J., Otter, G., Claas, J., Eskes, H. J., de Haan, J. F., Kleipool, Q., van Weele, M., Hasekamp, O., Hoogeveen, R., Landgraf, J., Snel, R., Tol, P., Ingmann, P., Voors, R., Kruizinga, B., & Levelt, P. F. (2012). TROPOMI on the ESA Sentinel-5 Precursor: A GMES mission for global observations of the atmospheric composition for climate, air quality, and ozone layer applications. *Remote Sensing of Environment*, *120*, 70–83. DOI: 10.1016/j.rse.2011.09.027

Wang, L., & Chen, X. (2021). Real-time detection of air pollutants using multichannel gas sensors: A review. *Atmospheric Environment*, *245*, 118023.

Wang, Y., Li, J., & Zhang, X. (2019). Design and implementation of a low-cost particulate matter sensor for air quality monitoring. *Sensors (Basel)*, *19*(12), 2765. PMID: 31226728

Zhang, Y., & Liu, H. (2019). Design and implementation of a portable power system for IoT devices. *Journal of Power Sources*, *420*, 1–10. DOI: 10.1016/j.jpowsour.2019.03.100

KEY TERMS AND DEFINITIONS

I2C: This refers to the communication protocol which is synchronous in nature and is used to communicate between micro-controllers and peripheral devices.

Internet of Things (IoT): This refers to a network of interconnected devices equipped with sensors and various software tools to collect data and communicate with each other via the Internet.

LSTM: This refers to the recurrent neural network architecture and is mostly used to handle sequential data.

Node.js: This is an open-source runtime environment that allows developers to run JavaScript on the server side.

Vehicular Sensing Network (VSN): This refers to a network system where vehicles are equipped with sensors or IoT devices to collect and share data. The vehicle acts as a mobile data node and is effective for large-scale data collection.

Chapter 6
Performance Evaluation of Various Machine Learning Models and Its Implications for Informed Air Policy Decisions: A Comparative Study for Delhi

Vikram Ranjan

School of Engineering and Technology, Vivekananda Institute of Professional Studies, Delhi, India

Garima Chanana

https://orcid.org/0000-0002-2745-8375

School of Engineering and Technology, Vivekananda Institute of Professional Studies, Delhi, India

ABSTRACT

Machine learning (ML) models are powerful tools for predicting the Air Quality Index (AQI). This study presents a comparative analysis of several regression models for AQI prediction in Delhi, including Gradient Boosting,

DOI: 10.4018/979-8-3693-9030-6.ch006

XGBoost, LightGBM, CatBoost, Elastic Net, K-Nearest Neighbors, Linear Regression, and Random Forest. Models were assessed using Mean Absolute Error (MAE), Root Mean Squared Error (RMSE), and R-squared (R^2). The results show that the Random Forest model outperforms others with an R^2 of 0.932, RMSE of 0.293, and MAE of 0.216. Random Forest's ability to capture intricate correlations and resilience to noise and outliers makes it ideal for AQI prediction. Based on these findings, the authors recommend measures such as expanding urban green spaces, implementing pollution control for vehicles, and preventing agricultural biomass burning. These initiatives will help policymakers effectively mitigate Delhi's air pollution.

1. INTRODUCTION

Globally, air pollution is a serious concern. According to previous research studies (Suk et al., 2016), it has been observed that environmental air pollution affects approximately 8.9 million people worldwide. It causes a variety of health problems, including respiratory system disorders such as bronchitis, asthma, skin infections, heart issues, diseases of the throat and eyes, and lung cancer, (Manisalidis et al., 2020). The emission of various harmful gases and particles, such as CO, O_3, SO_2, $PM_{2.5}$, and PM_{10}, is the major cause of air pollution. The combustion of fossil fuels, industrial emissions, wildfires, transportation, and agricultural practices all contribute to the production of these pollutants, (AbdelSattar, 2019).

In this study, we aim to perform a thorough investigation of Delhi's air quality using the AQI dataset, using multiple machine learning models. The data set selected has 6 columns i.e. O_3 (concentration of ozone gas), $PM_{2.5}$ (concentration of $PM_{2.5}$), PM_{10} (concentration of PM_{10}), CO (concentration of carbon monoxide gas) and AQI. Each column has 15,862 rows for different dates. Each row represent date of which the concentration is given. The dataset contains the record concentration of mentioned pollutants of 2 years in Delhi. The objective of our work is to use machine learning models in developing an informed policy for mitigating air pollution. The article also explores the role of key sources of pollution for CO, O_3, SO_2, $PM_{2.5}$, and PM_{10}. Additionally, the interdependencies among these pollutants and contributing factors are investigated, leading to the development of policies aimed at reducing these dependencies and ultimately decreasing pollutant emissions.

Machine Learning (ML) consists of state-of-the-art methods by use of which a model can learn on its own by analyzing the patterns and trends. With an explosion of monitoring data using sensors and the increasing demand for fast and accurate prediction, ML models have been rapidly developed and applied in air pollution research, (Li et al., 2023). There are many ML algorithms that can be used to analyze large data sets and extract some useful information from data set. These models can derive connections between data, mitigating the influence of outliers, (Ozel et al., 2020), enhancing prediction accuracy and robustness, particularly in the handling of extensive datasets, (Yuchi et al., 2019). They generate a more precise fit to the data, yielding a smaller root mean square error (RMSE), particularly in nonlinear data, (Chen et al., 2022). These advantages contribute to the growing popularity of ML models in atmospheric science research. They serve as essential components for various tasks such as short-term forecasting, analysis of chemical behavior of pollutants, and climate impact assessment.

Making informed policy decisions guided by ML is gaining significant popularity. Using these models, it is possible to optimize policy design, foster sustainable behaviors, and enable continuous improvement in air pollution mitigation efforts. By leveraging data-driven insights, policies initiatives can be developed for addressing air pollution effectively.

For reducing the air pollution problem in Delhi there have been many different policies that have been implemented over the years. One of the earliest air pollution control policies is the Odd-Even Scheme which was introduced in 2016. The "Odd-Even Scheme" (9) is a traffic control measure implemented in various cities, including Delhi, to address air pollution and reduce traffic congestion. Under this scheme, vehicles are allowed to travel on specific days based on the last digit of their license plate number. For example, on "odd" days (like 1st, 3rd, 5th of the month), vehicles with license plate numbers ending in an odd digit are permitted to operate, while on "even" days (like 2nd, 4th, 6th), vehicles with license plate numbers ending in an even digit are allowed. The scheme is typically implemented as a temporary measure during periods of poor air quality or high pollution levels, often during the winter months when Delhi experiences severe smog. An analysis of AQI statistics revealed that Delhi's air quality did not improve during odd-even days that year. The average AQI from 4 to 15 November was 362, whereas in 2018, the average AQI for the same period in absence of odd-even was 335. In other words, Delhi's air quality was 8 percent worse in odd-even days compared to the previous year, (Dutta & Jinsart, 2021).

In 2017, Graded Responses Action Plan (Laura et al., 2018) was introduced in Delhi which is a comprehensive strategy aimed at addressing the city's severe air pollution issues. The Commission for Air Quality Management notified the Graded Response Action Plan (GRAP) to address poor air quality in Delhi. GRAP classifies air quality into four levels on the basis of Air Quality Index (AQI), triggering corresponding actions and restrictions. Stage I is for 'Poor' Air Quality (AQI ranging between 201-300), Stage II is for 'Very Poor' Air Quality (AQI ranging between 301-400), Stage III is for 'Severe' Air Quality (AQI ranging between 401-450) and Stage IV is for 'Severe+' Air Quality (AQI greater than 450). Air control measures have been specified in this policy depending on the stage of air pollution levels.

The National Clean Air Program (NCAP) (Chatterji et al., 2021) launched in 2019 is a nationwide initiative in India, and Delhi is one of the key focus areas due to its significant air pollution challenges. NCAP sets ambitious air quality improvement targets for Delhi, aiming to reduce the concentration of particulate matter (PM_{10} and $PM_{2.5}$) in the city's ambient air. These targets are designed to achieve a substantial reduction in pollution levels over a five-year period. NCAP emphasizes the importance of real-time air quality monitoring and data collection. It seeks to establish a robust network of monitoring stations to track pollution levels and assess the effectiveness of pollution control measures. The plan aligns with existing policies and programs, including the National Action Plan on Climate Change, initiatives on electric vehicles, and the Smart Cities Mission.

The Delhi government has also initiated its 'Red Light On, Gaadi Off' anti-pollution campaign, deploying 2,500 civil defense volunteers at 100 traffic signals throughout the city, (Saadat et al., 2021). The aim is to raise awareness and mitigate vehicular pollution. Encouraging drivers to turn off their engines during red lights or traffic not only improves local air quality by reducing emissions but also conserves fuel. Excessive idling is estimated to waste a significant amount of fuel over time, making engine shutdowns during brief stops environmentally beneficial. This campaign aims to save fuel, cut greenhouse gas emissions, and provides immediate health benefits by lowering exposure to harmful pollutants. This reduction in emissions can decrease the risk of respiratory and cardiovascular diseases, especially in densely populated urban areas like Delhi, (Charan, 2022).

Smog towers are tall cylindrical towers incorporate advanced air filtration technology, including HEPA filters and activated carbon, capable of capturing particulate matter and harmful pollutants from the surrounding air. A smog tower was erected in Delhi's Lajpat Nagar market, featuring a capacity of 600,000 m^3/day, (Guttikunda & Jawahar, 2020). Another was set-up in Connaught Place with 40 large fans. These towers were part of a broader effort to alleviate Delhi's severe smog and its health impacts. However, in the present time, smog towers are not widely regarded as an efficient technique for mitigating air pollution.

In the present work, we used different machine learning models such as K-Nearest Neighbors, Random Forest, Extreme Gradient Boosting, Gradient Boosting, Support Vector Regression, Kernal Ridge Regression, Elastic Net, Light Gradient Boosting Regression, Categorical Regression, and Linear Regression, and applied them on Delhi's AQI dataset that contains the concentration of different pollutants (CO, SO_2, $PM_{2.5}$, PM_{10}, O_3) to predict the AQI. We used various performance metrics, such as Mean Absolute Error (MAE), Root Mean Absolute Error (RMSE), and R-squared (R^2) to compare the accuracy of those models. The result reported in this study may assist in making effective strategies for air pollution mitigation.

The article follows a structured format comprising four key sections: Section 2 describes the literature review and provides an overview of current ML models being implemented to study the air quality. Section 3 describes the theoretical framework and delves into the foundational aspects of the machine learning models utilized in the study, elucidating their core concepts and methodologies. Section 4 includes results and discussion and presents the research findings, and discusses their significance and comparisons with previous works. Section 5 includes clean air initiatives for mitigating air pollution in Delhi and lastly, Section 6 concludes the study highlighting the key results and future research avenues in this field.

2. LITERATURE REVIEW

Research in the area of air quality prediction and pollution mitigation is a rich field of investigation. This section outlines the key research studies that have been reported in the literature. Research study by Ravindiran et al. (2023) examined the AQI dataset of Visakhapatnam, Andhra Pradesh, India. They applied various ML models, including LightGBM, Random Forest, Catboost, Adaboost, and XGBoost. The analysis focused on 12 contaminants and 10 meteorological parameters spanning from July 2017 to September 2022. Their results show that Catboost model surpassed others in performance, achieving an R^2 correlation coefficient of 0.9998. The model Mean Absolute Error (MAE), Mean Squared Error (MSE), and Root Mean Squared Error (RMSE) were 0.60, 0.58, and 0.76 respectively. Conversely, Adaboost exhibited the lowest effectiveness among the models, with an R^2 correlation coefficient of 0.9753.

Halsana (2020) studied the AQI utilizing the concentrations of $PM_{2.5}$, PM_{10}, SO_2, NO_2, CO, along with weather conditions such as temperature, humidity, and pressure. The researchers employed several supervised machine learning algorithms and evaluated their performance using various accuracy metrics. These algorithms included Linear Regression, Support Vector Regression, Decision Tree Regression, and Random Forest Regression. To compare the effectiveness of these algorithms, they assessed metrics such as R^2 score, MSE, and MAE. Among the algorithms tested, Random Forest Regression exhibited superior performance, achieving an R^2 score of 0.99985, MSE of 0.00013, and MAE of 0.00373.

In a study by Juarez and Petersen (2021) the performance of eight machine learning models in forecasting ozone concentrations 24 hours ahead is investigated. Utilizing hourly data for 12 pollutant and 5 meteorological variables. Notably, the models demonstrated R^2 values of XGBoost ($R^2 = 0.6161$), Random Forest ($R^2 = 0.6041$), K-Nearest Neighbors Regression ($R^2 = 0.5126$), Support Vector Regression ($R^2 = 0.4633$), Decision Trees (models $R^2 = 0.4023$), Linear Regression ($R^2 = 0.3937$), Adaboost ($R^2 = 0.3523$), LSTM ($R^2 = 0.16$). Random Forest Regression performed most effectively with year-long training. Further analysis indicated that training the models separately by seasons enhanced their performance, with winter yielding the most reliable results. In winter, the top-performing models were XGBoost ($R^2 = 0.755$), Random Forest ($R^2 = 0.747$), and K-Nearest Neighbors Regression ($R^2 = 0.704$). Interestingly, the Long Short-Term Memory model exhibited poor performance with annual training but emerged as the most effective model for summer and post-monsoon periods with seasonal training. In this study, Delhi was selected due to its availability of high-quality measurements, yet this presents a significant constraint for numerous other cities.

Research study by Mallegowda et al. (2021) explored the application of XGBoost, Random Forest, and Decision Tree models to forecast the $PM_{2.5}$ levels and AQI values of a city based on environmental conditions. The parameters considered for predicting $PM_{2.5}$ includes temperature (T), maximum temperature (T_M), minimum temperature (T_m), humidity (H), atmospheric pressure (PP), visibility (VV), wind speed (V), and maximum wind speed (VM). The results indicated that XGBoost outperformed the other models, as determined by the evaluation metrics. XGBoost exhibited superior performance with an RMSE value of 9.46, MSE value of 89.56, and MAE value of 4.56.

Research work by Kumar and Pande (2023) explores the air pollution data from 23 Indian cities over a six-year period. They utilize correlation-based feature selection to identify key pollutants affecting AQI and apply logarithmic transformations to skewed features. Exploratory data analysis reveals hidden patterns within the dataset, notably a significant decrease in pollutants in 2020. They tackle data imbalance using Synthetic Minority Over-sampling Technique (SMOTE) analysis, followed by splitting the dataset into 75-25% train-test subsets. Machine learning-based AQI predictions are made in their study using both with and without SMOTE resampling, leading to a detailed comparative analysis. Their study reveals that XGBoost is a top performer for both training and testing phases, while the Random Forest model shows promise in the training phase with SMOTE. The testing phase highlights the GNB model's strong performance in R^2 predictions. Additionally, classical statistical error metrics such as MAE, RMSE, RMSLE, and R^2 are employed to evaluate and compare the performance of machine learning models, confirming XGBoost as the overall best performer having MAE value of 0.472, RMSE of 1.027, RMSLE of 0.156, R^2 of 0.834 without SMOTE and MAE value of 0.174, RMSE of 1.008, RMSLE of 0.026, R^2 of 0.325 with SMOTE.

Singh et al. (2023) explored the relationship between AQI and lung cancer mortality rates in India. This study involves predictive modeling and impact assessment. To establish this relationship, various predictive models, including Linear Regression, K-Nearest Neighbors (KNN), Decision Tree, Artificial Neural Network (ANN), Random Forest Regression, and XGBoost Regression, were employed to estimate pollutant levels and AQI in India. Among them, XGBoost Regression demonstrated the highest accuracy, achieving a Mean Absolute Error (MAE) of 31.73, Mean Squared Error (MSE) of 1998.23, Root Mean Squared Error (RMSE) of 44.70, and an overall accuracy of 81.23%. Furthermore, the pollutant level estimations during training and testing phases reached an accuracy range of 81% to 98%. Following closely, Random Forest attained the second-highest accuracy range with MAE (24.25), RMSE (39.01), MSE (1522.14) and accuracy of 78.88. Additionally, the article examines the repercussions of escalating pollution levels on the increasing mortality rate among lung cancer patients in India.

In an effort to develop an effective method for predicting Air Quality Index (AQI) to aid in climate control efforts Gupta et al. (2023) utilized Synthetic Minority Over-sampling Technique (SMOTE) technique. Three distinct methods, namely Support Vector Regression (SVR), Random Forest Regression (RFR), and CatBoost regression, were employed to predict AQI levels in New Delhi, Bangalore, Kolkata, and Hyderabad. The results revealed that RFR consistently produced the lowest Root Mean Square Error (RMSE) values in Bangalore (0.5674), Kolkata (0.1403), and Hyderabad (0.3826), along with higher accuracy compared to SVR and CatBoost regression for Kolkata (90.9700%) and Hyderabad (78.3672%). Conversely, in New Delhi, CatBoost regression achieved the lowest RMSE value of 0.2792 and the highest accuracy of 79.8622%, while in Bangalore, the accuracy was 68.6860%. When applying the SMOTE algorithm to the dataset, Kolkata and Hyderabad exhibited the lowest RMSE values of 0.0988 and 0.0628, respectively, with high accuracies of 93.7438% and 97.6080% when using Random Forest regression. Conversely, CatBoost regression performed best for New Delhi with an accuracy of 85.0847%, and 90.3071% in Bangalore.

The preceding analysis suggests that the accuracy of different ML models varies based on the state under study and the allied techniques employed, such as SMOTE resampling. This study aims to specifically evaluate the performance of ten ML models in modeling the AQI of Delhi.

3. MACHINE LEARNING MODELS: THEORETICAL FRAMEWORK

3.1 Linear Regression

Linear Regression is a straight forward, linear relationship between the independent variable X and the dependent variable Y. The relationship is represented by the mathematical formula for a straight line, (Bangdiwala, 2018).

$$Y = \beta_0 X + \beta_1 \quad (1)$$

where β_0 is called the intercept and β_1 is called the slope. In the Cartesian plane, the intercept refers to the point where the line intersects the Y-axis. Meanwhile, the slope represents the rate of change along the Y-axis for a one-unit change in the X-axis. Linear regression aims to find the best-fitting line through the data points by minimizing the sum of the squared differences between the observed and predicted values.

3.2 Kernel Ridge Regression

Kernel ridge regression (KRR) (Vovk, 2013) is a regression technique that combines the regularization approach of ridge regression with the flexibility of kernel methods. Unlike traditional linear regression models, which assume a linear relationship between features and target variables, KRR can capture non-linear patterns in the data by mapping the features into a higher-dimensional space using a kernel function. This kernel function computes the similarity between pairs of data points, allowing KRR to learn complex relationships that may not be evident in the original feature space. The regularization parameter in KRR controls the trade-off between fitting the training data and penalizing large coefficients, thereby preventing overfitting. Despite its ability to capture non-linear relationships, KRR requires careful selection of the kernel function and its hyperparameters, and it can be computationally intensive for large datasets due to the need to compute the kernel matrix.

3.3 K-Nearest Neighbor Regression

K-Nearest Neighbors (KNN) Regression (Kramer, 2011) is a non-parametric method used for regression tasks. Unlike linear regression, which assumes a linear relationship between the independent and dependent variables, KNN regression doesn't make any assumptions about the underlying data distribution. Instead, it estimates the value of the dependent variable for a new data point by averaging the values of the k nearest neighbors in the feature space. In this method, the distance between the new data point and all other data points in the training set is calculated. This distance can be calculated using various metrics where the most commonly used is the Euclidean distance (d) defined as follows:

$$d(x,y) = \sqrt{\sum_{i=1}^{N}(x_i - y_i)^2} \tag{2}$$

where N is the number of data points. Based on the distance value, the k nearest neighbors of the new data point is identified. These k data points with the smallest distances to the new data point are used to make predictions about the new value (y_{new}) using the following equation, (Vovk, 2013):

$$y_{new} = \frac{1}{k}\sum_{i=1}^{k} y_i \tag{3}$$

One of the challenges associated with KNN is the selection of hyperparameters. The primary hyperparameters include the number of neighbors (k) and the choice of distance function (d), (Kramer, 2011). First, for small values of k, it focuses on capturing local data structures, making it sensitive to noise, while larger k values prioritize global data structures, reducing the impact of noise. Second, the choice of distance function d determines how distances between input vectors are calculated, with nearby instances having higher relevance. Common distance functions for KNN include Manhattan, Euclidean, and Mahalanobis distances.

3.4 Elastic Net Regression

The Elastic-Net regression model (Zou & Hastie, 2005) is a hybrid of Lasso (L1 regularization) and Ridge (L2 regularization) regression techniques. Elastic-Net regression combines L1 (Lasso) and L2 (Ridge) regularization to leverage the benefits of both, offering improved variable selection, handling correlated predictors, and balancing bias-variance tradeoff for better model performance. During regression tasks, the cost function evaluates the disparity between the model's predicted values and the actual dataset values, and regression aims to minimize this cost function to optimize model performance.

For linear regression, the cost function is defined as:

$$C.F. = \frac{1}{m}\sum_{i=1}^{m}(y^{(i)} - h(x)^{(i)})^2 \tag{4}$$

where m is the total number of training examples in the dataset, $h(x)^{(i)}$ represents the hypothetical function for prediction and $y^{(i)}$ represents the value of target variable for i^{th} training example.

In elastic net model, the cost function is defined as:

$$C.F. = \frac{1}{m}\left[\sum_{i=1}^{m}\left(y^{(i)} - h(x)^{(i)}\right)^2 + \lambda_1\sum_{i=1}^{n}w_j + \lambda_2\sum_{j=1}^{n}w_j^2\right] \tag{5}$$

Here, w_j represents the weight for j^{th} feature, n is the number of features in the dataset, λ_1 is the regularization strength for L-1 norm, and λ_2 is the regularization strength for L-2 norm.

Combining L1 and L2 regularization in Elastic-Net seeks to strike a balance between bias and variance. L1 regularization tends to induce higher bias, while L2 regularization typically reduces bias but increases variance.

This integration enhances generalization performance by mitigating the extremes of bias and variance inherent in each penalty alone.

3.5 Support Vector Regression

In SVM regression, support vectors are those data points for which the absolute difference between the predicted value and the actual target value is equal to the margin parameter ϵ. These data points lie either on the margin or within the margin region, and they define the boundaries of the margin.

The basic idea behind SVM regression (Shevade et al., 2000) is to find the hyper plane that best fits the data while still maximizing the margin. The hyper plane equation in SVM regression can be represented as:

$$\hat{y} = w.x + b \tag{6}$$

where $\hat{y}$ is the predicted output, w is the weight vector, x is the feature vector and b is the bias term.

The weight vector (w) and the bias term (b) are learned during the training process. The weight vector represents the coefficients corresponding to each feature in the input feature vector, while the bias term represents the intercept.

During the training process, the following cost function is optimized:

$$C.F. = min_{a,b} \frac{1}{2} \left| |w| \right|^2 + C \sum_{i=1}^{n} \left(\max\left(0, \left| y_i - \left(w.x_i + b\right) \right| - \varepsilon\right) \right)^p \tag{7}$$

The objective is to find the optimal values of w and b that minimize the cost function while satisfying the constraints. This is done using optimization methods like gradient descent, quadratic programming etc.

3.6 Random Forest Regression

Random Forest (RF) (Ishwaran & Lu, 2019) is ensemble learning method that operates by constructing a multitude of decision trees during training and outputs the mean prediction of the individual trees for regression problem. It consists of a collection of randomized tree predictors $\{h(x,\theta_m,L),\ m=1,\ldots,M\}$.

Here, $h(x,\theta_m,L)$ is the mth random tree predictor of $h(x)$ and $\{\theta_m\}$ are independent identically distributed random quantities encoding the randomization needed for constructing a tree. θ_m is selected prior to growing the tree and is independent of the learning data, L. The tree predictor is combined to form the finite forest estimator of $h(x)$ (Ishwaran & Lu, 2019)

$$h\left(x,\Theta_1,..\mathscr{L}.,\Theta_m,\right) = \frac{1}{M}\sum_{m=1}^{M} h\left(x,\Theta_m,\mathscr{L}\right) \tag{8}$$

The infinite forest estimator is obtained by taking the limit as $M^{\circ}\rightarrow\infty$ and equals

$$h\left(x,\mathscr{L}\right) = E_{\Theta}\left[h\left(x,\Theta_m,\mathscr{L}\right)\right] \tag{9}$$

3.7 Gradient Boosting

Gradient boosting (Bentéjac, Csörgő, & Martínez-Muñoz, 2021) is an ensemble learning technique. In this model, an initial simple model, often the mean is calculated for regression problem. The model then calculates the residuals between the actual and predicted values, which are termed as pseudo-residuals. A weak learner, typically a decision tree, is then trained on these residuals, focusing on areas where the current model performs poorly. The predictions of this weak learner are then added to the ensemble, scaled by a learning rate that determines the contribution of each learner. This process is iteratively repeated, with each subsequent learner trained to correct the errors of the ensemble formed by the previous models. By continuously refining the predictions through the addition of weak learners, gradient boosting constructs a robust and accurate final model capable of capturing intricate patterns and relationships within the data. To enhance the model, regularization techniques, such as limiting tree depth and early stopping, can be applied to prevent overfitting and improve model generalization.

3.8 XGBoost Regression

eXtreme Gradient Boosting (XGBoost) (Chen & Guestrin, 2016), builds upon the principles of gradient boosting while introducing several key enhancements. At its core, XGBoost follows the iterative process of sequentially training weak learners, typically decision trees, to correct the errors of the previous models as described above. However, it incorporates regularization techniques such as L1 and L2 regularization to control model complexity and prevent overfitting. Additionally, XGBoost employs tree pruning to remove splits that contribute minimally to improving model performance, leading to simpler and more interpretable models. Another notable feature is its ability to handle missing values during the tree construction process, eliminating the need for preprocessing steps. Furthermore, XGBoost is designed for scalability and efficiency, leveraging parallel and distributed computing techniques to process large datasets swiftly. Therefore, XGBoost's consists of a combination of enhancements results in superior performance, scalability, and flexibility compared to traditional gradient boosting implementations.

3.9 Light GBM Regression

Light Gradient Boosting Machine (LightGBM) (Ke et al., 2017) implements a novel tree-building strategy known as leaf-wise growth, in contrast to the traditional level-wise growth used by other gradient boosting implementations. This distinctive approach involves expanding the tree by adding new leaves sequentially, rather than layer by layer. By doing so, LightGBM can prioritize splitting nodes that yield the greatest reduction in the loss function, resulting in faster training times and reduced memory consumption. It also includes both regularization techniques, i.e. L1 and L2 regularization, to prevent overfitting and improve model generalization. These regularization methods help ensure that the trained models maintain high predictive performance on unseen data. One important feature of

LightGBM is that it uses histogram-based algorithms for feature discretization during training. This technique involves combining continuous features into discrete bins, which accelerates the computation of the best split points for each leaf. Therefore, LightGBM significantly reduces the computational burden associated with training gradient boosting models.

3.10 CatBoost Regression

CatBoost (Prokhorenkova et al., 2018) is a cutting-edge gradient boosting algorithm designed specifically for regression tasks, offering efficient handling of categorical features and delivering accurate predictions. Unlike traditional approaches, CatBoost eliminates the need for manual preprocessing of categorical variables by directly incorporating them into the training process. It employs an innovative technique called ordered boosting, which simultaneously grows multiple trees in parallel, enhancing the efficiency of the training process. Furthermore, CatBoost integrates various regularization techniques, such as L1 and L2 regularization, to prevent overfitting and improve model generalization. Its dynamic learning rate adjustment based on gradient magnitudes enables faster convergence and better performance. CatBoost is optimized for speed and memory efficiency, making it capable of handling large-scale regression tasks with millions of samples and features. It provides built-in cross-validation functionality for evaluating model performance and fine-tuning hyperparameters.

4. RESULTS AND DISCUSSION

4.1 Dataset

In this work we have used a data set which contains concentration of various pollutants. The data set selected has 6 columns i.e. Date, O_3 (concentration of ozone), $PM_{2.5}$ (concentration of $PM_{2.5}$), PM_{10} (concentration of PM_{10}), CO (concentration of Carbon monoxide) and AQI. Each column has 15862 rows for different dates. Each row represent date of which the concentration is given. The dataset contains the record concentration of mentioned pollutants from 12 May 2021 to 2 December 2022.

The Air Quality Index (AQI) is a comprehensive measure that evaluates air quality by considering the concentrations of various pollutants, including O_3, $PM_{2.5}$, PM_{10}, CO, sulfur dioxide (SO_2), and nitrogen dioxide (NO_2). It offers a standardized method for communicating air quality to the public, with distinct AQI categories signaling varying levels of health risks. There are several factors that impact the AQI of the city. Seasonal predictors such as temperature, humidity, wind speed, and pressure contribute to air quality. The effect of these variables might not be explicitly included independent columns but may be assumed to influence the parameters of the dataset. For example, elevated temperatures increase the rate of ozone (O_3) formation, while higher humidity helps particulate matter such as PM2.5 to take up water and settle. Wind speed and direction are also vital, with weaker wind speeds increasing pollutant accumulation and more powerful winds facilitating dispersion. Rainfall further cleanses the air by washing out the pollutants, allowing for the temporary improvement in AQI. Because the dataset involves several seasons, variability in the pollutant concentration indirectly reflects seasonal effects. Nonetheless, rather than targeting seasonal parameters, we directly examined the concentration of O_3 (ozone), PM2.5 (particulate matter 2.5), PM10 (particulate matter 10), and CO (carbon monoxide) in order to estimate their direct influence on AQI.

The data also accounts for the impacts of several policy interventions undertaken in Delhi to manage air pollution. Initiatives like the odd-even rule for traffic, where the use of vehicles is restricted on the basis of registration numbers, has resulted in short-term declines in PM2.5, PM10, and CO levels. Likewise, the impact of Diwali firecracker bans can be accounted for in the form of spikes in pollution in the data. Also, the adoption of the Graded Response Action Plan (GRAP), which imposes limitations on construction and industrial activities depending on AQI levels of the city, would have impacted the trends in reported air pollution data. Even though the dataset does not contain meteorological conditions or policy-related variables explicitly, it indirectly accounts for their impact through daily pollutant concentration data. By amalgamating multiple pollutants into a unified index, the AQI facilitates policymakers, health authorities, and the public in comprehending overall air quality conditions and devising suitable strategies to safeguard health. Hence, in this study, we employ various machine learning models to discern which one performs optimally in predicting AQI.

4.2 Data Preprocessing

4.2.1 Removing Missing Values

Data preprocessing analysis is conducted. Analyzing data preprocessing is crucial for assessing data quality, a prerequisite for effective visualization and ML model creation. Preprocessing reduces noise, enhancing processing speed and model generalization. Common issues include outliers and missing data. We checked if our dataset contains missing values or not. The data analysis revealed the presence of missing values. Through Figure1, we can see that one row of $PM_{2.5}$ and 16 rows of O_3 contain missing values. Given that the proportion of rows with missing values is insignificant compared to the total dataset size, we opted to remove these rows to ensure data integrity and completeness.

Figure 1. Number of rows containing missing values

```
In [11]: df.isnull().sum()

Out[11]: date      0
         pm2_5     1
         pm10      0
         o3       16
         co        0
         so2       0
         aqi       0
         dtype: int64

In [12]: df=df.dropna()
```

4.2.2 Outlier Detection and Removal

Outliers within a dataset are data points that deviate significantly from the rest of the observations and can have significant impact on the distribution of data and model performance. Managing outliers is therefore essential for improving accuracy of predictions to ensure that the model is not affected by the extreme values while training. In the selected dataset, outlier identification is done using boxplot (Figure 2) which graphically shows the extreme values beyond the typical range of observations. The presence of outliers in the air pollution data can be attributed to sudden environmental changes, extreme weather conditions, or sporadic emission events such as industrial activities, vehicular congestion, or fireworks during festive periods.

To systematically handle these outliers, we employed the Interquartile Range (IQR) method, a widely used statistical technique that helps detect and remove extreme values by defining thresholds based on the first (Q1) and third quartile (Q3) values. The formula used for outlier detection is IQR=Q3-Q1. Figure 2 illustrates that both PM2.5 and PM10 exhibit a significant number of outliers, indicating fluctuations in particulate matter concentrations beyond typical levels. Such variations may be caused by short-term pollution spikes due to local emissions or weather condition variations. However, in Figure 3, these outliers are effectively addressed and resolved using the IQR method, resulting in a more refined dataset with reduced variability and improved reliability for model training. This preprocessing step ensures that our predictive model gives more accurate AQI predictions.

Figure 2. Boxplot with outliers

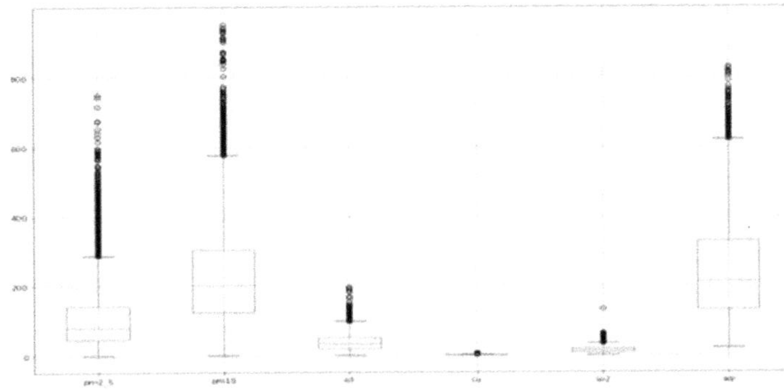

Figure 3. Boxplot without outliers

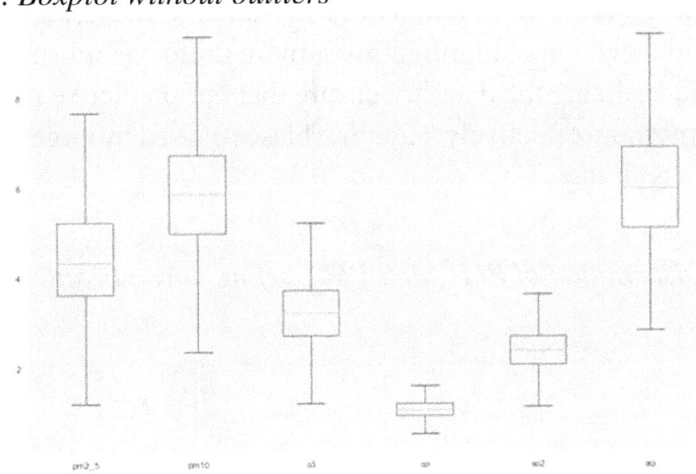

4.2.3 Data Normalization

Normalization helps in transforming the data into a standardized scale, thereby improving model performance and stability. This is an important data preprocessing step for dealing with features of the dataset that exhibit non-normal distributions. In the selected dataset, PM2.5 and PM10 concentrations showed a non-normal distribution, as depicted in Figure 4. Such variations can lead to wide-ranging values that may negatively impact model training, especially for algorithms sensitive to magnitude differences among features.

To enhance prediction accuracy and improve model convergence, normalization was applied to the dataset. Normalization scales the data within a specific range ensuring that all features contribute equally to the learning process. The formula for Min-Max normalization, which was used in our study, is as follows:

$$X_{normalized} = \frac{X - X_{min}}{X_{max} - X_{min}}$$

where $X_{normalized}$ is the normalized value, X_{min} is the minimum value, X_{max} is the maximum value, and X is the is the original value of the dataset. Figure 5 illustrates the distribution of PM2.5 and PM10 after applying the normalization technique, highlighting a more uniform and standardized scale. By normalizing the data, we ensure that our predictive models can learn patterns more effectively, reducing biases caused by large variations in feature magnitudes.

Figure 4. Distribution of $PM_{2.5}$ and PM_{10} before normalization

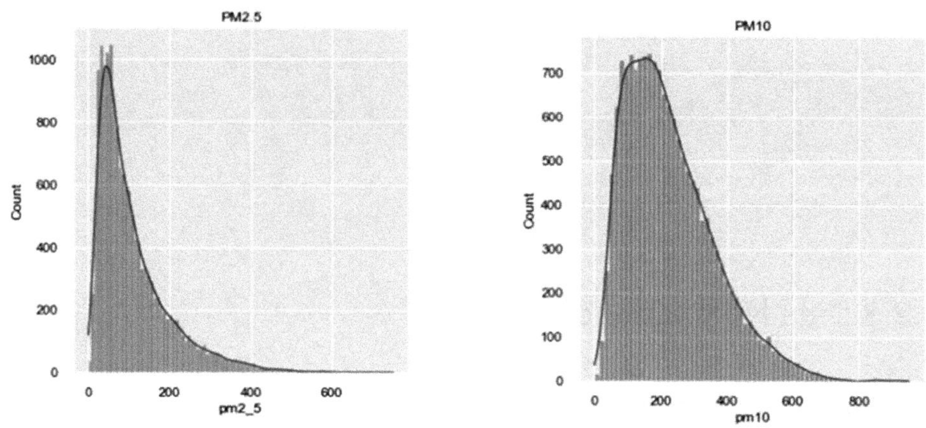

Figure 5. Distribution of $PM_{2.5}$ and PM_{10} after normalization

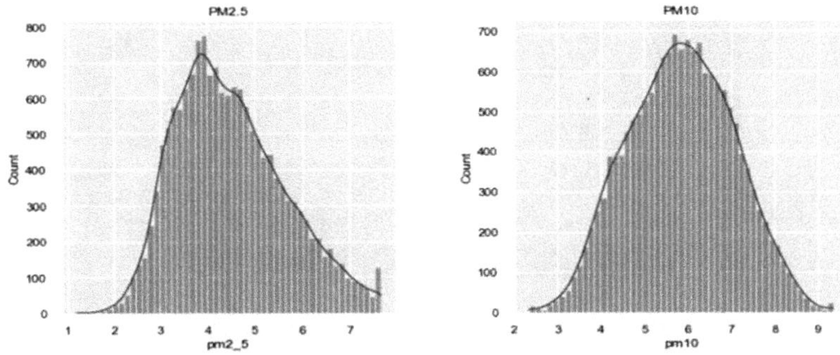

4.2.4 Data Standardization or Data Scaling

After data preprocessing successfully removing outliers, the next step involves data transformation, such as standardization or scaling. The dataset exhibits a wide range of values, with some features ranging from 0 to 10^3, while others have values up to a maximum of 10^2. To ensure consistency and comparability across features, it is necessary to scale them to a uniform range. While standardization is commonly employed, in certain cases, data scaling yields superior results. For this particular dataset, data scaling is chosen as the preferred transformation method.

4.3 Correlation Analysis

After, exploratory data analysis (EDA) was conducted on our dataset. Exploratory data analysis (EDA) represents the initial stage of data analytics, conducted prior to the application of any machine learning models. Each independent variable (CO, O_3, SO_2, $PM_{2.5}$, and PM_{10}) influences the value of the dependent variable i.e. AQI. In Figure 6, the importance of features for AQI can be observed. From this analysis, it can be concluded that $PM_{2.5}$ and PM_{10} exhibit high importance in determining AQI levels.

Figure 6. Plot showing the feature importance of each variable

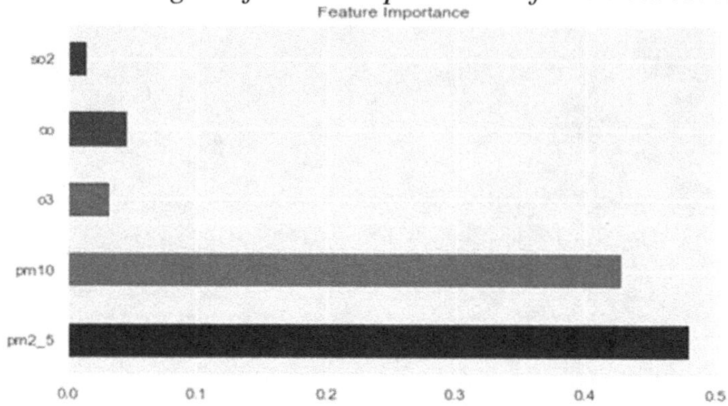

Correlation checking is a crucial preprocessing step as it identifies highly correlated features, which can introduce redundancy and affect prediction quality. Heatmap visualization offers an effective way to assess and evaluate correlations among features, providing clear insights into their relationships.

Figure 7. Heatmap of co-relation among variables

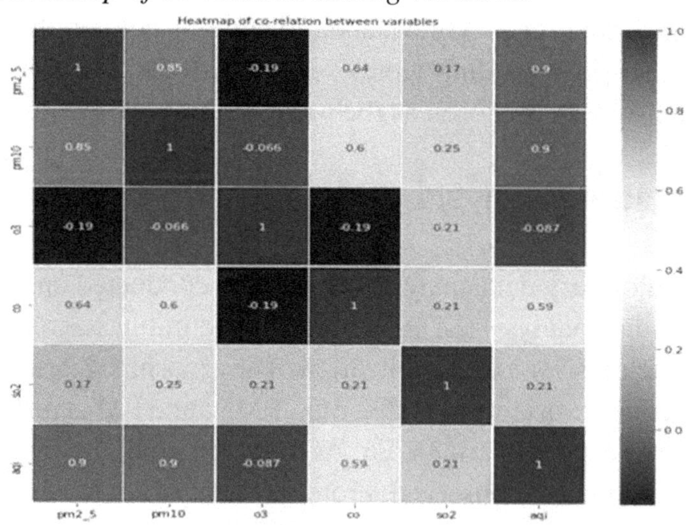

Figure 7 shows the heatmap of correlation coefficient between two variables. Upon inspection of the heatmap, it is evident that $PM_{2.5}$ and PM_{10}, exhibit strong correlations with AQI, with correlation coefficients of 0.9, and 0.9 respectively.

4.4 Comparative Analysis of Various Machine Learning Algorithms

In this section, we discuss the predictive power of machine learning models for predicting AQI for Delhi state. To do that, the dataset is divided into training and testing subsets before assessing machine learning models. Training set contains 75% and testing set contains 25% of data as shown in Figure 8. The model is trained using the training set, and its predictions are compared against the testing set to evaluate the accuracy of the model.

Figure 8. Splitting dataset into training and testing sets

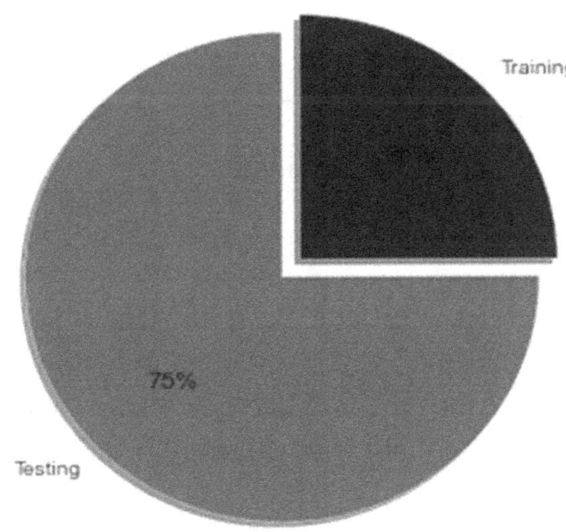

These models include Regression models such as Linear Regression and Kernel Ridge Regression, Elastic Net, boosting techniques like Gradient Boosting, XGBoost, and LightGBM, as well as Random Forest and KNN (K-Nearest Neighbors). We applied various performance metrics such as Root Mean Square Error (RMSE), Mean Absolute Error (MAE), and R-squared (R^2) on the models to evaluate their performance. The results indicate that Random Forest gave better performance out of the 10 selected machine learning methods with RMSE values of 0.293, MAE value of 0.216, and R^2 accuracy of 0.932. This was followed by categorical boosting with an RMSE value of 0.294, MAE value of 0.216, and R^2 accuracy of 0.931. A detailed summary of each model's performance is presented in Table 1.

Table 1. Mean Average Error (MAE), Root Mean Square Error (RMSE) and R^2 values for all selected ML models

S.No.	Model	MAE	RMSE	R^2
1	K-Nearest Neighbor Regression	0.245	0.331	0.913
2	**Random Forest Regression**	**0.216**	**0.293**	**0.932**
3	Extreme Gradient Boosting Regression (XGBoost)	0.228	0.310	0.925
4	Gradient Boosting Regression	0.226	0.308	0.925
5	Support Vector Regression	0.287	0.372	0.891
6	Kernel Ridge Regression	0.272	0.352	0.902
7	Elastic Net Regression	0.292	0.375	0.889
8	Light Gradient Boosting Regression	0.219	0.298	0.930
9	Categorical Boosting (CatBoost) Regression	0.216	0.294	0.931
10	Linear Regression	0.292	0.375	0.889

Figure 9 displays a scatter plot illustrating the relationship between predicted and true values of AQI. As the points on the scatter plot are aligned closely around the diagonal line (y = x), it suggests a strong correlation between predicted and true values, indicating high accuracy in the model predictions.

Figure 9. Scatter plot between predicted values and true values of AQI

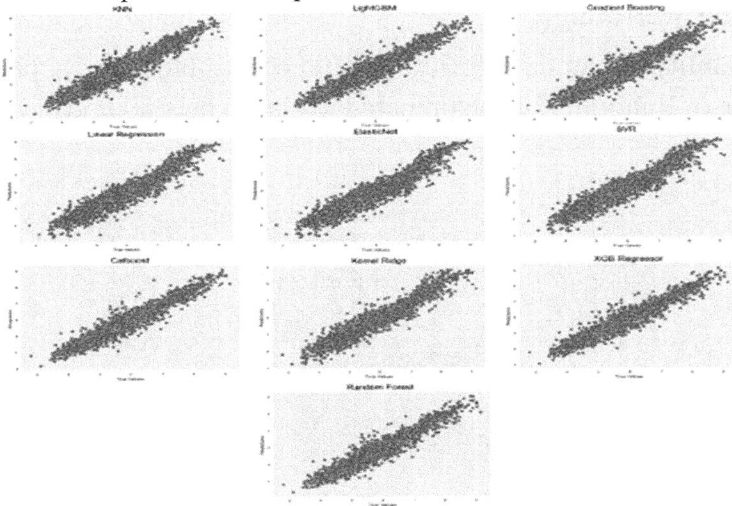

Visualization plots help enhance our understanding of the results and expedite decision-making. Here, we present plots depicting the performance metrics (MAE, RMSE, and R-squared) for all implemented models.

Figure 10. Bar graph of Mean Absolute Error for each model

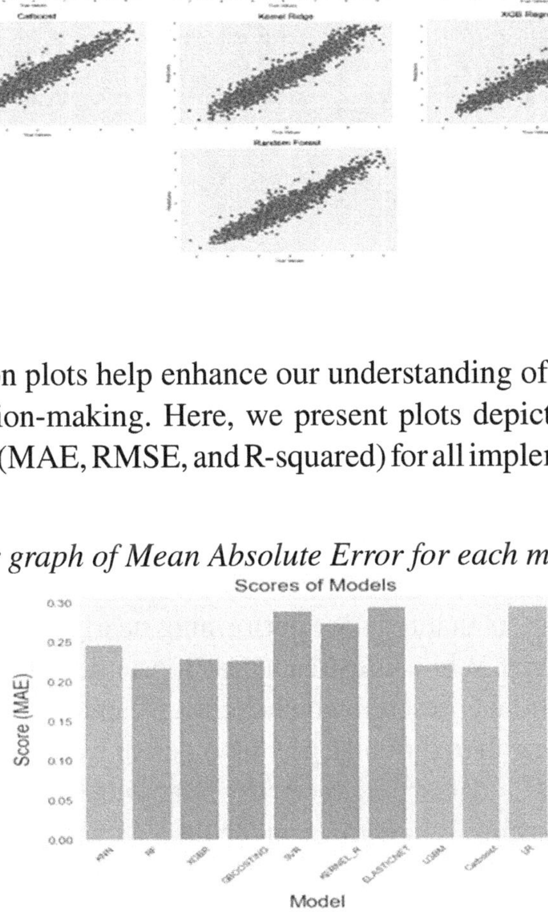

Figure 10 shows the Mean Absolute Error of all implemented model from which we can conclude that Random Forest has lowest MAE value of 0.216 and highest MAE value of 0.292 is obtained by both Elastic Net and Linear Regression. While both elastic net and linear regression models may be susceptible to overfitting, Random Forest has a built-in capability to mitigate overfitting.

This ability to handle overfitting could contribute to the superior performance of Random Forest compared to elastic net and linear regression models.

Figure 11. Bar graph of root mean square error for each model

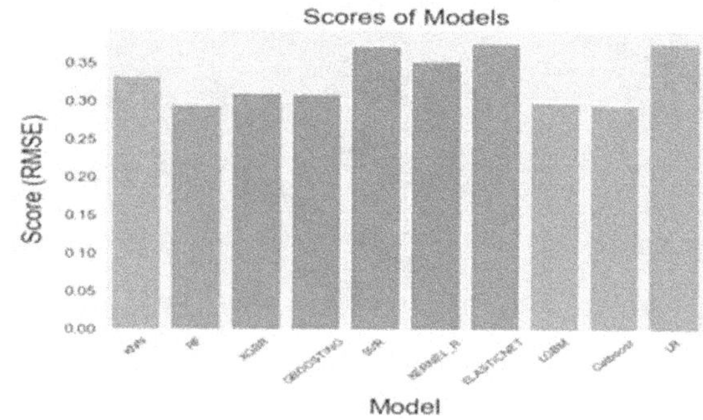

From Figure 10, it is evident that LGBM, CatBoost, and Random Forest exhibit similar RMSE values of 0.298, 0.294, and 0.293, respectively. Moreover, in Figure 11, we can observe that the R-squared scores for each model are also similar, with scores of 0.930, 0.930, and 0.930, respectively. This suggests that they are performing nearly equally in terms of predictive accuracy. While LGBM and CatBoost utilize gradient boosting techniques, Random Forest relies on bagging. Despite the algorithmic disparities, all three aim to diminish prediction error by integrating multiple weak learners. The dataset characteristics facilitate effective utilization of ensemble learning by all three algorithms, leading to the observed similarity in RMSE values.

Figure 12. Bar graph of R-squared accuracy score for each model

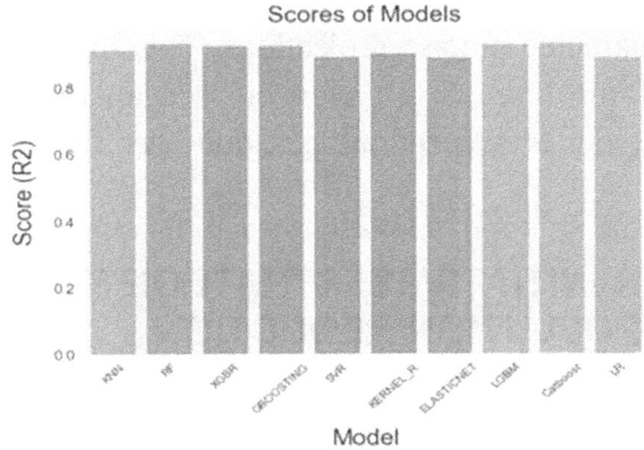

In our study, we found that Random Forest and CatBoost models outperformed other methods in predicting AQI. This superiority can be attributed to various factors. Firstly, air quality is influenced by a multitude of variables such as weather conditions, pollutants, geography, and human activities. Decision tree-based models like Random Forest and CatBoost excel at capturing the intricate non-linear relationships between these factors and AQI, which may be challenging for linear methods to model effectively.

Moreover, air quality data often contains noise from measurement errors or outliers. Decision tree-based models are known for their robustness to such noise and outliers, enabling them to provide stable predictions even with imperfect data.

Another advantage of Random Forest and CatBoost is their ensemble nature, where multiple decision trees are combined to make predictions. This approach tends to yield better generalization performance compared to individual decision trees, making these models particularly well-suited for AQI prediction tasks.

The analysis presented in the current study trains the model on Delhi's dataset but may not generalize well to regions with different pollution dynamics. Nevertheless, our findings can be generalized to other metropolitan cities with comparable urban activity, traffic, industrial emissions, and climatic factors. Cities having similar sources of pollution and seasonal fluctuation are likely to show comparable AQI trends. However, for those cities with unique environmental and socio-economic determinants, further region-specific information as well as model modification would be needed to guarantee precise projections. This limitation presents an opportunity for future research to explore model adaptability across diverse geographical regions by incorporating region-specific factors.

5. CLEAN AIR INITIATIVES: STRATEGIES FOR EFFECTIVE POLLUTION REDUCTION

Our trained model can be used to forecast air quality levels in Delhi. These predictions can help policymakers anticipate pollution hotspots and take proactive measures to mitigate their impact. In this article, we suggest three-fold synergistic measures that can be taken for improving air quality in Delhi.

5.1 Development of Urban Green Spaces

By harnessing the predictive capabilities of machine learning models for predicting ambient air quality, cities can strategically identify pollution hotspots with elevated levels of air pollutants. The machine learning models serve as invaluable tools guiding policymakers in prioritizing interventions at these pollution hotspots. One such intervention strategy involves the development of urban green spaces (Ramaiah & Avtar, 2019) through innovative urban planning initiatives in lieu of the pollution hotspots.

Urban green spaces encompass both public and private open areas within urban environments, characterized primarily by their vegetation cover. These spaces serve as vibrant hubs for mitigation of ambient air pollutants through absorption of carbon dioxide, and reduction of the urban heat island effect, thereby enhancing overall environmental quality and livability. According to research conducted by Knight et al. (2021), green spaces have been shown to effectively decrease levels of heat, ozone, and ultraviolet (UV) radiation, thereby leading to enhancements in air quality. On average, urban green spaces reduce the urban heat island (UHI) effect by cooling the air by approximately 1 degree Celsius and providing shade, (Vargas-Hernández, Pallagst, & Zdunek-Wielgołaska, 2023)

The use of machine learning models can assist in identifying ideal locations for parks, gardens, and green belts within these pollution-affected zones. Using this data, urban planners can design tailored green space projects aimed at mitigating the adverse effects of pollution while enhancing residents' access to nature and recreational facilities. Through proactive implementation of these initiatives, cities can not only combat pollution but also foster healthier, more sustainable urban environments. Ongoing monitoring and evaluation, driven by ML model analysis, will ensure the effectiveness of these green space interventions, enabling cities to adapt and refine their strategies for long-term pollution reduction and environmental resilience.

5.2 Integrating Pollution Control Devices for Cleaner Vehicles

In addition to the establishment of urban green spaces, the integration of various pollution control devices into vehicles presents a promising avenue for reducing air pollution emissions and enhancing fuel efficiency. This integration is particularly crucial given the findings of previous studies, such as those conducted by Goyal et al. (2006), which indicate that, the transport sector's contribution to pollution in cities like Delhi can be as high as 72%. Among the key pollution control devices are Catalytic Converters, Exhaust Gas Recirculation (EGR) Systems, Selective Catalytic Reduction (SCR) systems, and Particulate Filters.

Catalytic converters (Robles-Lorite et al., 2023) play a vital role in reducing harmful emissions by facilitating chemical reactions that convert toxic gases like carbon monoxide, nitrogen oxides, and hydrocarbons into less harmful substances. EGR (Piqueras et al., 2020) systems contribute to nitrogen oxide reduction by recirculating a portion of exhaust gases back into the engine cylinders, thereby lowering combustion temperatures and minimizing the formation of nitrogen oxides. Similarly, SCR systems utilize a catalyst to convert nitrogen oxides into nitrogen and water vapor by injecting a urea-based solution (AdBlue) into the exhaust stream, commonly used in diesel vehicles to meet stringent emission standards. This system has demonstrated average NOx reductions (deNOx) of 82.8%, 91.7%, and 85.5% for SCR-inlet gas temperatures below, within, and above the thermal window of 220–340 °C, respectively, (Mera et al., 2020). Diesel particulate filters (DPFs) (Guan et al., 2015) are designed to trap and remove soot particles from the exhaust stream, thereby reducing emissions of particulate matter (PM) and black carbon. This integration will be particularly useful, as our analysis shows that PM2.5 and PM 10 emitted from vehicular emissions are major causes of pollution.

In addition to integration of pollution control devices, the adoption of electric vehicles (Alanazi, 2023) offers a significant reduction in emissions compared to traditional internal combustion engine vehicles. The integration of oxygen sensors (Ramamoorthy, Dutta, & Akbar, 2003) within the vehicles will aid in monitoring oxygen levels in exhaust gases which can be used as feedback to optimize fuel combustion. This will help in further reducing emissions and enhancing fuel efficiency. Fuel vapor recovery systems (Irivama et al., 2005) are also instrumental in capturing and recirculating fuel vapors from the fuel tank to the engine intake system, preventing their release into the atmosphere and mitigating emissions of volatile organic compounds (VOCs). The integration of these pollution control devices and systems into vehicles holds promise for significantly reducing emissions, improving air quality, and mitigating the environmental impact of transportation.

In addition to pollution control devices, the use of biodiesel-diesel blends (Hasan & Rahman, 2017) in internal combustion engines has gained significant attention for its potential to improve both performance and emissions characteristics. In particular, studies have shown that the optimal blend ratio, such as B20 (20% biodiesel, 80% diesel), combined with enhancements in operating parameters and the use of catalytic converters, can lead to notable improvements. In a research study conducted by Ramalinga, Rajendra, and Ganesan. (2018) it is demonstrated that employing B20 in conjunction with optimized operating conditions and catalytic converter technology resulted in enhanced engine performance and a substantial reduction in emissions compared to conventional diesel engines. These findings underscore the promising role of biodiesel blends in achieving cleaner and more efficient combustion processes in internal combustion engines.

5.3 Measures for Effective Prevention of Agricultural Biomass Burning

Another major cause of ambient air pollution in Delhi is transboundary pollutant transport. This significantly contributes to seasonal air quality deterioration in Delhi. Burning agricultural stubble can result in the significant emission of various air pollutants, including CO_2, N_2O, CH_4, CO, NO_x, SO_2, and particulate matter (PM2.5 and PM10), such as elemental carbon. Sahai et al. (2011) showed in his work that burning 63 million tons of stubble biomass releases approximately 91 million tons of CO2, 3.4 million tons of CO, 0.6 million tons of CH4, 0.1 million tons of NOx, and about 1.2 million tons of particulate matter into the atmosphere. In a recent study by Nirwan et al. (2024), they studied the spatial distribution of contributing areas for gaseous criteria air pollutants, particularly focusing on stubble burning. The research shows that there is a sudden increase in CO levels in the National Capital Territory (NCT) coinciding with peaks in stubble burning in Punjab during the post monsoon season. Meteorological conditions were also found to be a key factor which exacerbates the problem. It has been observed in their studies that winter contributes to a larger area transporting pollutants, despite more CO being generated during the post monsoon season due to stubble burning.

To address the issue of crop residue burning which is a significant contributor to air pollution and environmental degradation requires comprehensive strategies encompassing both in-situ and ex-situ crop residue management initiatives. In-situ Crop Residue Management (CRM) (Singh et al., 2019) involves the procurement of specialized machinery such as happy seeders, straw choppers, and mulchers, enabling farmers to manage crop residues effectively without resorting to burning. Promoting the adoption of high-yield and short-duration paddy varieties encourages practices like direct seeding of rice (DSR) (Farooq et al., 2011), reducing the volume of crop residue post-harvest. Moreover, staggering the harvesting schedule among farmers helps decrease the concentration of crop residues and facilitates better utilization of CRM machinery.

Ex-situ Crop Residue Management (Kurinji & Kumar, 2021) initiatives include utilizing paddy straw as biomass feedstock for power generation in biomass power projects, co-firing paddy straw in thermal power plants alongside coal, and converting it into second-generation (2G) ethanol feedstock. Additionally, paddy straw serves as feedstock in compressed biogas (CBG) plants, providing clean-burning fuel for vehicles and cooking, reducing emissions and reliance on traditional fuels. Employing paddy straw as fuel in industrial boilers and establishing waste-to-energy plants utilizing it as feedstock contribute to sustainable waste management and clean energy production, (Harun, Hanafiah, & Noor, 2022). Moreover, rice husk finds applications in various industries, including construction, fuel production, and water pollutant removal, further enhancing its utility and sustainability, (Shukla et al., 2022). These initiatives in synergy will promote sustainable agricultural practices and help in mitigating air pollution. This will help in achieving India's objectives of environmental conservation and renewable energy development.

6. CONCLUSION

The research delves into evaluating the efficacy of various regression models for predicting air quality parameters such as CO, O_3, SO_2, PM 2.5, and PM 10 concentrations for Delhi AQI dataset. Through a thorough examination, including metrics like Mean Absolute Error (MAE), Root Mean Squared Error (RMSE), and R-squared (R^2), we aim to identify the most accurate model. Our findings reveal that the Random Forest model emerges as the top performer, with an R^2 value of 0.932, RMSE of 0.293, and MAE of 0.216. CatBoost model perform well due with R^2 value of 0.931, RMSE of 0.294, and MAE of 0.216. Random Forest and CatBoost stand out due to their ability to capture intricate relationships within air quality data, resilience against noise and outliers, and the ensemble approach that enhances predictive capabilities. To mitigate the impact of air pollutants some key initiatives can be taken such as development of urban green spaces, integration of pollution control devices in vehicles, and implementing measures to prevent agricultural biomass burning effectively.

Credit Authorship Contribution Statement:

Vikram Ranjan: Writing – original draft, Data Curation, Investigation, Visualization, Software.

Garima Chanana: Conceptualization, Methodology, Investigation, Formal analysis, Writing – review & editing, Supervision.

Funding Declaration: The authors are thankful to Vivekananda Institute of Professional Studies - Technical Campus for their support. This research did not receive any specific grant from funding agencies.

Data Availability: The link to the dataset used for training the models is https://github.com/sagar118/H2OHackathon-AQI-Prediction/blob/main/data/train.csv. All the calculated data is reported within the manuscript.

REFERENCES

AbdelSattar, A. (2019), Monitoring air pollution using satellite data, *Proceedings of the International Conference on Industrial Engineering and Operations Management*, 772-780 https://www.ieomsociety.org/gcc2019/papers/126.pdf

Alanazi, F. (2023). Electric Vehicles: Benefits, Challenges, and Potential Solutions for Widespread Adaptation. *Applied Sciences (Basel, Switzerland), 13*(10), 6016. DOI: 10.3390/app13106016

Bangdiwala, S. I. (2018). Regression: Simple linear. *International Journal of Injury Control and Safety Promotion, 25*(1), 113–115. DOI: 10.1080/17457300.2018.1426702 PMID: 29400125

Bentéjac, C., Csörgő, A., & Martínez-Muñoz, G. (2021). A comparative analysis of gradient boosting algorithms. *Artificial Intelligence Review, 54*(3), 1937–1967. DOI: 10.1007/s10462-020-09896-5

Charan, A. (2022). Marketing communication and awareness on sustainable consumption of fossil fuel in Delhi and NCR. *International Journal of Multidisciplinary Education Research, 11*,http://ijmer.in.doi./2022/11.06.23

Chatterji, A. (2021). Air pollution in Delhi: filling the policy gaps, *Massachusetts Undergraduate Journal of Economics, 17(1)*https://www.umass.edu/economics/sites/default/files/MUJE2021.pdf

Chen, T., & Guestrin, C. (2016). Xgboost: A scalable tree boosting system. In *Proceedings of the 22nd acm sigkdd international conference on knowledge discovery and data mining* (pp. 785-794). DOI: 10.1145/2939672.2939785

Chen, X., Zheng, H., Wang, H., & Yan, T. (2022). Can machine learning algorithms perform better than multiple linear regression in predicting nitrogen excretion from lactating dairy cows. *Scientific Reports, 12*(1), 12478. DOI: 10.1038/s41598-022-16490-y PMID: 35864287

Dutta, A., & Jinsart, W. (2021). Air quality, atmospheric variables and spread of COVID-19 in Delhi (India): An analysis. *Aerosol and Air Quality Research, 21*(3), 200417. DOI: 10.4209/aaqr.2020.07.0417

Farooq, M. K. H. M., Siddique, K. H., Rehman, H., Aziz, T., Lee, D. J., & Wahid, A. (2011). Rice direct seeding: Experiences, challenges and opportunities. *Soil & Tillage Research, 111*(2), 87–98. DOI: 10.1016/j.still.2010.10.008

Goyal, S. K., Ghatge, S. V., Nema, P. S. M. T., & Tamhane, , S. (2006). Understanding urban vehicular pollution problem vis-a-vis ambient air quality–case study of a megacity (Delhi, India). *Environmental Monitoring and Assessment, 119*, 557–569. DOI: 10.1007/s10661-005-9043-2 PMID: 16741810

Guan, B., Zhan, R., Lin, H., & Huang, Z. (2015). Review of the state-of-the-art of exhaust particulate filter technology in internal combustion engines. *Journal of Environmental Management, 154*, 225–258. DOI: 10.1016/j.jenvman.2015.02.027 PMID: 25743879

Gupta, N. S., Mohta, Y., Heda, K., Armaan, R., Valarmathi, B., & Arulkumaran, G. (2023). Prediction of Air Quality Index Using Machine Learning Techniques: A Comparative Analysis. *Journal of Environmental and Public Health, 2023*, 1–26. Advance online publication. DOI: 10.1155/2023/4916267

Guttikunda, S., & Jawahar, P. (2020). Can we vacuum our air pollution problem using smog towers? *Atmosphere (Basel), 11*(9), 922. DOI: 10.3390/atmos11090922

Halsana, S. (2020). Air quality prediction model using supervised machine learning algorithms. International Journal of Scientific Research in Computer Science. *Engineering and Information Technology, 8*, 190–201. DOI: 10.32628/CSEIT206435

Harun, S. N., Hanafiah, M. M., & Noor, N. M. (2022). Rice straw utilisation for bioenergy production: A brief overview. *Energies, 15*(15), 5542. DOI: 10.3390/en15155542

Hasan, M. M., & Rahman, M. M. (2017). Performance and emission characteristics of biodiesel–diesel blend and environmental and economic impacts of biodiesel production: A review. *Renewable 5and Sustainable Energy Reviews, 74*, 938-948 .DOI: 10.1016/j.rser.2017.03.045

Iriyama, Y., Kobayashi, M., Matsubara, T., Nishimura, Y., Nomura, R., & Ishikawa, T. (2005). Design of a fuel vapor-containment system (FVS) to meet zero evaporative emissions requirements in a hybrid electric vehicle. *SAE Transactions*, 1551–1558. DOI: 10.4271/2005-01-3825

Ishwaran, H., & Lu, M. (2019). Standard errors and confidence intervals for variable importance in random forest regression, classification, and survival. *Statistics in Medicine*, *38*(4), 558–582. DOI: 10.1002/sim.7803 PMID: 29869423

Juarez, E. K., & Petersen, M. R. (2021). A comparison of machine learning methods to forecast tropospheric ozone levels in Delhi. *Atmosphere (Basel)*, *13*(1), 46. DOI: 10.3390/atmos13010046

Ke, G., Meng, Q., Finley, T., Wang, T., Chen, W., Ma, W., & Liu, T. Y. (2017). Advances in neural information processing systems: Vol. 30. Lightgbm: A highly efficient gradient boosting decision tree. Academic Press.

Knight, T., Price, S., Bowler, D., Hookway, A., King, S., Konno, K., & Richter, R. L. (2021). How effective is 'greening' of urban areas in reducing human exposure to ground-level ozone concentrations, UV exposure and the 'urban heat island effect'? An updated systematic review. *Environmental Evidence*, *10*(1), 1–38. DOI: 10.1186/s13750-021-00226-y

Kramer, O. (2011). Unsupervised K-nearest neighbor regression. arXiv preprint arXiv:1107.3600. /arXiv.1107.3600DOI: 10.48550

Kumar, K., & Pande, B. P. (2023). Air pollution prediction with machine learning: A case study of Indian cities. *International Journal of Environmental Science and Technology*, *20*(5), 5333–5348. DOI: 10.1007/s13762-022-04241-5 PMID: 35603096

Kurinji, L. S., & Kumar, S. (2021). *Is Ex-situ Crop Residue Management a Scalable Solution to Stubble Burning? A Punjab Case Study*. Council on Energy, Environment and Water.

Laura, D. V., Chatterton, T., Namdeo, A., Shivanagendra, S. G., Goyal, S., Bell, M., Goodman, P., Longhurst, J., Hayes, E., Kumar, R., Sethi, V., Ramadurai, S. B. G., Majumder, S., Menon, J., Turamari, M. N., & Barnes, J. (2018). Air pollution in Delhi: A review of past and current policy approaches. *Air Pollution.* DOI: 10.2495/AIR180411

Li, Y., Sha, Z., Tang, A., Goulding, K., & Liu, X. (2023). The application of machine learning to air pollution research: A bibliometric analysis. *Ecotoxicology and Environmental Safety, 257*, 114911. DOI: 10.1016/j.ecoenv.2023.114911 PMID: 37154080

Mallegowda, M., Kanavalli, A., Verma, Y., Vamsi, S. J. K., Mukesh, T., & Saxena, V. (2021). Prediction of air quality index using machine data learning on atmospheric. *NVEO-Natural Volatiles & Essential Oils Journal,* 7544-7552.

Manisalidis, I., Stavropoulou, E., Stavropoulos, A., & Bezirtzoglou, E. (2020). Environmental and health impacts of air pollution: A review. *Frontiers in Public Health, 8*, 14. DOI: 10.3389/fpubh.2020.00014 PMID: 32154200

Mera, Z., Matzer, C., Hausberger, S., & Fonseca, N. (2020). Performance of selective catalytic reduction (SCR) system in a diesel passenger car under real-world conditions. *Applied Thermal Engineering, 181*, 115983. DOI: 10.1016/j.applthermaleng.2020.115983

Nirwan, N., Siddiqui, A., Kannemadugu, H. B. S., Chauhan, P., & Singh, R. P. (2024). Determining hotspots of gaseous criteria air pollutants in Delhi airshed and its association with stubble burning. *Scientific Reports, 14*(1), 986. DOI: 10.1038/s41598-023-51140-x PMID: 38200112

Piqueras, P., Morena, J. D. L., Sanchis, E. J., & Pitarch, R. (2020). Impact of exhaust gas recirculation on gaseous emissions of turbocharged spark-ignition engines. *Applied Sciences (Basel, Switzerland), 10*(21), 7634. DOI: 10.3390/app10217634

Prokhorenkova, L., Gusev, G., Vorobev, A., Dorogush, A. V., & Gulin, A. (2018). Advances in neural information processing systems: Vol. 31. CatBoost: unbiased boosting with categorical features. Academic Press.

Ramaiah, M., & Avtar, R. (2019). Urban green spaces and their need in cities of rapidly urbanizing India: A review. *Urban Science (Basel, Switzerland), 3*(3), 94. DOI: 10.3390/urbansci3030094

Ramalingam, S., Rajendran, S., & Ganesan, P. (2018). Performance improvement and exhaust emissions reduction in biodiesel operated diesel engine through the use of operating parameters and catalytic converter: A review. *Renewable & Sustainable Energy Reviews, 81*, 3215–3222. DOI: 10.1016/j.rser.2017.08.069

Ramamoorthy, R., Dutta, P. K., & Akbar, S. A. (2003). Oxygen sensors: Materials, methods, designs and applications. *Journal of Materials Science, 38*(21), 4271–4282. DOI: 10.1023/A:1026370729205

Ravindiran, G., Hayder, G., Kanagarathinam, K., Alagumalai, A., & Sonne, C. (2023). Air quality prediction by machine learning models: A predictive study on the indian coastal city of Visakhapatnam. *Chemosphere, 338*, 139518. DOI: 10.1016/j.chemosphere.2023.139518 PMID: 37454985

Robles-Lorite, L., Dorado-Vicente, R., Torres-Jiménez, E., Bombek, G., & Lešnik, L. (2023). Recent Advances in the Development of Automotive Catalytic Converters: A Systematic Review. *Energies, 16*(18), 6425. DOI: 10.3390/en16186425

() Saadat, M. N., Das, S., Nandy, S., Pandey, D., Chakraborty, M., Mina, U., & Sarkar, A. (2021). Can the nation-wide COVID-19 lockdown help India identify region-specific strategies for air pollution?. *Spatial Information Research*, 1-15. .DOI: 10.1007/s41324-021-00426-1

Sahai, S., Sharma, C., Singh, S. K., & Gupta, P. K. (2011). Assessment of trace gases, carbon and nitrogen emissions from feld burning of agricultural residues in India. *Nutrient Cycling in Agroecosystems, 89*(2), 143–157. DOI: 10.1007/s10705-010-9384-2

Shevade, S. K., Keerthi, S. S., Bhattacharyya, C., & Murthy, K. R. K. (2000). Improvements to the SMO algorithm for SVM regression. *IEEE Transactions on Neural Networks, 11*(5), 1188–1193. DOI: 10.1109/72.870050 PMID: 18249845

Shukla, S. S., Chava, R., Appari, S., Bahurudeen, A., & Kuncharam, B. V. R. (2022). Sustainable use of rice husk for the cleaner production of value-added products. *Journal of Environmental Chemical Engineering*, *10*(1), 106899. DOI: 10.1016/j.jece.2021.106899

Singh, A. K., Alagusundaram, K., Kumar, A., Singh, R., Sehgal, V. K., Chahal, V. P., . . . Singh, S. K. (2019). In-Situ Crop Residue Management: Key Outcome and Learning. *Division of Agricultural Extension, ICAR, New Delhi, 30.*

Singh, T., Kaur, A., Katyal, S. K., Walia, S. K., Dhand, G., Sheoran, K., Mohanty, S. N., Khan, M. I., Awwad, F. A., & Ismail, E. A. (2023). Exploring the relationship between air quality index and lung cancer mortality in India: Predictive modeling and impact assessment. *Scientific Reports*, *13*(1), 20256. DOI: 10.1038/s41598-023-47705-5 PMID: 37985855

Suk, W. A., Ahanchian, H., Asante, K. A., Carpenter, D. O., Diaz-Barriga, F., Ha, E. H., Huo, X., King, M., Ruchirawat, M., da Silva, E. R., Sly, L., Sly, P. D., Stein, R. T., Berg, M. V. D., Zar, H., & Landrigan, P. J. (2016). Environmental pollution: An under-recognized threat to children's health, especially in low-and middle-income countries. *Environmental Health Perspectives*, *124*(3), A41–A45. DOI: 10.1289/ehp.1510517 PMID: 26930243

Ucun Ozel, H., Gemici, B. T., Gemici, E., Ozel, H. B., Cetin, M., & Sevik, H. (2020). Application of artificial neural networks to predict the heavy metal contamination in the Bartin *River.Environmental Science and Pollution Research International*, *27*(34), 42495–42512. DOI: 10.1007/s11356-020-10156-w PMID: 32705560

Vargas-Hernández, J. G., Pallagst, K., & Zdunek-Wielgołaska, J. (2023). Urban green spaces as a component of an ecosystem. In *Sustainable Development and Environmental Stewardship: Global Initiatives Towards Engaged Sustainability* (pp. 165–198). Springer International Publishing. DOI: 10.1007/978-3-031-28885-2_8

Vovk, V. (2013). Kernel ridge regression. In *Empirical Inference: Festschrift in Honor of Vladimir N. Vapnik* (pp. 105-116). Berlin: Springer Berlin Heidelberg. DOI: 10.1007/978-3-642-41136-6_11

Yuchi, W., Gombojav, E., Boldbaatar, B., Galsuren, J., Enkhmaa, S., Beejin, B., Naidan, G., Ochir, C., Legtseg, B., Byambaa, T., Barn, P., Henderson, S. B., Janes, C. R., Lanphear, B. P., McCandless, L. C., Takaro, T. K., Venners, S. A., Webster, G. M., & Allen, R. W. (2019). Evaluation of random forest regression and multiple linear regression for predicting indoor fine particulate matter concentrations in a highly polluted city. *Environmental Pollution*, *245*, 746–753. DOI: 10.1016/j.envpol.2018.11.034 PMID: 30500754

Zou, H., & Hastie, T. (2005). Regularization and variable selection via the elastic net. *Journal of the Royal Statistical Society. Series B, Statistical Methodology*, *67*(2), 301–320. DOI: 10.1111/j.1467-9868.2005.00503.x

Chapter 7
Ethical Considerations and Challenges of Leveraging IoT and Machine Learning in Smart Urban Planning

Mahad Mohtashim
https://orcid.org/0009-0003-7990-049X
National University of Sciences and Technology, Islamabad, Pakistan

ABSTRACT

Smart cities are the future for urban areas. Integrating the IoT network into urban settlements can generate streams of varying data. This data is then utilized by powerful machine learning models capable of extracting insights to significantly improve urban planning decisions. However, as this technology evolves, multiple ethical and technical issues arise. These will be discussed extensively in this chapter, accompanied by case studies to show the dangers of not eliminating them. In addition, modern tools will be explained to mitigate these challenges and establish an inclusive and efficient city ripe with the opportunity to innovate.

DOI: 10.4018/979-8-3693-9030-6.ch007

INTRODUCTION

The advent of computers in the mid-20th century and their rapid evolution since then have fundamentally changed human society. From the introduction of the first programmable computer, the ENIAC (Swaine & Freiberger, 2024), to the development of AI in more recent years, advances in computing have been made at an unprecedented rate. These developments have not been limited to the confines of technical institutions or government organizations but have had widespread implications on all facets of life (Ma et al., 2021). Almost everywhere, whether it's ordering food, chatting with a friend, or researching to write a chapter, technology has become an integral part of our daily lives. Recently, with the rapid innovation in the field of AI, our routines are taking another shift as we start to rely on machine learning models to make our tasks not just easier but to explore our existing avenues in ways we have never done before. AI has allowed us to see trends in data that were previously hidden (Donovan, 2023), enabling breakthroughs in fields ranging from healthcare to urban planning. It has empowered us to predict the future with greater accuracy by providing insights that shape policy decisions, business strategies, and personal choices. By analyzing patterns in large datasets, AI can forecast economic trends, anticipate public health crises, and even model climate change scenarios.

Furthermore, the introduction of the IoT (Internet of Things) has made the collection of real-time data much simpler and more efficient (Villamil et al., 2020). Gone are the days of conducting strenuous surveys and sifting through historical records. IoTs instantly capture data, sending it to data warehouses capable of storing terabytes of data and then being fed to powerful machine learning models capable of comprehensive analysis.

It was only a matter of time before these technologies transitioned from being restricted to affording organizations to being deployed all over an urban landscape, conceiving the concept of smart cities (Mohanty et al., 2016). By harnessing the power of AI and IoT, smart cities can leverage the continuous streams of data generated across an urban area. It can allow for more informed decision-making that optimizes infrastructure, enhances quality of life, and promotes sustainability (Chang & Smith, 2023). Smart cities utilize data from various sources, such as traffic sensors, public transportation systems, environmental monitors, and energy grids, to predict and implement the next best steps for the benefit of the community (Ullah et al., 2023). This is an incredible boon for urban planners, as it allows for data-driven decision-making that is proactive, adaptive, and highly efficient in addressing the complexities of modern urban life.

"With great power comes great responsibility" aptly describes the role of urban planners leveraging machine learning and IoT in smart cities. These technologies offer immense capabilities to optimize urban life, but this power comes with the ethical obligation to ensure that these advancements are used inclusively, equitably, and sustainably, all while addressing critical challenges like data privacy, algorithmic bias, and environmental impact (Sanchez et al., 2024). Throughout this chapter, we will explore the many ethical issues and challenges that arise in smart urban planning and corresponding case studies on how they affect the people under smart city initiatives. Furthermore, we will explore many methods, tools, and frameworks that can mitigate these issues effectively and ensure that smart city projects are implemented responsibly and in the best way possible!

CHALLENGES

In this section, we will explore the many ethical and technical problems that arise from using IoTs and machine learning in urban planning. An IoT (Internet of Things) refers to the network created by using devices embedded with software and sensors that capture, process, and transmit data (IBM, n.d.). The devices in an IoT work autonomously and collect a certain type of data for a specific time interval. Examples include security cameras, temperature or light sensors, and air quality sensors (Berte, 2018). These devices have now shifted from being mere smart home devices to becoming an integral part of the development of smart cities, acting as endpoints to gather data for further processing (Berte, 2018).

Machine learning is a subset of artificial intelligence that empowers computers to learn and improve from experience without being explicitly programmed. (Alam, 2023; Mahesh, 2020b) The algorithm programs itself by taking in data as input. This data is coupled with features (a measurable property of data) that the algorithm attributes to the parameters (patterns) it extracts from the data while training. This then creates a function, the algorithm's mathematical interpretation of the data, concluding the training phase (Stanly et al., n.d.). Test inputs are given from an unseen test set to check the accuracy of the predictions generated by this function. A high testing accuracy is usually a good indicator that the training performed well. A low testing accuracy means the data or the algorithm needs to be tweaked as the function predicts incorrectly.

Deep learning is a branch of machine learning. (Sarker, 2021) It originated from the introduction of the ANN (Artificial Neural Network). (Sarker, 2021) This structure resembles a human brain, a mesh of neurons that transmit information between them. Deep learning algorithms use these complex neural networks with multiple layers to find trends in large, unstructured datasets. Different neural networks serve different tasks ranging from image generation to natural language processing (Mosavi et al., 2020), which, after training, generate a model capable of predicting when given test data.

Throughout this chapter, the distinction between machine learning and deep learning has not been made to maintain simplicity and to address the main points rather than differentiate.

1) Data Privacy Concerns

Big tech companies have always come under intense scrutiny after multiple incidents of potential misuse of user data. Google's privacy policy has extended from 600 words in 1999 to 4000 words in 2019 (Warzel & Ngu, n.d.), reflecting the increasing range and amount of what Google collects. Similarly, as cities become increasingly interconnected through IoTs, vast amounts of data are collected, ranging from pollution levels to more personal everyday activities of citizens (Siman et al., 2023). This would inadvertently put at risk individual privacy, raising concerns about how that data is being used, what measures are being taken to secure it and how decisions are being made based on that data. Urban planners need to identify what sort of privacy concerns can arise.

1.1 Lack of Transparency in Data Collection and Usage

The opacity surrounding the data collection process and its subsequent use in models makes the entire system questionable (Balasubramaniam et al., 2022). Many urban IoT systems and the urban planners who deploy them fail to disclose the practices involved in data capture and usage. As a result, citizens remain largely unaware of what data is being collected, how it is being used, and how decisions are being derived from it (Hudson-Smith et al., 2021). This concern will be explored later in detail.

1.2 Dataveillance

Such continuous monitoring without complete disclosure leads to 'dataveillance'. While these systems may offer benefits to citizens' daily lives, they also create a pervasive surveillance network that tracks individuals without their explicit consent (Clarke, 1988; Connolly & Fox, 2017). Dataveillance, or data-driven surveillance, fuels the fear that you're always being watched and causes discomfort in citizens, making them act in unease rather than being their natural selves (Büchi et al., 2022).

1.3 Reidentification of Individuals

Even if the data collected from IoTs is anonymized, the continuous stream of information may still enable the re-identification of individuals. With advancements in cross-referencing and data analytics, the aggregation of data from multiple sources can create detailed individual profiles (Curelariu & Lodie, 2024). Though it can prove useful for criminal apprehension, however, this profiling can result in discrimination of people with characteristics the authorities may deem undesirable (van Zoonen, 2016).

Case Study: Sidewalk Labs' Quayside Project

The Quayside project, proposed by Sidewalk Labs as part of its Master Innovation and Development Plan (MIDP), aimed to create an innovative urban community on the Toronto waterfront. Sidewalk Labs is an Alphabet Inc. subsidiary focused on urban innovation (Ramaswami, 2022) and aims to reimagine urban living by developing futuristic smart cities. Waterfront Toronto is a government organization overseeing the development of Toronto's waterfront and ensuring city planning goals were met for this project. Quayside's project model was tightly integrated around its digital layer, which involved advanced digital infrastructure and digitally enabled services. These services were designed to meet Waterfront Toronto's key innovation and community development objectives. The project proposed using modern technologies such as Software-Defined Networks (SDN) and Super Passive Optical Networks (Super-PON) for high-speed internet and privacy-preserving Distributed Verifiable Credentials (Lim, 2020). These innovations supported core systems managing mobility, energy, waste, and other essential urban functions, which were coordinated via the Urban Data Platform (UDP) to enable interoperability and data integration (Lim, 2020). The project envisioned modular buildings, heated pavements and autonomous transportation systems for improved connectivity and efficiency. Sustainability was a cornerstone of this project as it came equipped with plans to integrate energy-efficient systems, renewable energy sources, and reduced waste strategies.

Even though it was a promising venture, Sidewalk Labs officially shut down the Quayside project in May 2020, citing economic uncertainties worsened by the COVID-19 pandemic as the primary reason (Doctoroff, 2020). The decision came after years of planning, public consultations and mounting criticism from local communities. Despite the efforts to address concerns and refine their proposals, the combination of public opposition and financial viability challenges ultimately led Sidewalk Labs to withdraw from the Toronto waterfront initiative. Public opposition stemmed mainly from the growing concern about data misuse.

Data secrecy was a primary concern in the Quayside project due to the large volume of personal information collected from citizens as part of the smart city infrastructure. Sidewalk Labs proposed an "Urban Data Trust" to oversee and protect this data, ensuring it was anonymized and not sold to third parties without authorization. However, public trust was eroded by Sidewalk Labs' lack of transparency in not disclosing their data collection and privacy protocols during the early stages of the project (Austin & Lie, 2021). Concerns about the potential data re-identification of individuals through advanced algorithms like neural networks raised alarms. Even though Sidewalk Labs claimed to minimize and secure the data, critics argued that the possibility of re-identification was high, making the data vulnerable to misuse. The Urban Data Trust remained a conceptual framework and lacked clear management structures (Walker, 2019). It deepened scepticism about the handling of sensitive urban data.

Another significant factor in the failure was Canada's privacy laws. They were outdated and insufficient to address the concerns raised by the scale of data collection proposed by Sidewalk Labs. Laws like the Privacy Act failed to protect personal travel and real-time movement data — key data points for Sidewalk Labs' initiative (Scassa, 2019). This legal gap left many citizens uneasy about the potential for data misuse. The consent-based approach in the Personal Information Protection and Electronic Documents Act (PIPEDA) was inadequate for the scale of data usage envisaged by the project, and the overall fragmented legal framework hindered effective regulation.

The Quayside project faced significant data privacy concerns because of the large-scale collection of personal and movement data. Despite the efforts to safeguard privacy, it continued to fuel unease. Many felt that the existing legal framework did not protect residents' data, especially given the project's potential for excessive surveillance. This lack of confidence in data protection ultimately played a significant role in the project's failure.

2) Algorithmic Bias

Similar to humans, machine learning models also carry biases. They can make irrational decisions based on preconceived notions, often from skewed datasets (Kartal, 2023). Since humans curate datasets, some biases will inevitably creep in, leading to predictions that may reinforce existing inequalities. For instance, a machine learning model trained on historical data of tech-role hiring is more likely to predict a male candidate as the most suitable for subsequent hiring. Of course, the model will have no awareness of the current waves made by women in the tech industry (Apollo Solutions, n.d.). As cities become more reliant on IoT and machine learning, failure to address these biases may create a vicious cycle of disadvantages that is difficult to break, entrenching inequities in urban systems and policies (Fountain, 2022). Urban planners and algorithm designers must be aware of the biases (Ferrara, 2023) they may face when utilizing such technology.

2.1 Measurement Bias

Measurement bias is particularly relevant to this chapter as the use of IoT devices comes with inherent inaccuracies and sensitivities (Gaddam et al., 2020). It is the distorted measurement of key values (Zumbrun, 2023). These variabilities are then reflected in the model's predictions, potentially skewing the output. For instance, sensor calibration is essential for consistent readings, as changes in temperature, humidity, and pollution may lead to inaccurate data collection. Additionally, different generations of sensors have varying sensitivities, with modern devices capable of capturing highly intricate data that older sensors might fail to detect, resulting in inconsistencies across datasets. It can also extend into “Seasonal Bias” (Ho & Beyan, 2020), where, for example, data taken in the summer cannot generate an accurate prediction for the winter.

2.2 Representation Bias

Representation bias occurs when the data collection process fails to consider outliers, anomalies and the potential diversity of a population (Shahbazi et al., 2023), creating a narrow scope that does not reflect the true complexity of an urban environment. For instance, uneven deployment and maintenance of IoTs across regions can distort urban planning decisions. Sensors in wealthier districts are more likely to be adequately maintained than those in rural areas, leading to the misrepresentation of marginalized communities and depriving people of the resources they need most (Bosworth & Venhorst, 2017).

2.3 Sampling Bias

When selecting data points for training, it is essential that these points adequately represent the population. Sampling bias can occur when the data used to train a machine learning model is not representative of the full spectrum of a city's population (M. Mitchell, 2021). In that case, the outcomes of those models may favor certain groups over others, widening the urban inequality gap.

2.4 Confirmation Bias

Confirmation bias is the tendency to seek or interpret evidence that supports expectations or hypotheses (Nickerson, 1998). Individuals often prioritize information supporting their preconceptions while disregarding contradictory evidence (Koriat et al., 1980). In machine learning, it is crucial to recognize that model predictions should not be treated as definitive (Barbierato & Gatti, 2024), particularly when addressing critical governance and urban planning decisions. Urban planners might unconsciously favour predictions from machine learning models that align with their preconceptions, potentially resulting in biased or irrational decisions that fail to serve the broader public interest.

Case Study: COMPAS (Correctional Offender Management Profiling for Alternative Sanctions)

A major pillar of smart cities is smart governance (Augustyn, 2013). Its purpose is to harness technology to make intelligent, data-driven decisions about many administrative and judicial cases (Abdullah Kaiser, 2024). It also extends into public security systems to maintain a safe and crime-free environment. For this, an important aspect is predictive policing. It refers to using statistical algorithms and machine learning models to forecast potential criminal activities and individuals at risk of reoffending (Kim, 2022). These systems aim to assist law enforcement agencies in security resource allocation and judicial decision-making by analyzing data such as criminal records, location patterns, and socioeconomic indicators.

COMPAS was a case management tool used in pretrial detention, trial, sentencing and guiding parole steps in the justice system (Brennan & Dieterich, 2017). It was manufactured by Northpointe in the US and used in New York, Wisconsin, California, and Florida's Broward County, which we will infer throughout this section. It derived its assessment based on more than 15 factors, an important one being recidivism, the tendency of a criminal to commit an offence again while having already faced punishment. This relapse rate helps identify individuals at a higher risk of being apprehended again; therefore, it was a valuable metric for this tool.

These factors were grouped into five main categories, each consisting of multiple scales to provide an extensive selection of the criminal's characteristics. These scales were based on empirical evidence from official records and interviews with clients, forming the basis of the data for this model. The five assessment categories and their corresponding scales were:

1. **Criminal Involvement:** Criminal involvement, history of non-compliance, history of violence and current violence
2. **Relationships/Lifestyle:** Criminal associates/peers, criminal opportunity, leisure and recreation, social isolation and substance abuse
3. **Personality/Attitudes:** Criminal personality, negative social cognitions, criminal thinking observation, criminal thinking self-report, anger/violence and a cognitive behaviour scale
4. **Family:** Family criminality and socialization failure
5. **Social Exclusion:** Financial problems, vocational/educational profile, social environment, residential instability and social adjustment problems.

These factors created a digital profile, guiding law enforcement agencies in predicting future misbehaviour. A risk category was assigned, highlighting a low, medium or high probability of committing a crime in the future.

Broward County's initial validation study (Blomberg et al., 2010) demonstrated COMPAS to be a reliable system and a good predictor of general recidivism (likelihood of reoffending of any nature). The report concluded, "While the COMPAS risk assessment instrument is very predictive of actual recidivism among offenders released from jail, it is particularly accurate in identifying high-risk offenders."

ProPublica, an investigative journalism organization based in the US, analyzed the COMPAS system and its validity (Larson et al., 2016). They examined over 7,000 defendants from Broward County between 2013 and 2014 and examined the relationship between COMPAS scores, race, and actual outcomes. Their findings revealed significant concerns about the fairness and accuracy of COMPAS, particularly concerning racial bias. A higher number of false positives were attributed to the people of the black community, wrongfully considered twice as likely as a high risk when compared to white defendants. Furthermore, the tool did not actively consider race as an input but relied on factors closely correlated with race, such as neighbourhood characteristics and employment status. It reflected systematic inequalities and, hence, disproportionate outcomes. Furthermore, being a proprietary software, Northpointe did not disclose how the scores were calculated. This lack of transparency hindered efforts to identify and correct biases.

Algorithmic bias can significantly threaten a diverse setting (Kontokosta & Hong, 2021). By implementing biased technology in smart cities, there is an imminent threat of instigating social conflicts and reinforcing existing inequalities, leading to prejudiced outcomes in areas like law enforcement, hiring practices or resource allocation (Noble, 2018). The reliance on data that may already reflect historical biases worsens the problem, particularly when machine learning models are trained on this data without addressing underlying issues of fairness. It is an ethical imperative to consider race, gender, age, and socioeconomic conditions when constructing such models and to ensure a safe and inclusive environment that is equitably distributed across all demographics in a smart city.

3) Lack of Transparency

In a nutshell, a machine learning model uses algorithms to train on data to recognize patterns and then make predictions. To those unfamiliar with artificial intelligence, the process seems not only complex but also untrustworthy. The 'black box' nature of these models raises public suspicion as they lack insight into how their data decides their fate (Larsson & Heintz, 2020). Moreover, with sensors constantly collecting data on every movement and action of people, many would feel this level of monitoring to be invasive (Nower, 2019). It is crucial for governments and administrative bodies to adopt open and transparent practices regarding their use of modern technology in urban planning. Such transparency will garner trust, fostering acceptance of innovation and the harmonious integration of technology to create smarter cities. By exploring the three levels of AI transparency (Haresamudram et al., 2023), urban planners and algorithm designers can better understand how to implement them.

3.1 Algorithmic Transparency

Algorithmic transparency is a well-researched and well-documented aspect of AI, but also one of the most challenging to implement. It focuses on explaining the logic and processes used to reach a final decision and the factors that influenced them. A proprietary codebase, often considered intellectual property, cannot be disclosed publicly without risking the loss of competitive advantage (Dalle et al., 2002). However, the lack of transparency in these algorithms has resulted in biased outcomes, sometimes unintended by their developers. For instance, Amazon's AI recruiting tool was found to discriminate against women due to biases present in the training data (Dastin, 2018). Therefore, it is essential to promote openness through accountability and trust. This requires granting access to code for auditing purposes and scrutinizing datasets to uncover hidden biases and errors (Larsson & Heintz, 2020).

3.2 Interaction Transparency

Interaction transparency deals with communication between humans and AI systems, ensuring users understand how these systems make decisions or provide recommendations. The problem with modern-day explainability tools is that they often fail to convey the explanation in an intuitive or comprehensible manner, leaving the users just as uninformed as before the interaction (Gilpin et al., 2019). To address these issues, urban planners and AI developers must incorporate principles from human-computer interaction (HCI) into the design of interfaces, ensuring the public's clarity of the AI processes (Liao & Vaughan, 2023)

3.3 Social Transparency

Social transparency extends beyond understanding and communicating the processes of AI. It looks at the broader societal implications of deploying AI, which can impact citizens (Ehsan et al., 2021). It expands into topics concerning data security, privacy, and biases, which are pivotal for the ethical usage of AI. This transparency is relevant not only to algorithm experts and policymakers but also to the collective acknowledgement of the people of the ethical practices and regulations that govern these technologies. Social transparency will be elaborated on when discussing social sustainability.

As the IoT network continues to grow and cities become more reliant on this technology, it is the need of the hour to make citizens aware of this trend. Smart cities are the future, and it is equally important to have smart citizens who are mindful of their data being collected and assured that this data will be used only for their benefit. This can be instilled through open policies on algorithmic education, clear communication and transparent development.

4) Issues with Data Compatibility

When training machine learning models, especially supervised ones, the input features must maintain a consistent structure, e.g. fixed dimensions of images with the exact resolution (Zhang, 2013). Ensuring this consistency with millions of IoTs, each collecting different sorts of data, can be challenging as the heterogeneity demands tedious pre-processing until it is ready for training.

4.1 Annotation Overhead

Each IoT device operates with distinct standards and protocols for data collection and processing. When data is not harmonized, it tends to be stored in inconsistent formats (Asghari et al., 2019), which will require tedious re-annotation and often require human intervention. Therefore, with fragmented features derived from a multitude of sources for data, these inconsistencies demand a massive re-configuration overhead.

4.2 Silo Systems

Moreover, by abstracting singular IoTs to an isolated network, siloed systems emerge as a byproduct. These fragmented technological infrastructures have no interoperability (Komninos et al., 2022). Collaboration is hindered by a lack of communication and compatibility among systems and cohesive insights may be lost (Soe, 2018). An example may be the lack of coordination between flood sensors and disaster management systems. If water levels rise to a hazardous level and are not addressed immediately, it may result in delayed crisis response, incurring more devastating damages.

As cities grow, the scalability of AI will be essential. However, using legacy systems lacking cohesion between units, the delay caused by shaping them into a uniform standard will prove to be a bottleneck in handling the exponential growth of data.

5) Scalability of IoTs and AI

The emerging discipline of modern AI engineering is firmly grounded on three principles: human-centred algorithms, robust and secure models, and, lastly, scalable AI—the ability of the models and data to operate at the required speed and complexity (Barmer et al., 2021).

Increasing urbanization in smart cities calls for greater connectivity of newly expanded areas. It requires the large-scale installation of IoTs like traffic lights, cameras, and environmental sensors, as well as subsequent maintenance. As these areas become a part of the IoT mesh, the sheer scale of data increases rapidly. The large volume and velocity require immense computational resources and time to be processed and train a machine learning model. Therefore, as cities continue to expand, a new set of challenges hinder scalability.

5.1 Infrastructure Development Expense

To truly connect a city, ubiquitous sensor installations are a necessity (Hoang, 2024). However, this involves a substantial portion of funds to be allocated solely to develop this technological infrastructure. Furthermore, the networking infrastructure will have to be significantly upgraded, incorporating low latency 5G connectivity and cloud hosting to ensure smooth and rapid transmission of massive volumes of data (Car et al., 2022). Continuous operational expenses, e.g. maintenance and electricity, must also be accounted for. Hence, creating a new or updating an existing infrastructure requires a hefty investment, which may not be possible for resource-barren areas. Insufficient funds greatly hinder scalability, leaving a stagnant implementation with a growing need to ameliorate the system.

5.2 High Computational Demands

Advanced AI algorithms, especially deep learning networks, require extensive computational resources (Sun et al., 2017), which increase exponentially with data. Training state-of-the-art models, like those used in urban planning, consume vast amounts of energy and therefore require a large budget. OpenAI, the company running ChatGPT, noted a tenfold annual increase in the computing resources required for training large AI models (OpenAI, n.d.). Urban planners should carefully expand their computational resources while expanding the IoT network, as it will be futile; otherwise, the models cannot train with such massive data streams.

5.3 Hardware Constraints of IoT Devices

IoT devices are generally designed to be small, low-cost, and low-power devices. Their computing and memory capacities are limited and not meant for intense computation (Yuan, 2024). On the other hand, machine learning models are resource-intensive and run several iterations to train large volumes of data. It demands innovation in optimizing the models through compression techniques and eliminating redundant parameters. Algorithm designers should create models which do not overwhelm the capabilities of the underlying, lightweight hardware for effective and quick transmission.

6) Cybersecurity Risks

As smart cities continue to evolve, more and more sensors join the mesh of connectivity. In 2023, 16.6 billion IoT devices were connected, with an estimated 30 billion IoTs by 2025 (IoT Analytics, n.d.). With this many endpoints collecting and analyzing data every second, it invites more sinister attention. Cybersecurity attacks have rampaged the technical industry by exploiting vulnerabilities and causing unprecedented damage. Whether it's a data breach or denial of service attacks, these actions bring critical systems to a halt, which can significantly impact the lives of citizens and the services they utilize.

Furthermore, recovering from these attacks is a costly endeavor. In 2017, Maersk, the world's largest shipping company, fell victim to the NotPetya ransomware attack (Steinberg et al., 2021). A combination of two powerful and virulent hacking tools, the malware affected the IT infrastructure by encrypting data and rendering more than 49,000 devices, including laptops, unusable. The operational paralysis caused delays and incoordination, losing the company more than $200 million in recovery efforts and lost revenue. The stakes are much higher in smart cities as the lives of citizens and essential services can be greatly impacted by these attacks. Urban planners must be aware of such attacks and take appropriate measures to avoid unfortunate incidents.

6.1 DoS – Denial of Service

DoS arises from overloading a network with fake requests (Kumar, 2016). This massive volume of network traffic makes them inaccessible to legitimate users. Hackers can flood IoT networks with requests and hinder their communication with other devices or the central server they're connected to (Kalinin et al., 2021). DDoS (Distributed DoS) is done through multiple attacking devices, causing rapid disruption in the network. PDoS (Permanent DoS) targets IoTs to cause lasting damage to their hardware, forcing them to be reinstalled and burdening cities with downtime and replacement costs (IDB, n.d.).

6.2 Man in the Middle Attack

While DoS disrupts the quality of transmission, Man in the Middle can compromise a system's privacy and security facets (Mallik, 2019). A perpetrator takes control of the communication channels by manipulating the original transmission channel. Through this, it can intercept and even alter information exchanged between IoT devices (Fereidouni et al., 2023).

6.3 Illusion Attack

An intruder device can act as a part of the network and falsify information (Kalinin et al., 2021). It can manipulate the devices around it and hinder the sensing efforts, as incorrect data will be accounted for. This can be hazardous for smart transportation systems as malicious autonomous vehicles can manipulate other vehicles causing traffic jams and accidents (Zaidi, 2019).

6.4 Ransomware

Ransomware is malicious software which blocks any services on a device until a sum of money is paid to revert it. Perpetrators can hijack devices and install this software to disrupt networks and encrypt essential data, demanding ransom for the decryption key (Wani & Sathiya, 2020). This can also lead to the creation of botnets, a network of devices infected with malware, and can further propagate the ransomware into the network (Kirubavathi & Anitha, 2014).

6.5 Phishing Attacks

Perpetrators can send seemingly authentic links to people to trick them into accessing them. Victims can lose sensitive information or download malware from these links (IBM, n.d.). It can lead to a data breach as employees at data centers can give up their credentials, thereby allowing access to smart city data. Malware downloads can also lead to botnets in sensitive networks, disrupting critical systems.

Case Study: Atlanta Ransomware Attack

In March 2018, the Atlanta Ransomware Attack occurred, targeting vulnerabilities in the city's IT infrastructure and crippling municipal services (Kraszewski, 2019). The malware used was the SamSam ransomware, which is known for exploiting such technological infrastructure. It utilized a brute-force approach to gain access instead of phishing employees for credentials. It used algorithmic password-cracking tactics to guess weak passwords and secure credentials.

The ransomware infected other hosts in the network, encrypting multiple city systems and locking out employees from their computers. It affected departments like customer billing, police, court information, utilities, traffic tickets and business licenses or renewals (CoverLink, 2021), forcing the government to shut down its technical infrastructure as a precaution, including the court system database and the Wi-Fi at Hartsfield–Jackson Atlanta International Airport. The attackers demanded $50,000 in Bitcoin as ransom before restoring any technology or decrypting any data.

The government decided not to comply with the attackers and denied paying the ransom to avoid encouraging any future cyber-attacks. Resorting to recover all access and data independently, the government spent $2.7 million in these efforts (later estimated to be $9.5 million). This attack was the largest successful breach of ransomware in a major American city, affecting up to an estimated 6 million people. Many legal documents and police dashcam video files were permanently deleted, and the government could not restore its online payment programs until May.

IoTs are notorious for having poor security and default passwords, making them an easy target for cyber-attacks (Baho & Abawajy, 2023). With IoTs scattered all over smart cities, it takes one vulnerability to sabotage an entire technological system on which so many depend. An audit performed 2 months before the Atlanta attack revealed that between 1,500 and 2,000 total vulnerabilities were identified within the Atlanta government's digital operations and technology (City Auditor's Office,

2018), highlighting the authorities' complacency regarding cybersecurity. Urban planners should prioritize implementing stringent security protocols and investing in advanced cybersecurity solutions to safeguard the IoT networks and technological infrastructure on which they increasingly rely. With sensitive citizen data and critical city operations at stake, a single security breach could result in catastrophic consequences, including compromised privacy, disrupted services, and widespread public harm.

7) Scarce Data

A machine learning model scans for trends in data and uses those trends to make a prediction. With the lack of complete and high-quality data, the prediction, too, will lack quality. The scarcity of data in machine learning models can lead to issues like overfitting (Bansal et al., 2022), where the model maps itself too strictly to the training data, leaving no room for generalization and causing low accuracy when predicting the test data.

7.1 Disproportionate Data

Scare data is not just the lack of data but also an uneven spread, leading to a scarcity of categories. It can arise from the uneven distribution of IoTs. The installation and maintenance of IoTs will likely occur more often in more affluent parts of the city than in rural regions (Yaacoub & Alouini, 2020). It would create an unbalanced data distribution, and the subsequent trained model cannot apply to the whole city. This specified model training will lead to geographical disparity as decisions will be unfair for the areas not considered in the training dataset (Franklin et al., 2024).

7.2 Privacy Regulations

In domains lacking proper monitoring infrastructure, there is an inherent likelihood of sparsity in the data (Alzubaidi et al., 2023). This can also be derived from privacy regulations like Europe's GDPR (General Data Protection Regulation) Law that limits the collection of detailed data in domains like public safety (European Parliamentary Research Service [EPRS], 2020). This can obscure granularity and reduce precision in predictions. The lack of a 360-degree view of data can hinder comprehensive training.

7.3 Poor Annotation

This issue also extends into poorly labelled data. Data lacking proper annotation is equally useless. Machine learning models need to classify data in order to make predictions based on those categories. If the said classes are scarce, the model will generate a vague prediction (IBM, n.d.).

8) Lack of human-centric design principles

The inhabitants of a city will be the ones most affected by algorithmic urban planning. With the integration of IoTs and machine learning into urban infrastructure, a recurring issue is how the collected data is used to benefit the major stakeholders i.e. the people. Rather than focusing on residents' needs, values, and experiences, these systems prioritize efficiency, uniformity and cost-saving (Chib et al., 2021).

Striking a balance between optimizing resources and addressing the needs of people lies at the heart of effective urban planning. For instance, it is futile to conserve energy in streetlights to the extent that pedestrians feel unsafe or struggle to see (Hawkins, 2020). Smart lighting systems should adjust to pedestrian traffic and neighborhood safety concerns rather than solely focus on energy efficiency.

In addition, urban planners should avoid a one-size-fits-all design. Implementing generic strategies in diverse metropolitan areas without considering their unique socio-economic and cultural characteristics will likely lead to inequitable outcomes, failing to meet the needs of all residents (Esposito et al., 2021).

It is essential for urban planners to avoid technochauvinism. It is the idea that predictions generated by the model are the final answer to our problems (Broussard, 2018). This unquestioning optimism and lack of caution can significantly impact social issues (Cobbe, 2022). Rather than assuming it is just our fault, intense scrutiny of the model should be conducted in cases of unusual outputs.

Therefore, citizens should be the priority when designing such algorithms, adhering to principles that emphasize their comfort, safety, and overall well-being. By incorporating human feedback at critical stages of training, societal values can be upheld, and many of these issues can be prevented.

9) AI Literacy

Rapid technological advancement makes it hard for everyone to keep up with the latest innovations. The issue of AI illiteracy transcends age, as it is no longer confined to older generations lagging behind younger, tech-savvy individuals. Instead, a lack of dynamic motivation or the necessity to stay informed has contributed to a gap in understanding among people of all ages. This lack of awareness and familiarity with AI tools and their applications hinders individuals from effectively leveraging these technologies in their daily lives, workplaces, and decision-making processes (Ackerman, 2021). Similarly, for urban planners, the race to stay up to date has become a cause for concern.

In order to leverage these technologies, urban planners must understand what they are implementing. Not doing so leads to over-reliance on vendors or external consultants who may not achieve the expected product as it may be fraught with issues like bias. Policymakers and urban planners lacking this knowledge will be unable to critically evaluate these implementations.

AI illiteracy extends into a lack of transparency. Not having a functional understanding of AI may lead to distrust among citizens. The 'black box' view will raise doubts about its working, and the spread of misinformation about the fear of losing jobs to AI or constant surveillance will heighten tensions between the people and administrative bodies (Cao et al., 2023).

10) Sustainability Impacts

To ensure the successful integration of IoTs and machine learning in urban planning, it is crucial to establish sustainable protocols maintained over time with consistent quality and accuracy (Kuhlman & Farrington, 2010). Current smart cities have yet to fully meet the three key pillars of sustainability: environmental, economic, and social (Salha et al., 2020). Many of these implementations face challenges such as high resource consumption, lack of equitable access, and insufficient consideration of long-term environmental impact. As cities grow and technological demands increase, addressing these sustainability concerns becomes essential to ensure that smart cities benefit all residents while minimizing their ecological footprint and ensuring economic viability (Joss, 2015).

10.1 Environmental Sustainability

Environmental sustainability strives to protect and maintain environmental assets for current and future generations (Stepping, 2019). This includes an eco-friendly urban settlement with a minimal ecological footprint, working towards diminishing any further emissions. With machine learning and IoTs being the foundations of a smart city, these technologies can bring about efficiency in processes but also come with their own set of adverse environmental impacts (Ligozat et al., 2022).

IoT devices are made to deal with a specific set of instructions. It makes them more optimized for latency and energy consumption. In a city, however, thousands of IoTs are deployed, each capturing data at regular intervals. As a whole, this demands high energy allocation (Ejaz et al., 2017), and the required energy source varies from country to country. In some cases, these devices may be attached to a greener energy source like solar panels, while others may be connected to a power grid. These power grids may get their energy from thermal power plants, which actively contribute to climate change (Penmetsa & Holbert, 2021). Furthermore, the processing, transmission and storing of data requires significant amounts of energy. Then, the eventual training of a machine learning model makes up its environmental footprint, owing to its energy-demanding training process on massive datasets (Ligozat et al., 2022).

Improper e-waste disposal (electronic waste) is also a harbinger of the deteriorating environment (Averda, n.d.). The short lifespan of current IoTs can be attributed to hardware obsolescence or rapid technological advancement, demanding continuous replacement. As an IoT reaches the end of its useful life, it is replaced, and any useful components are removed. If recklessly disposed of, the remaining parts lead to harmful substances, such as heavy metals and plastics, leaching into the soil and water. The UN estimates that over 50 million metric tons of e-waste are generated worldwide every year (UNEP, 2019), and this figure is rising as smart cities become the norm.

While using IoTs and machine learning will allow for optimization in various aspects of urban planning, a smart city will only be worth it if it reduces the environmental impact and promotes ecological sustainability.

10.2 Economic Sustainability

Economic sustainability refers to promoting long-term economic growth while not negatively impacting other aspects of society (Jeronen, 2020). It focuses on ensuring financial stability through conserving resources and their efficient use by harnessing technology and thorough financial analysis. In the long term, smart cities have the potential to reduce inefficiencies and innovate solutions to establish a circular economy. However, achieving this vision requires urban planners to address significant barriers, including resource misallocation, inequitable investment strategies, and the challenges of integrating scalable technologies that are both cost-effective and inclusive (Kumar & Dahiya, 2016).

Smart cities require a hefty initial investment (Puron-Cid & Gil-Garcia, 2022). It includes deploying IoT devices, advanced data centers and high-speed communication networks. Installing smart utilities such as intelligent water meters, energy grids, and transportation systems also demands significant financial resources. In addition, these cities require ongoing operational costs to manage, maintain and upgrade these technologies, creating a continuous financial burden (Macomber, 2018).

Furthermore, machine learning models of the scale that must cater to cities require a lot of resources, including energy, storage, and skilled professionals who will continuously innovate and implement these models. It is more than likely that citizens will resist such a substantial investment and would advocate spending on other avenues where it would be better utilized. Urban planners should ensure an acceptable level of infrastructure transparency to educate the people on this investment and how it will benefit them and other societal avenues in the long run (Ionescu et al., 2023).

Ill-managed smart cities will likely exacerbate the divide between affluent and economically disadvantaged communities (Radchenko, 2023). The expensive infrastructure required, such as IoT devices, smart utilities, and high-speed networks, is more likely to be implemented in wealthier areas where maintenance and returns on investment are more straightforward to justify. Residents in less affluent neighborhoods may be unable to benefit from enhanced public services like efficient transportation or reduced energy costs, further entrenching socioeconomic disparities (Ševčík et al., 2022). With richer neighborhoods providing better quality education and technical training programs, these technical jobs will then continue to be offered to people who reside in such areas and can afford to enroll in such programs, which provide the necessary skills to maintain a smart city (Wang et al., 2022).

10.3 Social Sustainability

Social sustainability aims to foster an inclusive environment that enhances the quality of life for all citizens, regardless of socioeconomic status (Chen et al., 2022). A smart city should ensure equal access to resources, opportunities, and the benefits of technological advancements. It emphasizes the integration of the physical and digital dimensions of urban planning with the design of a socially cohesive and supportive structure (Sugandha et al., 2022). As smart cities evolve, many issues arise, whether it is the socioeconomic gap in availing of technological opportunities or looming privacy concerns that hinder the progress towards a socially sustainable environment.

The rapid adoption of IoT and AI technologies may leave technologically underserved communities behind. This gap will lead to unfair availability of opportunities, causing a "digital divide" between communities (Caragliu & Del Bo, 2023). Automation and use of AI can cause job losses in traditional roles, disproportionately affecting low-skilled workers and further impacting such communities. This can socially exclude vulnerable groups like the elderly and people with disabilities if adequate measures are not taken to make these opportunities more accessible (Zhou et al., 2023).

Data privacy and the lack of transparency are major concerns impeding social sustainability in smart cities (Layode et al., 2024). As discussed above, both issues significantly hinder public trust and engagement. Data privacy concerns stem from continuously collecting sensitive personal data through IoT devices, smart infrastructure, and AI systems. Citizens fear that their data may be misused by both private companies and government entities, leading to breaches of trust and the potential for discrimination or surveillance. Furthermore, the 'black box' view of AI will continue to raise suspicion among citizens as they fear becoming clients of a city that no longer belongs to them (Mancebo, 2020). A lack of proper data governance frameworks and policies exacerbates these fears, leaving individuals vulnerable and disempowered.

This literature review has explored the multifaceted challenges arising from integrating AI and IoT technologies in urban planning. Issues such as data privacy concerns and the risks of invasive surveillance and unauthorized data usage were highlighted. The review also addressed algorithmic bias, which showcased how underrepresented or skewed datasets can lead to unfair outcomes. The lack of transparency in AI systems raises skepticism, as opaque algorithms often leave the public unaware of how decisions are made.

Additional challenges included data compatibility issues, where fragmented systems and non-standardized data formats hinder integration, and scalability concerns as cities struggle to manage the exponential growth of IoT data within existing infrastructure. Cybersecurity risks highlight the potential for catastrophic failures if exploited. Furthermore, data scarcity in underserved regions can skew decision-making, while the absence of human-centric design principles risks alienating the populations these technologies aim to serve. Finally, the environmental, economic, and social dimensions of sustainability present ongoing challenges as cities strive to balance technological advancement with ecological and societal well-being.

While this review has outlined the current hurdles, it is crucial to acknowledge that new challenges will undoubtedly emerge with technological evolution. These will require innovative solutions and adaptive frameworks to ensure that the future smart cities are not only technologically advanced but also equitable, ethical and sustainable. In the next section, we will discuss current tools and frameworks essential in the arsenal of smart urban planners.

SOLUTIONS

This section will discuss frameworks and methodologies to supplement AI systems. These can mitigate the problems we discussed earlier and provide direction in finding solutions to newer problems. These can range from helping urban planners implement their projects efficiently to guiding citizens in how these systems will work. They can also be valuable for developers who can incorporate these techniques when developing machine learning models for smart cities.

1) eXplainable AI (XAI): Ensuring transparency through literacy

The integration of technology into daily organizational tasks has become the norm. It has revolutionized operations through computers, software, and data systems. With advancements like ChatGPT and other large language models (LLMs), problem-solving approaches have significantly evolved, enhancing content creation, customer service, and data analysis (Northwest Education, 2024). IoT devices further enable real-time data collection, offering insights into operations with minimal human intervention (Vicci, 2024).

It was only a matter of time before these technologies extended to entire cities, where smart city initiatives leverage IoT and AI to optimize urban services and improve living standards. However, AI's "black box" nature raises concerns about transparency and fairness, especially in sensitive sectors like healthcare and law enforcement (Bathaee, 2018). Addressing these challenges through explainable AI (XAI) and robust transparency frameworks is crucial to ensure societal trust and acceptance of these transformative technologies.

XAI is a set of methods used to explain the inner workings of an AI model (IBM, n.d.). It is more relevant to deep learning models involving DNNs (Deep Neural Networks) rather than machine learning models, which are primarily intuitive. A deep learning model's complex workings and components, like the activation function and loss function, can be better explained using XAI. It includes a post hoc explanation of how the model worked and generated the prediction. XAI explanations can be classified into four categories (Laato et al., 2022):

1. **Explanation by simplification:** The AI system is explained by simplifying its architecture and other components
2. **Feature relevance explanation:** The relevance of features contributing to the specific model decision
3. **Local explanation:** Larger parts of the model are explained individually
4. **Visual explanation:** Visual support helps understand the factors on which the model was based.

1.1 SHAP (SHapley Additive exPlanations)

SHAP is an XAI framework rooted in game theory (Salih et al., 2024). It explains model predictions by treating each feature as a player and the model's output as the payoff. It offers local and global explanations, providing insights into the importance of features for a single instance and across all instances (Lundberg & Lee, 2017). It uses Shapley values, which provide a mathematically sound way to distribute contributions among features fairly (Li et al., 2024). SHAP calculates the impact of each feature by considering all possible combinations of features and measuring how much a particular feature changes the prediction.

1.2 LIME (Local Interpretable Model-Agnostic Explanations)

LIME is also a widely used XAI approach (Salih et al., 2024). It achieves this by approximating the model's behaviour locally around a specific instance using a more straightforward, interpretable surrogate model, such as linear regression. It generates explanations by perturbing the input data and observing changes in the model's output, thereby identifying the most influential features for a given prediction (Ribeiro et al., 2016). This method is particularly valued for its model-agnostic nature, allowing it to work with any machine learning algorithm.

Several other XAI frameworks, such as ELI5 in Python, Google's What-If Tool, and Oracle's Skater, offer diverse approaches to model explainability. These tools not only aid data scientists and decision-makers by revealing how machine learning models operate and ensure fairness but also significantly enhance end-user experience in smart cities. These frameworks foster trust and enable citizens to better understand public services by clearly explaining AI-driven decisions. This transparency ensures that smart city initiatives remain inclusive and accountable, allowing residents to interact confidently with technology-driven systems while benefiting from optimized urban solutions. These tools bridge the gap between complex algorithms and human comprehension, promoting innovation and social equity in modern urban environments.

2) Digital Twin Technology

Urban planners meticulously design and communicate proposals for new infrastructure, considering numerous factors such as budget, sustainability, and the impact on residents. Effective planning requires comprehensive data to assess these factors accurately. Conducting surveys and analyzing official records provide critical insights into community needs, environmental considerations, and economic feasibility. However, these sources have issues; surveys can be biased, and records can be historically obsolete (Sanchez, 2024).

A well-distributed IoT network can elevate the urban planning process by enabling the creation of digital twins—virtual replicas of physical environments that integrate real-time data from IoT devices (El-Agamy et al., 2024). With IoT and sensor technologies, it is possible to form dynamic connectivity between a virtual replica and its physical counterpart (Hämäläinen, 2021). Digital twin technology allows planners to simulate and analyze various scenarios without physical interventions. By mirroring urban environments digitally, planners can test infrastructure designs, predict outcomes, and identify potential inefficiencies or risks before implementing changes in the real world.

Digital twin technologies have the following characteristics (Zheng et al., 2018):

1. **Integration of Various Data Types:** Digital twins integrate multiple data sources from physical objects, including sensors, IoT devices, and other monitoring systems, to create an accurate and dynamic virtual model.
2. **Lifecycle Presence and Co-Evolution:** Digital twins exist throughout the entire lifecycle of physical objects, from design and construction to maintenance and decommissioning. They evolve in real-time alongside their physical counterparts, continuously accumulating knowledge about their status, performance, and changes.
3. **Optimization and Description:** These virtual models describe the physical entities and provide a platform for optimization. By simulating different scenarios and analyzing data, digital twins enable improvements in efficiency, sustainability, and performance.

Therefore, digital twin technologies offer tremendous potential in urban planning, where they can provide a comprehensive, real-time representation of a city's infrastructure.

Case Study: Virtual Singapore

Various governments have taken the initiative to construct virtual replicas of their cities. Virtual Singapore is a 3D digital model of Singapore that uses real-time and topographical data (Jeong et al., 2022). The project was divided into two phases. In the first phase, aerial photography and airborne LiDAR were used to record the country's topological surface data and develop digital models. In the second phase, vehicle-mounted laser scans augmented the aerial footage with street-level data, significantly improving the level of detail. The vehicular mapping survey acquired over 3 million photos of the 5500 km road network. Quick data collection and modification models were employed to manipulate large amounts of data, offering a modelling accuracy of 0.3 metres (Prime, 2022). The virtual city was supplemented with various platforms for simulating real-life scenarios like transport, disaster management and environmental monitoring (Stone, 2024). This initiative can allow relevant stakeholders to test their investment in infrastructure, helping them visualize the city's development and evolution in response to factors like population growth. Business owners can use the platform's data to perform business analytics, allowing more informed financial decisions. Planners can test solutions without taking too many risks and performing a deep feasibility study to ensure effective planning.

Digital twin cities are a critical asset for urban planners. They offer transformative potential for urban planning by enabling virtual replication of city environments. These replicas allow planners to analyze real-time data, simulate scenarios, and evaluate the impact of changes without disrupting real-world systems. As cities face increasing urbanization and climate change challenges, digital twin cities emerge as a crucial tool in building sustainable, resilient, and intelligent urban environments. Embracing this technology ensures that urban planning remains proactive, adaptive, and aligned with the needs of modern societies.

3) IBM Fairness 360 and Bias Mitigation Tools

As discussed in the literature review, algorithmic bias can be incredibly challenging to address, as human biases often infiltrate the data used for training models. Bias can originate from several sources, such as biased datasets, historical inequalities embedded in the data, and subjective judgments made by those creating the datasets. These biases can then propagate throughout the modelling process, leading to biased predictions (Chang & Shokri, 2023).

Several open-source libraries and tools have been developed to help detect, understand and mitigate biases in machine learning models. These tools provide valuable functionalities for addressing bias, making them essential for creating fairer AI systems. Some provide metrics and frameworks to identify inequities in data or predictions, helping developers and researchers understand the extent and nature of bias in their models.

1. **Fairness Measures** (Zehlike et al., 2017): These measures focus on detecting bias and provide fairness metrics such as difference of means, disparate impact, and odds ratio. They incorporate fairness-aware algorithms like FA*IR and DELTR, designed to promote equitable outcomes in ranked search results (Zehlike et al., 2017).
2. **FairML** (Adebayo, 2016): Audits predictive models by quantifying the relative effects of various inputs to assess fairness. It utilizes techniques like input perturbation and sensitivity analysis to assign relative importance scores to features, revealing potential biases in the model.
3. **FairTest** (Tramèr et al., 2017): Detects biases in datasets by checking associations between predicted labels and protected attributes. It runs a series of statistical tests to assess whether specific features correlate disproportionately with the algorithm's output, thereby identifying regions where errors might be unusually high.
4. **Aequitas** (Stevens et al., 2018): This auditing toolkit offers several fairness metrics, including demographic or statistical parity, along with a "fairness tree" to guide users in selecting the appropriate metric for their situation. However, it is not available for commercial use.
5. **Themis** (Galhotra et al., 2017): It is a bias toolbox that automatically generates test suites to measure discrimination in decision-making systems. This process enables uncovering subtle and complex patterns of discrimination that may not be immediately evident through traditional analysis methods. By simulating different scenarios and evaluating how model predictions vary, it can highlight regions where unfair outcomes are more likely to occur.

Others mitigate bias at various stages of the machine learning pipeline, including data preprocessing, model training, and post-processing.

1. **Themis-ML** (Bantilan, 2018) provides fairness metrics and bias mitigation algorithms. One such algorithm is relabeling (Kamiran & Calders, 2012). It adjusts the labels in the training dataset to ensure that predictions do not favour one demographic group over others. Another is the additive counterfactual fairness estimator (Kusner et al., 2017) that modifies predictions based on the potential counterfactual outcome (what would have happened if a sensitive attribute were

different) and then adds the resulting corrections to the final output. Reject option classification (Kamiran et al., 2012) is another method that provides an option to "reject" specific predictions when they are considered to be uncertain or potentially biased.

2. **Fairness Comparison** (Friedler et al., 2018) is one of the more extensive libraries. It features both bias detection metrics and mitigation methods, such as the disparate impact remover (Feldman et al., 2015) and prejudice remover (Kamishima et al., 2012). This library is designed as a testbed for comparing various metrics and algorithms and allows new methods and datasets to be added.

In an attempt to unify these diverse features, IBM Fairness 360 (AIF360) was created (Bellamy et al., 2018). It combines fairness metrics, algorithms for bias mitigation, and explainability features into a single open-source toolkit designed to be accessible to a broad range of users, including researchers, data scientists and policymakers. The tool's functionality is divided into four classes, each harbouring its features.

3.1 Dataset Class

This class structures and prepares the data for fairness analysis and bias mitigation. It identifies protected attributes, such as race, gender or age, which are often linked to discrimination so that the developer can be aware of them while modelling. It also offers extensive preprocessing techniques like normalization (to ensure consistent scales across features), binarization (to transform categorical variables for better analysis), and partitioning (to separate privileged and unprivileged groups for comparisons). Additionally, it supports data import and export in various formats, such as Pandas data frames and CSV files, making it highly compatible with popular data processing workflows. Pre-integrated datasets, such as COMPAS and Adult Census, are also available for experimentation.

3.2 Metrics Class

This class enables the assessment of fairness using a diverse range of statistical measures. It evaluates group fairness, such as statistical parity difference, which checks if positive outcomes are equally distributed across groups. It also includes disparate impact and the ratio of favourable outcomes for unprivileged versus privileged groups. Individual fairness metrics, like consistency, also assess whether similar individuals receive similar outcomes. Advanced evaluation methods provide deeper insights, including the Theil index (measuring inequality in predictions) and average odds difference (comparing error rates across groups). The class also supports custom metrics, offering flexibility for specific fairness requirements and making it a versatile tool for bias diagnostics.

3.3 Explainer Class

This class emphasizes interpretability, using techniques like SHAP and LIME for post-hoc explanations of model behaviour. These methods highlight feature contributions, helping to identify sources of bias. It provides tools for global interpretability, summarizing model tendencies, and local interpretability. By analyzing feature importance and error rates across groups, this class empowers users to understand how bias emerges in predictions. Its visualizations and numeric scores make fairness insights accessible, aiding in debugging and ethical assessment of machine learning systems.

3.4 Algorithms Class

This class encompasses techniques to mitigate bias at various stages of the machine learning pipeline. Preprocessing algorithms like reweighting adjust data representation to ensure balanced outcomes and disparate impact remover modifies feature distributions to eliminate potential biases. During training, in-processing techniques like adversarial debiasing incorporate adversarial networks to suppress discriminatory patterns. Post-training, post-processing methods such as equalized odds and reject option classification refine predictions to achieve fairness. These algorithms are tailored for different workflows and ensure that bias mitigation strategies are seamlessly integrated into model training and deployment phases.

Furthermore, AIF360 facilitates end-to-end fairness evaluations by integrating them with popular frameworks like scikit-learn, PyTorch, and TensorFlow to ensure that bias mitigation techniques can be incorporated into existing workflows. Its built-in benchmarking tools allow for comparing fairness metrics and mitigation strategies, helping practitioners assess the effectiveness of different approaches. This flexibility makes it an indispensable resource for deploying equitable AI systems across smart cities.

4) Human in the Loop

Human-in-the-loop (HITL) is a human-centric design principle that emphasizes the importance of human involvement throughout the development of an AI system (Wu et al., 2021). This approach ensures that technology remains aligned with human values in an automated process. It integrates human judgment at key stages, such as data labelling, model training, decision-making, and real-time monitoring (Emami et al., 2024). By incorporating human feedback, continuous correction of biased outputs makes AI more adaptable to diverse contexts and societal needs. Humans are often referred to as “oracles” in HITL because they provide critical knowledge and labels to the model. An oracle is essentially an entity with extensive domain knowledge that helps improve the model's performance by annotating data points that are uncertain or ambiguous to the machine learning model.

On the basis of who is controlling, and the level of control available, different approaches can be identified for HITL in machine learning (Holmberg et al. 2020; Bengio et al. 2009). These approaches are discussed briefly here but have been extensively discussed by Mosqueira-Rey et al. (2022).

4.1 Active Learning

This process begins with a set of labelled and unlabeled data. The learner queries an oracle (usually an expert) to label the most informative examples from the unlabeled set. This process repeats iteratively until the model reaches the desired performance level. The primary goal is to reduce the cost of labelling while maximizing the model's accuracy by selecting the most uncertain or important examples for annotation. By integrating human expertise in this way, active learning helps overcome challenges in data collection and can significantly reduce the time and effort required for training robust machine learning models.

4.2 Interactive Machine Learning

It builds upon active learning by emphasizing a closer, continuous interaction between users and the machine learning system. This interaction focuses on guiding the learning process through feedback loops, where users label data and refine the model based on their expertise. It provides a real-time and adaptive way for users to influence and improve the model as it learns.

4.3 Machine Teaching

This paradigm complements active and interactive learning by focusing on how humans can explicitly teach models using predefined examples or guidelines. A human instructor provides carefully chosen examples to "teach" the model the correct behavior. This approach shifts the focus from simply labelling data to actively structuring the teaching process, allowing the user to influence the model's learning trajectory directly. Machine teaching can be particularly valuable in situations where the task is highly specialized or when there is a clear need for a model to follow certain rules or constraints.

4.4 Curriculum Learning

It introduces a structured approach to training machine learning models by presenting the data in a sequence that progresses from simpler to more complex tasks. This approach mimics how humans learn by gradually increasing the difficulty of problems. It helps the model build a foundation of basic knowledge before tackling more challenging scenarios. Curriculum learning has been shown to improve the efficiency and performance of machine learning models by making the training process smoother and more organized. By starting with simpler tasks, models can learn the foundational concepts before being exposed to more complex and nuanced data.

HITL principles are critical to ensure human interaction throughout the training process and at the time of deployment. Urban planners should incorporate these guidelines in every model they develop so that they are accurate and more adaptable to real-world complexities. As cities increasingly turn to AI and machine learning to solve complex issues, human feedback and supervision will remain integral to achieving successful, impactful solutions. This collaborative approach ensures that the models evolve in ways aligned with human values and real-world needs.

The various methodologies and frameworks discussed in this section provide essential solutions to the challenges faced in leveraging AI within urban planning and other complex domains. XAI helps in the crucial aspect of garnering the trust of the public through explaining and visualizing models. The digital twin cities can provide a platform for urban planners to test and tinker with projects while paying close attention to Human In The Loop principles to create human-centric proposals. And finally eradicating bias by employing tools like IBM Fairness 360 to establish an inclusive and dynamic smart city.

CONCLUSION

Smart cities are not just a network of sensors and algorithms – they are living, breathing ecosystems shaped by their inhabitants. The fusion of IoT and machine learning offers unprecedented opportunities to build more efficient, sustainable, and intelligent cities. But true progress isn't measured by how much data we collect or how advanced our AI becomes. Instead, it's measured by how well technology serves humanity.

With great power comes great responsibility. Data privacy is not just a technical challenge; it's a fundamental human right. Algorithmic bias is not just a flaw in code; it dictates real-world inequalities. Cybersecurity failures don't just disrupt systems; they erode trust. If we allow technology to evolve without ethics, smart cities risk becoming tools of surveillance, exclusion, and systemic injustice.

However, these challenges are not insurmountable. Transparency-driven AI, human-in-the-loop decision-making, bias-mitigation frameworks, and sustainable urban policies are not optional add-ons but the backbone of ethical and resilient smart cities. The power to shape the future lies in our choices today: Will we allow technological advancement to outpace accountability, or will we set the foundation for cities that are not only intelligent but just?

The answer lies in innovation with intention: a smart city reflecting its people's needs, rights, and aspirations. If we harness technology responsibly, we won't just build better cities; we will create a future where progress and ethics walk hand in hand, forging urban landscapes that are as just as they are intelligent.

ACKNOWLEDGMENT

I want to thank Dr. Rafia Mumtaz for guiding me in writing this chapter and providing material to structure it. I would also like to thank Dr. Quratulain Mohtashim for answering my persistent queries with patience and clarity. Finally, I want to thank Ms. Arooba Hashmi for proofreading certain sections and assisting me with referencing.

REFERENCES

Abdullah Kaiser, Z. R. M. (2024). Smart governance for smart cities and nations. *Journal of Economy and Technology*, *2*, 216–234. DOI: 10.1016/j.ject.2024.07.003

Ackerman, D. (2021, May 18). Helping students of all ages flourish in the era of artificial intelligence. MIT News. https://news.mit.edu/2021/ai-education-raise-0518

Adebayo, J. A. (2016). FairML: Toolbox for diagnosing bias in predictive modeling. Master's thesis, Massachusetts Institute of Technology. Retrieved from https://github.com/adebayoj/fairml

Alam, A. (2023). What is machine learning? *Zenodo*. https://doi.org/DOI: 10.5281/zenodo.8231580

Alzubaidi, L., Bai, J., Al-Sabaawi, A., Santamaría, J., Albahri, A. S., Al-Dabbagh, B. S. N., Fadhel, M. A., Manoufali, M., Zhang, J., Al-Timemy, A. H., Duan, Y., Abdullah, A., Farhan, L., Lu, Y., Gupta, A., Albu, F., Abbosh, A., & Gu, Y. (2023). A survey on deep learning tools dealing with data scarcity: Definitions, challenges, solutions, tips, and applications. *Journal of Big Data*, *10*(1), 46. Advance online publication. DOI: 10.1186/s40537-023-00727-2

Asghari, P., Rahmani, A., & Javadi, H. (2019). Internet of Things applications: A systematic review. *Computer Networks*, *148*, 241–261. DOI: 10.1016/j.comnet.2018.12.008

Augustyn, A. (2013). Smart cities – brand cities of the future. In The Business of Place: Critical, Practical and Pragmatic Perspectives [Conference proceedings]. Retrieved from https://www.researchgate.net/publication/320555578_Smart_Cities_-_brand_cities_of_the_future

Averda. (n.d.). Smart cities: How they create a better environment. Retrieved from https://www.averda.com/rsa/news/smart-cities-better-environment

Baho, S., & Abawajy, J. (2023). Analysis of consumer IoT device vulnerability quantification frameworks. *Electronics (Basel), 12*(5), 1176. DOI: 10.3390/electronics12051176

Balasubramaniam, N., Kauppinen, M., Hiekkanen, K., & Kujala, S. (2022). Transparency and explainability of AI systems: Ethical guidelines in practice. In Requirements engineering: Foundation for software quality (Lecture Notes in Computer Science, pp. 1–16). Retrieved from https://www.researchgate.net/publication/359105897_Transparency_and_Explainability_of_AI_Systems_Ethical_Guidelines_in_Practice

Bansal, A., Sharma, R., & Kathuria, M. (2022). A Systematic Review on Data Scarcity Problem in Deep Learning: Solution and Applications. *ACM Computing Surveys, 54*(10s), 1–29. DOI: 10.1145/3502287

Bantilan, N. (2018). Themis-ml: A fairness-aware machine learning interface for end-to-end discrimination discovery and mitigation. *Journal of Technology in Human Services, 36*(1), 15–30. https://github.com/cosmicBboy/themis-ml. DOI: 10.1080/15228835.2017.1416512

Barbierato, E., & Gatti, A. (2024). The Challenges of Machine Learning: A Critical Review. *Electronics (Basel), 13*(2), 416. DOI: 10.3390/electronics13020416

Barmer, H., Dzombak, R., Gaston, M., Palat, J., Redner, F., Smith, T., & Wohlbier, J. (2021). National AI engineering initiative: Scalable AI. Retrieved from https://insights.sei.cmu.edu/library/scalable-ai/

Bathaee, Y. (2018). The Artificial Intelligence Black Box and the Failure of Intent and Causation. *Harvard Journal of Law & Technology, 31*(2). https://jolt.law.harvard.edu/assets/articlePDFs/v31/The-Artificial-Intelligence-Black-Box-and-the-Failure-of-Intent-and-Causation-Yavar-Bathaee.pdf

Bellamy, R. K. E., Dey, K., Hind, M., Hoffman, S. C., Houde, S., Kannan, K., Lohia, P., Martino, J., Mehta, S., Mojsilovic, A., Nagar, S., Ramamurthy, K. N., Richards, J., Saha, D., Sattigeri, P., Singh, M., Varshney, K. R., & Zhang, Y. (2018). AI fairness 360: An extensible toolkit for detecting, understanding, and mitigating unwanted algorithmic bias. arXiv. https://arxiv.org/pdf/1810.01943

Bengio, Y., Louradour, J., Collobert, R., & Weston, J. (2009). Curriculum learning. . https://doi.org/DOI: 10.1145/1553374.1553380

Berte, D.-R. (2018). Defining the IoT. *Proceedings of the International Conference on Business Excellence*, 12, 118–128. DOI: 10.2478/picbe-2018-0013

Bosworth, G., & Venhorst, V. (2017). Economic linkages between urban and rural regions – what's in it for the rural? *Regional Studies*, *52*(1), 1–12. DOI: 10.1080/00343404.2017.1339868

Brennan, T., & Dieterich, W. (2017). Correctional offender management profiles for alternative sanctions (COMPAS). In Handbook of Recidivism. Retrieved from https://www.researchgate.net/publication/321528262_Correctional_Offender_Management_Profiles_for_Alternative_Sanctions_COMPAS

Broussard, M. (2018). Artificial unintelligence. In The MIT Press eBooks. DOI: 10.7551/mitpress/11022.001.0001

Büchi, M., Festic, N., & Latzer, M. (2022). The chilling effects of digital dataveillance: A theoretical model and an empirical research agenda. *Big Data & Society*, *9*(1), 205395172110653. DOI: 10.1177/20539517211065368

Cao, Y., Hu, Y., Liu, Q., Lu, M., & Shan, Y. (2023). Job creation or disruption? Unraveling the effects of smart city construction on corporate employment in China. *Technological Forecasting and Social Change*, *195*, 122783. DOI: 10.1016/j.techfore.2023.122783

Car, T., Pilepić Stifanich, L., & Kovačić, N. (2022). The role of 5G and IoT in smart cities. ENTRENOVA - ENTerprise REsearch InNOVAtion, 8(1), 377–389. DOI: 10.54820/entrenova-2022-0032

Caragliu, A., & Del Bo, C. F. (2023). Smart cities and the urban digital divide. *NPJ Urban Sustainability*, *3*(1), 43. Advance online publication. DOI: 10.1038/s42949-023-00117-w

Chang, H., & Shokri, R. (2023). Bias propagation in federated learning. arXiv (Cornell University). /arxiv.2309.02160DOI: 10.48550

Chang, S., & Smith, M. K. (2023). Residents' Quality of Life in Smart Cities: A Systematic Literature review. *Land (Basel)*, *12*(4), 876. DOI: 10.3390/land12040876

Chen, T., Gil-Garcia, J. R., & Gasco-Hernandez, M. (2022). Understanding social sustainability for smart cities: The importance of inclusion, equity, and citizen participation as both inputs and long-term outcomes. *Journal of Smart Cities and Society*, *1*(2), 135–148. DOI: 10.3233/SCS-210123

Chib, A., Alvarez, K., & Todorovic, T. (2021). Critical Perspectives on the Smart City: Efficiency Objectives vs Inclusion Ideals. *Journal of Urban Technology*, *29*(4), 83–99. DOI: 10.1080/10630732.2021.2001712

City Auditor's Office. (2018, January). ISO/IEC 27001 ISMS precertification audit. City Auditor's Office. Retrieved from https://www.atlaudit.org/isoiec-27001-isms-precertification-audit---january-2018.html

Clarke, R. A. (1988). Information technology and dataveillance. *Communications of the ACM*, *31*(5), 498–512. DOI: 10.1145/42411.42413

Cobbe, J. (2022). *Technochauvinism*. Department of Computer Science and Technology, University of Cambridge.

Connolly, R., & Fox, G. (2017). Dataveillance and information privacy concerns. In *Biometrics: Concepts, methodologies, tools, and applications* (pp. 973–986). IGI Global. DOI: 10.4018/978-1-5225-0983-7.ch063

CoverLink. (2021, September 20). City of Atlanta ransomware. CoverLink. Retrieved from https://coverlink.com/case-study/city-of-atlanta-ransomware/

Curelariu, T., & Lodie, A. (2024). The lawfulness of re-identification under data protection law. In Annual Privacy Forum 2024 (pp. 112–131). ENISA; European Commission; Karlstads universitet. DOI: 10.1007/978-3-031-68024-3_6

Dastin, J. (2018, October 11). Insight: Amazon scraps secret AI recruiting tool that showed bias against women. Reuters. Retrieved from https://www.reuters.com

Donovan, M. (2023, April 20). How AI is helping historians better understand our past. MIT Technology Review. https://www.technologyreview.com/2023/04/11/1071104/ai-helping-historians-analyze-past/

Ehsan, U., Liao, Q. V., Muller, M., Riedl, M. O., & Weisz, J. D. (2021). Expanding explainability: Towards social transparency in AI systems. In *CHI Conference on Human Factors in Computing Systems (CHI '21)*. ACM. DOI: 10.1145/3411764.3445188

Ejaz, W., Naeem, M., Shahid, A., Anpalagan, A., & Jo, M. (2017). Efficient energy management for the internet of things in smart cities. *IEEE Communications Magazine*, *55*(1), 84–91. DOI: 10.1109/MCOM.2017.1600218CM

El-Agamy, R. F., Sayed, H. A., Akhatatneh, A. M. A., Aljohani, M., & Elhosseini, M. (2024). Comprehensive analysis of digital twins in smart cities: A 4200-paper bibliometric study. *Artificial Intelligence Review*, *57*(6), 154. Advance online publication. DOI: 10.1007/s10462-024-10781-8

Emami, Y., Almeida, L., Li, K., Ni, W., & Han, Z. (2024). Human-In-The-Loop Machine Learning for safe and ethical autonomous Vehicles: principles, challenges, and opportunities. arXiv (Cornell University). / arxiv.2408.12548DOI: 10.48550

Esposito, G., Clement, J., Mora, L., & Crutzen, N. (2021). One size does not fit all: Framing smart city policy narratives within regional socio-economic contexts in Brussels and Wallonia. *Cities (London, England)*, *118*, 103329. DOI: 10.1016/j.cities.2021.103329

European Parliamentary Research Service. (2020). The impact of the General Data Protection Regulation (GDPR) on artificial intelligence. European Parliament. https://www.europarl.europa.eu/RegData/etudes/STUD/2020/641530/EPRS_STU(2020)641530_EN.pdf

Feldman, M., Friedler, S. A., Moeller, J., Scheidegger, C., & Venkatasubramanian, S. (2015). Certifying and removing disparate impact. In *Proceedings of the ACM SIGKDD International Conference on Knowledge Discovery and Data Mining* (pp. 259–268). ACM.

Fereidouni, H., Fadeitcheva, O., & Zalai, M. (2023). IoT and man-in-the-middle attacks. arXiv. https://arxiv.org/abs/2308.02479

Ferrara, E. (2023). Fairness and bias in artificial intelligence: A brief survey of sources, impacts, and mitigation strategies. MDPI Electronics, 6(1), 3. https://www.mdpi.com/2413-4155/6/1/3

Fountain, J. E. (2022). The moon, the ghetto, and artificial intelligence: Reducing systemic racism in computational algorithms. *Government Information Quarterly*, *39*(2), 101645. Advance online publication. DOI: 10.1016/j.giq.2021.101645

Franklin, G., Stephens, R., Piracha, M., Tiosano, S., Lehouillier, F., Koppel, R., & Elkin, P. (2024). The Sociodemographic Biases in Machine Learning Algorithms: A Biomedical Informatics perspective. *Life (Chicago, Ill.)*, *14*(6), 652. DOI: 10.3390/life14060652 PMID: 38929638

Friedler, S. A., Scheidegger, C., Venkatasubramanian, S., Choudhary, S., Hamilton, E. P., & Roth, D. (2018). A comparative study of fairness-enhancing interventions in machine learning. https://github.com/algofairness/fairness-comparison

Gaddam, A., Wilkin, T., Angelova, M., & Gaddam, J. (2020). Detecting sensor faults, anomalies, and outliers in the Internet of Things: A survey on the challenges and solutions. *Electronics (Basel)*, *9*(3), 511. Advance online publication. DOI: 10.3390/electronics9030511

Galhotra, S., Brun, Y., & Meliou, A. (2017). Fairness testing: testing software for discrimination. DOI: 10.1145/3106237.3106277

Gilpin, L. H., Bau, D., Yuan, B. Z., Bajwa, A., Specter, M., & Kagal, L. (n.d.). Explaining explanations: An overview of interpretability of machine learning. Computer Science and Artificial Intelligence Laboratory, Massachusetts Institute of Technology. Retrieved from https://arxiv.org/abs/1806.00069

Hämäläinen, M. (2021). Urban development with dynamic digital twins in Helsinki city. *IET Smart Cities*, *3*(4), 201–210. DOI: 10.1049/smc2.12015

Haresamudram, K., Larsson, S., & Heintz, F. (2023). Three levels of AI transparency. *Computer*, *56*(2), 93–100. DOI: 10.1109/MC.2022.3213181

Hartley, K. (2023). Public Perceptions about Smart Cities: Governance and Quality-of-Life in Hong Kong. *Social Indicators Research*, *166*(3), 731–753. DOI: 10.1007/s11205-023-03087-9 PMID: 36999130

Hawkins, C. (2020). The challenges and opportunities of urban planning in the age of artificial intelligence. California Polytechnic State University. https://digitalcommons.calpoly.edu/cgi/viewcontent.cgi?article=1294&context=crpsp

Ho, D.-A., & Beyan, O. (2020). Biases in the data science lifecycle. arXiv. /arXiv.2009.09795DOI: 10.48550

Hoang, T. V. (2024). Impact of integrated artificial intelligence and Internet of Things technologies on smart city transformation. *Journal of Technical Education Science*, *19*(1), 64–73. DOI: 10.54644/jte.2024.1532

Holmberg, L., Davidsson, P., & Linde, P. (2020). A feature space focus in machine teaching. In 2020 IEEE International Conference on Pervasive Computing and Communications Workshops (PerCom Workshops), 1–2. DOI: 10.1109/PerComWorkshops48775.2020.9156175

IBM. (n.d.-a). Explainable AI (XAI). https://www.ibm.com/topics/explainable-ai

IBM. (n.d.-b). Internet of Things (IoT). IBM. Retrieved December 15, 2024, from https://www.ibm.com/topics/internet-of-things

IBM. (n.d.-c). Machine learning. IBM. https://www.ibm.com/topics/machine-learning

IBM. (n.d.-d). Phishing. IBM. Retrieved December 7, 2024, from https://www.ibm.com/topics/phishing

IDB. (n.d.). What are the cybersecurity risks for smart cities? Inter-American Development Bank. Retrieved from https://www.idb.org/what-are-the-cybersecurity-risks-for-smart-cities/

Ionescu, R., Zlati, M. L., & Antohi, V. (2023). Smart cities from low cost to expensive solutions under an optimal analysis. *Financial Innovation*, *9*(1), 60. Advance online publication. DOI: 10.1186/s40854-023-00448-8 PMID: 36883188

Javed, A. R., Ahmed, W., Pandya, S., Maddikunta, P. K. R., Alazab, M., & Gadekallu, T. R. (2023). A survey of Explainable artificial intelligence for smart cities. *Electronics (Basel)*, *12*(4), 1020. DOI: 10.3390/electronics12041020

Jeong, D., Baek, M., Lim, T., Kim, Y., Kim, S., Lee, Y., Jung, W., & Lee, I. (2022). Digital Twin: Technology evolution stages and implementation layers with technology elements. *IEEE Access : Practical Innovations, Open Solutions*, *10*, 52609–52620. DOI: 10.1109/ACCESS.2022.3174220

Jeronen, E. K. (2020). *Economic sustainability*. Summary. In Encyclopedia of Sustainable Management. DOI: 10.1007/978-3-030-02006-4_197-1

Joss, S. (2015, February). Smart cities: From concept to practice. Reflections, 9.

Kalinin, M., Krundyshev, V., & Zegzhda, P. (2021). Cybersecurity risk assessment in smart city infrastructures. *Machines (Basel)*, *9*(4), 78. DOI: 10.3390/machines9040078

Kamiran, F., & Calders, T. (2011). Data preprocessing techniques for classification without discrimination. *Knowledge and Information Systems*, *33*(1), 1–33. DOI: 10.1007/s10115-011-0463-8

Kamiran, F., Karim, A., & Zhang, X. (2012). Decision Theory for Discrimination-Aware Classification. https://doi.org/DOI: 10.1109/ICDM.2012.45

Kartal, E. (2023). A comprehensive study on bias in artificial intelligence systems: Biased or unbiased AI, that's the question! *International Journal of Intelligent Information Technologies*, *18*(1), 1–15. DOI: 10.4018/IJIIT.309582

Khan, I. H., Khan, M. I., & Khan, S. (2020b). Challenges of IoT implementation in smart city development. In Lecture notes in civil engineering (pp. 475–486). DOI: 10.1007/978-981-15-2545-2_40

Kim, J. J. (2022). Predictions or validation of assumptions: Predictive policing (Bachelor of Science thesis, School of Engineering, University of Virginia, Charlottesville, VA). Retrieved from https://libraetd.lib.virginia.edu/downloads/pg15bg01b

Kirubavathi, G., & Anitha, R. (2014). Botnets: A study and analysis. *Advances in Intelligent Systems and Computing*, *246*, 203–214. DOI: 10.1007/978-81-322-1680-3_23

Komninos, N., Kakderi, C., Mora, L., & Sefertzi, E. (2022). Towards high impact smart cities: A universal architecture based on connected intelligence spaces. *Journal of the Knowledge Economy*, *13*(6), 1–29. DOI: 10.1007/s13132-021-00767-0

Kontokosta, C. E., & Hong, B. (2021). Bias in smart city governance: How socio-spatial disparities in 311 complaint behavior impact the fairness of data-driven decisions. *Sustainable Cities and Society*, *64*, 102503. DOI: 10.1016/j.scs.2020.102503

Koriat, A., Lichtenstein, S., & Fischhoff, B. (1980). Reasons for confidence. *Journal of Experimental Psychology. Human Learning and Memory*, *6*(2), 107–118. DOI: 10.1037/0278-7393.6.2.107

Kuhlman, T., & Farrington, J. (2010). What is Sustainability? *Sustainability (Basel)*, *2*(11), 3436–3448. DOI: 10.3390/su2113436

Kumar, G. (2016). Denial of service attacks – An updated perspective. *Systems Science & Control Engineering*, *4*(1), 285–294. DOI: 10.1080/21642583.2016.1241193

Kumar, T. M. V., & Dahiya, B. (2016). Smart economy in smart cities. In Advances in 21st century human settlements (pp. 3–76). DOI: 10.1007/978-981-10-1610-3_1

Kusner, M. J., Loftus, J. R., Russell, C., & Silva, R. (2017). Counterfactual fairness. In *Advances in Neural Information Processing Systems*. NIPS.

Laato, S., Tiainen, M., Islam, A. N., & Mäntymäki, M. (2022). How to explain AI systems to end users: A systematic literature review and research agenda. *Internet Research*, *32*(7), 1–31. DOI: 10.1108/INTR-08-2021-0600

Larsson, S., & Heintz, F. (2020). Transparency in artificial intelligence. *Internet Policy Review*, *9*(2). Advance online publication. DOI: 10.14763/2020.2.1469

Layode, N. O., Naiho, N. H. N. N., Adeleke, N. G. S., Udeh, N. E. O., & Labake, N. T. T. (2024). Data privacy and security challenges in environmental research: Approaches to safeguarding sensitive information. *International Journal of Applied Research in Social Sciences*, *6*(6), 1193–1214. DOI: 10.51594/ijarss.v6i6.1210

Li, M., Sun, H., Huang, Y., & Chen, H. (2024). Shapley value: From cooperative game to explainable artificial intelligence. *Autonomous Intelligent Systems*, *4*(1), 2. Advance online publication. DOI: 10.1007/s43684-023-00060-8

Liao, Q. V., & Vaughan, J. W. (2023). AI transparency in the age of LLMs: A human-centered research roadmap. Microsoft Research. https://arxiv.org/abs/2306.01941

Ligozat, A.-L., Bugeau, A., Lefèvre, J., & Combaz, J. (2022). Unraveling the Hidden Environmental Impacts of AI: Life Cycle Assessment of AI Solutions. https://arxiv.org/abs/2110.11822

Lundberg, S. M., & Lee, S. (2017). A unified approach to interpreting model predictions. arXiv (Cornell University). /arxiv.1705.07874DOI: 10.48550

Ma, Z., Zhang, G., & Wei, D. (2021). Application of Computer Technology in Life under the Background of Big Data. *Journal of Physics: Conference Series*, *1881*(3), 032068. DOI: 10.1088/1742-6596/1881/3/032068

Macomber, J. D. (2018, April 4). Smart Cities are Complicated and Costly: Here's How to Build Them. Harvard Business Review. Retrieved from https://hbr.org

Mahesh, B. (2020b). Machine Learning Algorithms - a review. *International Journal of Science and Research (Raipur, India)*, *9*(1), 381–386. DOI: 10.21275/ART20203995

Mallik, A. (2019). Man-in-the-middle attack: Understanding in simple words. *Cyberspace Jurnal Pendidikan Teknologi Informasi*, *2*(2), 109. DOI: 10.22373/cj.v2i2.3453

Mancebo, F. (2019). Smart city strategies: Time to involve people. Comparing Amsterdam, Barcelona and Paris. *Journal of Urbanism*, *13*(2), 133–152. DOI: 10.1080/17549175.2019.1649711

Mitchell, M. (2021). Bias in the vision and language of artificial intelligence. Retrieved from https://web.stanford.edu/class/archive/cs/cs224n/cs224n.1194/slides/cs224n-2019-lecture19-bias.pdf

Mohanty, S. P., Choppali, U., & Kougianos, E. (2016). Everything you wanted to know about smart cities: The Internet of things is the backbone. *IEEE Consumer Electronics Magazine*, *5*(3), 60–70. DOI: 10.1109/MCE.2016.2556879

Mosavi, A., Ardabili, S., & Varkonyi-Koczy, A. R. (2020). List of deep learning models. In *Engineering for Sustainable Future* (pp. 287–303). Springer. DOI: 10.1007/978-3-030-36841-8_20

Mosqueira-Rey, E., Hernández-Pereira, E., Alonso-Ríos, D., Bobes-Bascarán, J., & Fernández-Leal, Á. (2022). Human-in-the-loop machine learning: A state of the art. *Artificial Intelligence Review*, *56*(4), 3005–3054. DOI: 10.1007/s10462-022-10246-w

Nickerson, R. S. (1998). Confirmation bias: A ubiquitous phenomenon in many guises. *Review of General Psychology*, *2*(2), 175–220. DOI: 10.1037/1089-2680.2.2.175

Northwest Education. (2024). ChatGPT: Revolutionizing the Digital World Impact on Businesses. Author.

Nower, N. (2019). Privacy in IoT: Expectations, causes of concerns, and reasons for concern mitigation. *International Journal of Computer Applications*, *177*(25), 37–42. DOI: 10.5120/ijca2019919718

Open, A. I. (n.d.). AI and compute. OpenAI. Retrieved from https://openai.com/index/ai-and-compute/

Penmetsa, V., & Holbert, K. E. (2021). Climate Change Effects on Thermal Power Generation and Projected Losses in Generation and Income in the U.S. for the Period 2020–2050. DOI: 10.1109/NAPS50074.2021.9449688

Prime, G. W. (2022, March 7). Virtual Singapore – Building a 3D-Empowered Smart Nation. Geospatial World. Retrieved from https://www.geospatialworld.net

Puron-Cid, G., & Gil-Garcia, J. R. (2022). Are smart cities too expensive in the long term? Analyzing the effects of ICT infrastructure on municipal financial sustainability. *Sustainability (Basel)*, *14*(10), 6055. DOI: 10.3390/su14106055

Radchenko, K. (2023). The economic and social impacts of smart cities: Multi-stakeholder pre-study results. Smart Cities and Regional Development (SCRD). *Journal*, *7*(2), 25–38. DOI: 10.25019/71fq6q53

Ribeiro, M. T., Singh, S., & Guestrin, C. (2016). "Why should I trust you?": explaining the predictions of any classifier. arXiv (Cornell University). DOI: 10.1145/2939672.2939778

Richards, N. M. (2013). The dangers of surveillance. *Harvard Law Review*, *126*(7), 1934–1965. https://harvardlawreview.org/wp-content/uploads/2013/05/vol126_richards.pdf

Risk/Needs Assessment Tools. (n.d.). *Handbook of Correctional Assessment and Treatment* (1st ed.). DOI: 10.1002/9781119184256.ch3

Salha, R. A., Jawabrah, M. Q., Badawy, U. I., Jarada, A., & Alastal, A. I. (2020). Towards Smart, Sustainable, Accessible and Inclusive City for Persons with Disability by Taking into Account Checklists Tools. *Journal of Geographic Information System*, *12*(04), 348–371. DOI: 10.4236/jgis.2020.124022

Salih, A., Raisi-Estabragh, Z., Galazzo, I. B., Radeva, P., Petersen, S. E., Menegaz, G., & Lekadir, K. (2023). Commentary on explainable artificial intelligence methods: SHAP and LIME. arXiv (Cornell University). /arxiv.2305.02012DOI: 10.48550

SamSam and the Silent Battle of Atlanta. (2019). In *11th International Conference on Cyber Conflict (CyCon)* (pp. 1-16). DOI: 10.23919/CYCON.2019.8757090

Sanchez, T. W., Brenman, M., & Ye, X. (2024). The ethical Concerns of artificial intelligence in urban planning. *Journal of the American Planning Association*, 1–14. DOI: 10.1080/01944363.2024.2355305

Sarker, I. H. (2021). Deep learning: A comprehensive overview on techniques, taxonomy, applications, and research directions. *SN Computer Science*, *2*(5), 420. Advance online publication. DOI: 10.1007/s42979-021-00815-1 PMID: 34426802

Ševčík, M., Chaloupková, M., Zourková, I., & Janošíková, L. (2022). Barriers to the implementation of smart projects in rural areas, small towns, and the city in Brno Metropolitan area. *European Countryside*, *14*(4), 675–695. DOI: 10.2478/euco-2022-0034

Shahbazi, N., Lin, Y., Asudeh, A., & Jagadish, H. V. (2023). Representation bias in data: A survey on identification and resolution techniques. *ACM Computing Surveys*, *293*(13s), 1–39. DOI: 10.1145/3588433

Siman, E., Abiodun, J., Timothy, G., & Nandom, S. S. (2023). IoT-driven smart cities: Enhancing urban sustainability and quality of life. In 7th International Interdisciplinary Research & Development Conference. Retrieved from https://www.researchgate.net/publication/374090800_IoT-Driven_Smart_Cities_Enhancing_Urban_Sustainability_and_Quality_of_Life

Soe, R.-M. (2018). Smart cities: From silos to cross-border approach. *International Journal of E-Planning Research*, *7*(2), 70–88. DOI: 10.4018/IJEPR.2018040105

Solutions, A. (n.d.). Breaking barriers: Top female innovators in tech. Retrieved from https://www.apollo-solutions.com/resources/blog/breaking-barriers-top-female-innovators-in-tech/

Stanly, H., Shalinie, M. S., & Paul, R. (n.d.). A review of generative and non-generative adversarial attack on context-rich images. Engineering Applications of Artificial Intelligence. Retrieved from https://www.sciencedirect.com/science/article/pii/S0952197623007790

Steinberg, S., Stepan, A., & Neary, K. (2021). NotPetya: A Columbia University case study. Picker Center Digital Education Group, Columbia's School of International and Public Affairs (SIPA). https://www.sipa.columbia.edu/sipa-education/picker-center-executive-education/case-collection

Stepping, K. M. K. (2019). Environmental sustainability. In Social indicators research series (pp. 187–206). DOI: 10.1007/978-3-030-05023-8_10

Stevens, A., Anisfeld, A., Kuester, B., London, J., Saleiro, P., & Ghani, R. (2018). Aequitas: Bias and fairness audit. Center for Data Science and Public Policy, The University of Chicago. Retrieved from https://github.com/dssg/aequitas

Stone, A. (2024). Virtual Singapore Is More Than Just a 3-D Model, It's an Intelligent Rendering of the City. GovTech. https://www.govtech.com

Sugandha, N., Freestone, R., & Favaro, P. (2022b). The social sustainability of smart cities: A conceptual framework. *City, Culture and Society*, *29*, 100460. DOI: 10.1016/j.ccs.2022.100460

Sun, H., Chen, X., Shi, Q., Hong, M., Fu, X., & Sidiropoulos, N. D. (2017). Learning to optimize: Training deep neural networks for wireless resource management. 2017 IEEE 18th International Workshop on Signal Processing Advances in Wireless Communications (SPAWC), 1–6. DOI: 10.1109/SPAWC.2017.8227766

Swaine, M. R., & Freiberger, P. A. (2024, December 11). ENIAC | History, Computer, Stands For, Machine, & Facts. Encyclopedia Britannica. https://www.britannica.com/technology/ENIAC

Tang, X., Li, X., Ding, Y., Song, M., & Bu, Y. (2020). The pace of artificial intelligence innovations: Speed, talent, and trial-and-error. *Journal of Informetrics*, *14*(4), 101094. DOI: 10.1016/j.joi.2020.101094

Tramer, F., Atlidakis, V., Geambasu, R., Hsu, D., Hubaux, J., Humbert, M., Juels, A., & Lin, H. (2017). FairTest: Discovering Unwarranted Associations in Data-Driven Applications. DOI: 10.1109/EuroSP.2017.29

Ullah, A., Anwar, S. M., Li, J., Nadeem, L., Mahmood, T., Rehman, A., & Saba, T. (2023). Smart cities: The role of Internet of Things and machine learning in realizing a data-centric smart environment. *Complex & Intelligent Systems*, *10*(1), 1607–1637. DOI: 10.1007/s40747-023-01175-4

United Nations Environment Programme. (2019, January 24). UN report: Time to seize opportunity, tackle challenge of e-waste. Chemicals & Pollution Action. Retrieved from https://www.unep.org/news-and-stories/press-release/un-report-time-seize-opportunity-tackle-challenge-e-waste

van Zoonen, L. (2016). Privacy concerns in smart cities. *Government Information Quarterly*, *33*(3), 472–480. DOI: 10.1016/j.giq.2016.06.004

Vicci, H. (2024). The Impact of IoT on the Modern World A review and evaluation study. SSRN Electronic Journal. https://doi.org/DOI: 10.2139/ssrn.4818308

Villamil, S., Hernandez, C., & Tarazona, G. (2020). An overview of internet of things. *Telkomnika*, *18*(5), 2320. DOI: 10.12928/telkomnika.v18i5.15911

Wang, Q., Luo, S., Zhang, J., & Furuya, K. (2022). Increased attention to smart development in rural areas: A scientometric analysis of Smart Village research. *Land (Basel)*, *11*(8), 1362. DOI: 10.3390/land11081362

Wani, A., & Sathiya, R. (2020). Ransomware protection in IoT using software defined networking. *International Journal of Electrical and Computer Engineering*, *10*(3), 3166–3175. DOI: 10.11591/ijece.v10i3.pp3166-3175

Warzel, C., & Ngu, A. (n.d.). Google's 4,000-word privacy policy is a secret history of the internet. The Privacy Project. https://www.nytimes.com/interactive/2019/07/10/opinion/google-privacy-policy.html

Wu, X., Xiao, L., Sun, Y., Zhang, J., Ma, T., & He, L. (2021). A survey of human-in-the-loop for machine learning. arXiv. /arXiv.2108.00941DOI: 10.48550

Yaacoub, E., & Alouini, M. (2020). Efficient fronthaul and backhaul connectivity for IoT traffic in rural areas. *IEEE Internet of Things Magazine*, *4*(1), 60–66. DOI: 10.1109/IOTM.0001.1900061

Yuan, P. (2024). Artificial intelligence in the Internet of Things: Integrating and optimizing AI algorithms for real-time data processing and decision-making. *Proceedings of the 2nd International Conference on Machine Learning and Automation*. DOI: 10.54254/2755-2721/102/20241015

Zaidi, T. (2019). An overview: Various attacks in VANET. In 2018 4th International Conference on Computing Communication and Automation (ICCCA), Noida, India. Retrieved from https://www.researchgate.net/publication/334760930_An_Overview_Various_Attacks_in_VANET

Zehlike, M., Bonchi, F., Castillo, C., Hajian, S., Megahed, M., & Baeza-Yates, R. (2017). FA*IR. DOI: 10.1145/3132847.3132938

Zehlike, M., Castillo, C., Bonchi, F., Hajian, S., & Megahed, M. (2017). Fairness Measures: Datasets and Software for Detecting Algorithmic Discrimination. Retrieved from http://fairness-measures.org/

Zhang, D. (2013, July). Inconsistencies in big data. In 2013 12th IEEE International Conference on Cognitive Informatics & Cognitive Computing (ICCICC) (pp. 176–182). IEEE. DOI: 10.1109/ICCI-CC.2013.6622226

Zhou, S., Loiacono, E. T., & Kordzadeh, N. (2023). Smart cities for people with disabilities: A systematic literature review and future research directions. *European Journal of Information Systems*, 1–18. DOI: 10.1080/0960085X.2023.2297974

Zumbrun, H. (2023, February). Let's talk about bias: Measurement bias. Presented at NCSLI 2023, Orlando, FL. Retrieved from https://mhforce.com/wp-content/uploads/2023/10/ASQ-Lets-Talk-about-Bias-Measurement-Bias.pdf

Compilation of References

Aazam, M., Huh, E. N., St-Hilaire, M., Lung, C. H., & Lambadaris, I. (2015). Cloud of Things: Integration of IoT with Cloud Computing. *Robots and Sensor Clouds*, *36*, 77–94. DOI: 10.1007/978-3-319-22168-7_4

AbdelSattar, A. (2019), Monitoring air pollution using satellite data, *Proceedings of the International Conference on Industrial Engineering and Operations Management*, 772-780 https://www.ieomsociety.org/gcc2019/papers/126.pdf

Abdolrasol, M. G., Mohamed, R., Hannan, M. A., Al-Shetwi, A. Q., Mansor, M., & Blaabjerg, F. (2021). Artificial neural networkbased particle swarm optimization for microgrid optimal energy scheduling. *IEEE Transactions on Power Electronics*, *36*(11), 12151–12157. DOI: 10.1109/TPEL.2021.3074964

Abdullah Kaiser, Z. R. M. (2024). Smart governance for smart cities and nations. *Journal of Economy and Technology*, *2*, 216–234. DOI: 10.1016/j.ject.2024.07.003

Abdur, M., Habib, S., Ali, M., & Ullah, S. (2017). Security Issues in the Internet of Things (IoT): A Comprehensive Study. *International Journal of Advanced Computer Science and Applications*, *8*(6), 383–388. DOI: 10.14569/IJACSA.2017.080650

Ackerman, D. (2021, May 18). Helping students of all ages flourish in the era of artificial intelligence. MIT News. https://news.mit.edu/2021/ai-education-raise-0518

Adebayo, J. A. (2016). FairML: Toolbox for diagnosing bias in predictive modeling. Master's thesis, Massachusetts Institute of Technology. Retrieved from https://github.com/adebayoj/fairml

Ahmad, R. W., Salah, K., Jayaraman, R., Yaqoob, I., & Omar, M. (2021). Blockchain for waste management in smart cities: A survey. *IEEE Access : Practical Innovations, Open Solutions*, *9*, 131520–131541. DOI: 10.1109/ACCESS.2021.3113380

Alam, A. (2023). What is machine learning? *Zenodo*. https://doi.org/DOI: 10.5281/zenodo.8231580

Alanazi, F. (2023). Electric Vehicles: Benefits, Challenges, and Potential Solutions for Widespread Adaptation. *Applied Sciences (Basel, Switzerland)*, *13*(10), 6016. DOI: 10.3390/app13106016

Albino, V., Berardi, U., & Dangelico, R. M. (2015). Smart cities: Definitions, dimensions, performance, and initiatives. *Journal of Urban Technology*, *22*(1), 3–21. DOI: 10.1080/10630732.2014.942092

Alzubaidi, L., Bai, J., Al-Sabaawi, A., Santamaría, J., Albahri, A. S., Al-Dabbagh, B. S. N., Fadhel, M. A., Manoufali, M., Zhang, J., Al-Timemy, A. H., Duan, Y., Abdullah, A., Farhan, L., Lu, Y., Gupta, A., Albu, F., Abbosh, A., & Gu, Y. (2023). A survey on deep learning tools dealing with data scarcity: Definitions, challenges, solutions, tips, and applications. *Journal of Big Data*, *10*(1), 46. Advance online publication. DOI: 10.1186/s40537-023-00727-2

Ammari, C., Belatrache, D., Touhami, B., & Makhloufi, S. (2022). Sizing, optimization, control and energy management of hybrid renewable energy system—A review. *Energy and Built Environment*, *3*(4), 399–411. DOI: 10.1016/j.enbenv.2021.04.002

Anbarasan, M., Muthu, B. A., Sivaparthipan, C. B., Sundarasekar, R., Kadry, S., Krishnamoorthy, S., Samuel R, D. J., & Dasel, A. A. (2019). Detection of flood disaster system based on IoT, big data and convolutional deep neural network. *Computer Communications*, *150*, 150–157. Advance online publication. DOI: 10.1016/j.comcom.2019.11.022

Angelidou, M. (2014). Smart city policies: A spatial approach. *Cities (London, England)*, *41*, S3–S11. DOI: 10.1016/j.cities.2014.06.007

Angelidou, M., Psaltoglou, A., Komninos, N., Kakderi, C., Tsarchopoulos, P., & Panori, A. (2018). Enhancing sustainable urban development through smart city applications. *Journal of Science and Technology Policy Management*, *9*(2), 146–169. DOI: 10.1108/JSTPM-05-2017-0016

Anjomshoaa, F., Duarte, D., Rennings, T. J., Matarazzo, P., deSouza, P., & Ratti, C. (2018). City scanner: Building and scheduling a mobile sensing platform for smart city services. *IEEE Internet of Things Journal*, *5*(6), 4567–4579. DOI: 10.1109/JIOT.2018.2839058

Anrong, D., Li, G., Li, J., & Kong, X. (2016). Research on Smart Community Planning of Yishanwan, China towards New Urbanization. *International Review for Spatial Planning and Sustainable Development*, *4*(1), 78–90. DOI: 10.14246/irspsd.4.1_78

Anthopoulos, L., Janssen, M., & Weerakkody, V. (2016). A unified smart city model (USCM) for smart city conceptualization and benchmarking. *International Journal of Electronic Government Research*, *12*(2), 77–93. DOI: 10.4018/IJEGR.2016040105

Anttiroiko, A. V., Valkama, P., & Bailey, S. J. (2014). Smart cities in the new service economy: Building platforms for smart services. *AI & Society*, *29*(3), 323–334. DOI: 10.1007/s00146-013-0464-0

Anttiroiko, A.-V. (2016). City-as-a-Platform: The rise of participatory innovation platforms in Finnish cities. *Sustainability (Basel)*, *8*(9), 922. DOI: 10.3390/su8090922

ASCS24. AUSTRALIAN smart communities association. (2024). What is a Smart Community? https://www.australiansmartcommunities.org.au/smart-communities

Asghari, P., Rahmani, A., & Javadi, H. (2019). Internet of Things applications: A systematic review. *Computer Networks*, *148*, 241–261. DOI: 10.1016/j.comnet.2018.12.008

Augustyn, A. (2013). Smart cities – brand cities of the future. In The Business of Place: Critical, Practical and Pragmatic Perspectives [Conference proceedings]. Retrieved from https://www.researchgate.net/publication/320555578_Smart_Cities_-_brand_cities_of_the_future

Averda. (n.d.). Smart cities: How they create a better environment. Retrieved from https://www.averda.com/rsa/news/smart-cities-better-environment

Baho, S., & Abawajy, J. (2023). Analysis of consumer IoT device vulnerability quantification frameworks. *Electronics (Basel)*, *12*(5), 1176. DOI: 10.3390/electronics12051176

Balasubramaniam, N., Kauppinen, M., Hiekkanen, K., & Kujala, S. (2022). Transparency and explainability of AI systems: Ethical guidelines in practice. In Requirements engineering: Foundation for software quality (Lecture Notes in Computer Science, pp. 1–16). Retrieved from https://www.researchgate.net/publication/359105897_Transparency_and_Explainability_of_AI_Systems_Ethical_Guidelines_in_Practice

Bangdiwala, S. I. (2018). Regression: Simple linear. *International Journal of Injury Control and Safety Promotion*, *25*(1), 113–115. DOI: 10.1080/17457300.2018.1426702 PMID: 29400125

Bansal, A., Sharma, R., & Kathuria, M. (2022). A Systematic Review on Data Scarcity Problem in Deep Learning: Solution and Applications. *ACM Computing Surveys*, *54*(10s), 1–29. DOI: 10.1145/3502287

Bantilan, N. (2018). Themis-ml: A fairness-aware machine learning interface for end-to-end discrimination discovery and mitigation. *Journal of Technology in Human Services*, *36*(1), 15–30. https://github.com/cosmicBboy/themis-ml. DOI: 10.1080/15228835.2017.1416512

Barakat, S., Ibrahim, H., & Elbaset, A. A. (2020). Multi-objective optimization of grid-connected PV-wind hybrid system considering reliability, cost, and environmental aspects. *Sustainable Cities and Society*, *60*, 102178. DOI: 10.1016/j.scs.2020.102178

Barbierato, E., & Gatti, A. (2024). The Challenges of Machine Learning: A Critical Review. *Electronics (Basel)*, *13*(2), 416. DOI: 10.3390/electronics13020416

Barmer, H., Dzombak, R., Gaston, M., Palat, J., Redner, F., Smith, T., & Wohlbier, J. (2021). National AI engineering initiative: Scalable AI. Retrieved from https://insights.sei.cmu.edu/library/scalable-ai/

Bathaee, Y. (2018). The Artificial Intelligence Black Box and the Failure of Intent and Causation. *Harvard Journal of Law & Technology*, *31*(2). https://jolt.law.harvard.edu/assets/articlePDFs/v31/The-Artificial-Intelligence-Black-Box-and-the-Failure-of-Intent-and-Causation-Yavar-Bathaee.pdf

Batty, M. (2013). Big data, smart cities and city planning. *Dialogues in Human Geography*, *3*(3), 274–279. DOI: 10.1177/2043820613513390 PMID: 29472982

Bellamy, R. K. E., Dey, K., Hind, M., Hoffman, S. C., Houde, S., Kannan, K., Lohia, P., Martino, J., Mehta, S., Mojsilovic, A., Nagar, S., Ramamurthy, K. N., Richards, J., Saha, D., Sattigeri, P., Singh, M., Varshney, K. R., & Zhang, Y. (2018). AI fairness 360: An extensible toolkit for detecting, understanding, and mitigating unwanted algorithmic bias. arXiv. https://arxiv.org/pdf/1810.01943

Bengio, Y., Louradour, J., Collobert, R., & Weston, J. (2009). Curriculum learning. . https://doi.org/DOI: 10.1145/1553374.1553380

Bentéjac, C., Csörgő, A., & Martínez-Muñoz, G. (2021). A comparative analysis of gradient boosting algorithms. *Artificial Intelligence Review*, *54*(3), 1937–1967. DOI: 10.1007/s10462-020-09896-5

Berte, D.-R. (2018). Defining the IoT. *Proceedings of the International Conference on Business Excellence*, 12, 118–128. DOI: 10.2478/picbe-2018-0013

Bon, A., van den Nieuwenhuijzen, D., Akkermans, H., de Bour, W., Edoga, C., Hegeman, M., & Werdervoort, M. (2020). *Digital Divide, Citizenship and Inclusion in Amsterdam*. Pangea.

Bosworth, G., & Venhorst, V. (2017). Economic linkages between urban and rural regions – what's in it for the rural? *Regional Studies*, *52*(1), 1–12. DOI: 10.1080/00343404.2017.1339868

Brennan, T., & Dieterich, W. (2017). Correctional offender management profiles for alternative sanctions (COMPAS). In Handbook of Recidivism. Retrieved from https://www.researchgate.net/publication/321528262_Correctional_Offender_Management_Profiles_for_Alternative_Sanctions_COMPAS

Broussard, M. (2018). Artificial unintelligence. In The MIT Press eBooks. DOI: 10.7551/mitpress/11022.001.0001

Bryson, J. M., Crosby, B. C., & Bloomberg, L. (2014). Public administration's final exam: Integrating empirical research on public engagement. *American Review of Public Administration*, *44*(2), 225–241.

Büchi, M., Festic, N., & Latzer, M. (2022). The chilling effects of digital dataveillance: A theoretical model and an empirical research agenda. *Big Data & Society*, *9*(1), 205395172110653. DOI: 10.1177/20539517211065368

Cao, Y., Hu, Y., Liu, Q., Lu, M., & Shan, Y. (2023). Job creation or disruption? Unraveling the effects of smart city construction on corporate employment in China. *Technological Forecasting and Social Change*, *195*, 122783. DOI: 10.1016/j.techfore.2023.122783

Car, T., Pilepić Stifanich, L., & Kovačić, N. (2022). The role of 5G and IoT in smart cities. ENTRENOVA - ENTerprise REsearch InNOVAtion, 8(1), 377–389. DOI: 10.54820/entrenova-2022-0032

Caragliu, A., Del Bo, C., & Nijkamp, P. (2009). Smart Cities in Europe, Series Research Memoranda 0048. VU University Amsterdam, Faculty of Economics, Business Administration and Econometrics.

Caragliu, A., & Del Bo, C. F. (2023). Smart cities and the urban digital divide. *NPJ Urban Sustainability*, *3*(1), 43. Advance online publication. DOI: 10.1038/s42949-023-00117-w

Caragliu, A., Del Bo, C., & Nijkamp, P. (2011). Smart Cities in Europe. *Journal of Urban Technology*, *18*(2), 65–82. DOI: 10.1080/10630732.2011.601117

Casini, M. (2017). Green Technology for Smart Cities. *IOP Conference Series. Earth and Environmental Science*, *83*, 012014. DOI: 10.1088/1755-1315/83/1/012014

Castell, N., Kobernus, M., Liu, H.-Y., Schneider, P., Lahoz, W., Berre, A. J., & Noll, J. (2015). Mobile technologies and services for environmental monitoring: The citi-sense-mob approach. *Urban Climate*, *14*, 370–382. DOI: 10.1016/j.uclim.2014.08.002

Chang, S., & Smith, M. K. (2023). Residents' Quality of Life in Smart Cities: A Systematic Literature review. *Land (Basel)*, *12*(4), 876. DOI: 10.3390/land12040876

Charan, A. (2022). Marketing communication and awareness on sustainable consumption of fossil fuel in Delhi and NCR. *International Journal of Multidisciplinary Education Research, 11,*http://ijmer.in.doi./2022/11.06.23

Chatterji, A. (2021). Air pollution in Delhi: filling the policy gaps, *Massachusetts Undergraduate Journal of Economics, 17(1)*https://www.umass.edu/economics/sites/default/files/MUJE2021.pdf

Chen, T., Gil-Garcia, J. R., & Gasco-Hernandez, M. (2022). Understanding social sustainability for smart cities: The importance of inclusion, equity, and citizen participation as both inputs and long-term outcomes. *Journal of Smart Cities and Society*, *1*(2), 135–148. DOI: 10.3233/SCS-210123

Chen, T., & Guestrin, C. (2016). Xgboost: A scalable tree boosting system. In *Proceedings of the 22nd acm sigkdd international conference on knowledge discovery and data mining* (pp. 785-794). DOI: 10.1145/2939672.2939785

Chen, X., Zheng, H., Wang, H., & Yan, T. (2022). Can machine learning algorithms perform better than multiple linear regression in predicting nitrogen excretion from lactating dairy cows. *Scientific Reports*, *12*(1), 12478. DOI: 10.1038/s41598-022-16490-y PMID: 35864287

Chib, A., Alvarez, K., & Todorovic, T. (2021). Critical Perspectives on the Smart City: Efficiency Objectives vs Inclusion Ideals. *Journal of Urban Technology*, *29*(4), 83–99. DOI: 10.1080/10630732.2021.2001712

Chin, J., Callaghan, V., & Ben Allouch, S. (2019). The Internet-of-Things: Reflections on the Past, Present and Future from a User-Centered and Smart Environment Perspective. *Journal of Ambient Intelligence and Smart Environments*, *11*(1), 45–69. DOI: 10.3233/AIS-180506

Chourabi, H. (2012). Understanding Smart Cities: An Integrative Framework. 2012 45th Hawaii International Conference on System Sciences, 2289-2297. DOI: 10.1109/HICSS.2012.615

City Auditor's Office. (2018, January). ISO/IEC 27001 ISMS precertification audit. City Auditor's Office. Retrieved from https://www.atlaudit.org/isoiec-27001-isms-precertification-audit---january-2018.html

Clarke, R. A. (1988). Information technology and dataveillance. *Communications of the ACM*, *31*(5), 498–512. DOI: 10.1145/42411.42413

Clim, A., Toma, A., Zota, R. D., & Constantinescu, R. (2022). The Need for Cybersecurity in Industrial Revolution and Smart Cities. *Sensors (Basel)*, *23*(1), 120. DOI: 10.3390/s23010120 PMID: 36616718

Cobbe, J. (2022). *Technochauvinism*. Department of Computer Science and Technology, University of Cambridge.

Connolly, R., & Fox, G. (2017). Dataveillance and information privacy concerns. In *Biometrics: Concepts, methodologies, tools, and applications* (pp. 973–986). IGI Global. DOI: 10.4018/978-1-5225-0983-7.ch063

CoverLink. (2021, September 20). City of Atlanta ransomware. CoverLink. Retrieved from https://coverlink.com/case-study/city-of-atlanta-ransomware/

Cugurullo, F. (2018). The origin of the Smart City imaginary: from the dawn of modernity to the eclipse of reason. Academic Press.

Curelariu, T., & Lodie, A. (2024). The lawfulness of re-identification under data protection law. In Annual Privacy Forum 2024 (pp. 112–131). ENISA; European Commission; Karlstads universitet. DOI: 10.1007/978-3-031-68024-3_6

Dastin, J. (2018, October 11). Insight: Amazon scraps secret AI recruiting tool that showed bias against women. Reuters. Retrieved from https://www.reuters.com

De Lange, M., & De Waal, M. (2017). Owning the city: New media and citizen engagement in urban design. In *Urban land use* (pp. 109–130). Apple Academic Press. DOI: 10.1201/9781315365794-5

de Waal, M., & Dignum, M. (2017). The citizen in the smart city. How the smart city could transform citizenship. it -. *Información Tecnológica*, *59*(6), 263–273. Advance online publication. DOI: 10.1515/itit-2017-0012

Dinda, S. (2008). Social capital in the creation of human capital and economic growth: A productive consumption approach. *Journal of Socio-Economics*, *37*(5), 2020–2033. DOI: 10.1016/j.socec.2007.06.014

Dommett, K., Barclay, A., & Gibson, R. (2024). Just what is data-driven campaigning? A systematic review. *Information Communication and Society*, *27*(1), 1–22. DOI: 10.1080/1369118X.2023.2166794

Donovan, M. (2023, April 20). How AI is helping historians better understand our past. MIT Technology Review. https://www.technologyreview.com/2023/04/11/1071104/ai-helping-historians-analyze-past/

Duong, D., Le, Q. M., Nguyen-Tai, T. L., & Nguyen, H. D. (2021). An effective AQI estimation using sensor data and stacking mechanism. In *New Trends in Intelligent Software Methodologies, Tools and Techniques* (pp. 123–134). IOS Press. DOI: 10.3233/FAIA210040

Dutta, A., & Jinsart, W. (2021). Air quality, atmospheric variables and spread of COVID-19 in Delhi (India): An analysis. *Aerosol and Air Quality Research*, *21*(3), 200417. DOI: 10.4209/aaqr.2020.07.0417

Eger, J. M. (2005). Smart communities, universities, and globalization: Educating the workforce for tomorrow's economy. *Metropolitan Universities, 16*(4), 28–38.

Ehsan, U., Liao, Q. V., Muller, M., Riedl, M. O., & Weisz, J. D. (2021). Expanding explainability: Towards social transparency in AI systems. In *CHI Conference on Human Factors in Computing Systems (CHI '21)*. ACM. DOI: 10.1145/3411764.3445188

Ejaz, W., Naeem, M., Shahid, A., Anpalagan, A., & Jo, M. (2017). Efficient energy management for the internet of things in smart cities. *IEEE Communications Magazine, 55*(1), 84–91. DOI: 10.1109/MCOM.2017.1600218CM

El-Agamy, R. F., Sayed, H. A., Akhatatneh, A. M. A., Aljohani, M., & Elhosseini, M. (2024). Comprehensive analysis of digital twins in smart cities: A 4200-paper bibliometric study. *Artificial Intelligence Review, 57*(6), 154. Advance online publication. DOI: 10.1007/s10462-024-10781-8

Esposito, G., Clement, J., Mora, L., & Crutzen, N. (2021). One size does not fit all: Framing smart city policy narratives within regional socio-economic contexts in Brussels and Wallonia. *Cities (London, England), 118*, 103329. DOI: 10.1016/j.cities.2021.103329

European Parliamentary Research Service. (2020). The impact of the General Data Protection Regulation (GDPR) on artificial intelligence. European Parliament. https://www.europarl.europa.eu/RegData/etudes/STUD/2020/641530/EPRS_STU(2020)641530_EN.pdf

Farooq, M. K. H. M., Siddique, K. H., Rehman, H., Aziz, T., Lee, D. J., & Wahid, A. (2011). Rice direct seeding: Experiences, challenges and opportunities. *Soil & Tillage Research, 111*(2), 87–98. DOI: 10.1016/j.still.2010.10.008

Federal Ministry for the Environment, Nature Conservation, and Nuclear Safety. (2020). The German Government's Climate Action Programme 2030.

Fekih, M. A., Bechkit, W., Rivano, H., Dahan, M., & Rena, F. (2020). Participatory air quality and urban heat islands monitoring system. *IEEE Sensors Journal*, *20*(12), 6789–6800.

Feldman, M., Friedler, S. A., Moeller, J., Scheidegger, C., & Venkatasubramanian, S. (2015). Certifying and removing disparate impact. In *Proceedings of the ACM SIGKDD International Conference on Knowledge Discovery and Data Mining* (pp. 259–268). ACM.

Fereidouni, H., Fadeitcheva, O., & Zalai, M. (2023). IoT and man-in-the-middle attacks. arXiv. https://arxiv.org/abs/2308.02479

Ferrara, E. (2023). Fairness and bias in artificial intelligence: A brief survey of sources, impacts, and mitigation strategies. MDPI Electronics, 6(1), 3. https://www.mdpi.com/2413-4155/6/1/3

Foth, M. (2017). Some thoughts on digital placemaking. In Media Architecture Compendium? Digital Placemaking.DOI: 10.7238/d.v0i12.915.31

Fountain, J. E. (2022). The moon, the ghetto, and artificial intelligence: Reducing systemic racism in computational algorithms. *Government Information Quarterly*, *39*(2), 101645. Advance online publication. DOI: 10.1016/j.giq.2021.101645

Franklin, G., Stephens, R., Piracha, M., Tiosano, S., Lehouillier, F., Koppel, R., & Elkin, P. (2024). The Sociodemographic Biases in Machine Learning Algorithms: A Biomedical Informatics perspective. *Life (Chicago, Ill.)*, *14*(6), 652. DOI: 10.3390/life14060652 PMID: 38929638

Friedler, S. A., Scheidegger, C., Venkatasubramanian, S., Choudhary, S., Hamilton, E. P., & Roth, D. (2018). A comparative study of fairness-enhancing interventions in machine learning. https://github.com/algofairness/fairness-comparison

Gabbar, H. A., Abdussami, M. R., & Adham, M. I. (2020). Optimal planning of nuclear-renewable micro-hybrid energy system by particle swarm optimization. *IEEE Access : Practical Innovations, Open Solutions*, *8*, 181049–181073. DOI: 10.1109/ACCESS.2020.3027524

Gaddam, A., Wilkin, T., Angelova, M., & Gaddam, J. (2020). Detecting sensor faults, anomalies, and outliers in the Internet of Things: A survey on the challenges and solutions. *Electronics (Basel)*, *9*(3), 511. Advance online publication. DOI: 10.3390/electronics9030511

Galhotra, S., Brun, Y., & Meliou, A. (2017). Fairness testing: testing software for discrimination. DOI: 10.1145/3106237.3106277

Gao, W., Fan, L., Ushifusa, Y., Gu, Q., & Ren, J. (2016). Possibility and Challenge of Smart Community in Japan. *Procedia: Social and Behavioral Sciences*, *216*, 109–118. DOI: 10.1016/j.sbspro.2015.12.015

Ghazali, M., Okamura, T., Abdullah, T., Sunar, M. S., Mohamed, F., & Ismail, N. (2016). In the Quest of Defining Smart Digital City in Medini Iskandar Malaysia, Iskandar Puteri, Malaysia. Proceedings of the SEACHI 2016 on Smart Cities for Better Living with HCI and UX.

Ghosh, S., Sarkar, S. K., Roy, P., Roy, B., & Podder, A. (2025). Role of Libraries in Promoting Digital Literacy and Information Fluency. In Navigating AI in Academic Libraries: Implications for Academic Research (pp. 77-108). IGI Global.

Gil, O., & Navarro, C. (2013). Innovations of Governance in Cities and Urban regions: Smart Cities in China, Iskandar (Malaysia), Japan, New York and Tarragona (Spain). Paper presented at the EURA Conference: Cities as Sheedbeds for Innovation.

Gilpin, L. H., Bau, D., Yuan, B. Z., Bajwa, A., Specter, M., & Kagal, L. (n.d.). Explaining explanations: An overview of interpretability of machine learning. Computer Science and Artificial Intelligence Laboratory, Massachusetts Institute of Technology. Retrieved from https://arxiv.org/abs/1806.00069

Goldsmith, S. (2021). As the Chorus of Dumb City Advocates Increases, How Do We Define the Truly Smart City? datasmart.ash.harvard.edu

Goodman, N., Zwick, A., Spicer, Z., & Carlsen, N. (2020). Public engagement in smart city development: Lessons from communities in Canada's Smart City Challenge. *The Canadian Geographer. Geographe Canadien, 64*(3), 416–432. DOI: 10.1111/cag.12607

Goutam Mukherjee, A., Ramesh Wanjari, U., Chakraborty, R., Renu, K., Vellingiri, B., & George, A., C R, S. R., & Valsala Gopalakrishnan, A. (2021). A review on modern and smart technologies for efficient waste disposal and management. *Journal of Environmental Management, 297*, 113347. DOI: 10.1016/j.jenvman.2021.113347 PMID: 34314963

Goyal, S. K., Ghatge, S. V., Nema, P. S. M. T., & Tamhane, , S. (2006). Understanding urban vehicular pollution problem vis-a-vis ambient air quality–case study of a megacity (Delhi, India). *Environmental Monitoring and Assessment, 119*, 557–569. DOI: 10.1007/s10661-005-9043-2 PMID: 16741810

Guan, B., Zhan, R., Lin, H., & Huang, Z. (2015). Review of the state-of-the-art of exhaust particulate filter technology in internal combustion engines. *Journal of Environmental Management, 154*, 225–258. DOI: 10.1016/j.jenvman.2015.02.027 PMID: 25743879

Gubbi, J., Buyya, R., Marusic, S., & Palaniswami, M. (2013). Internet of Things (IoT): A Vision, Architectural Elements, and Future Directions. *Future Generation Computer Systems, 29*(7), 1645–1660. DOI: 10.1016/j.future.2013.01.010

Gupta, N. S., Mohta, Y., Heda, K., Armaan, R., Valarmathi, B., & Arulkumaran, G. (2023). Prediction of Air Quality Index Using Machine Learning Techniques: A Comparative Analysis. *Journal of Environmental and Public Health, 2023*, 1–26. Advance online publication. DOI: 10.1155/2023/4916267

Gupta, R., & Gupta, R. (2016). ABC of Internet of Things: Advancements, Benefits, Challenges, Enablers and Facilities of IoT. *Symposium on Colossal Data Analysis and Networking* (pp. 1–5). DOI: 10.1109/CDAN.2016.7570875

Gurstein, M. (2003). Effective use: A community informatics strategy beyond the Digital Divide. *First Monday*, *8*(12). Advance online publication. DOI: 10.5210/fm.v8i12.1107

Gurstein, M. (2014). Smart cities vs. smart communities: Empowering citizens not market economics. *The Journal of Community Informatics*, *10*(3). Advance online publication. DOI: 10.15353/joci.v10i3.3438

Guttikunda, S., & Jawahar, P. (2020). Can we vacuum our air pollution problem using smog towers? *Atmosphere (Basel)*, *11*(9), 922. DOI: 10.3390/atmos11090922

Halsana, S. (2020). Air quality prediction model using supervised machine learning algorithms. International Journal of Scientific Research in Computer Science. *Engineering and Information Technology*, *8*, 190–201. DOI: 10.32628/CSEIT206435

Ha, M. P., Nazari-Heris, M., Mohammadi-Ivatloo, B., & Seyedi, H. (2020). A hybrid genetic particle swarm optimization for distributed generation allocation in power distribution networks. *Energy*, *209*, 118218. DOI: 10.1016/j.energy.2020.118218

Hämäläinen, M. (2021). Urban development with dynamic digital twins in Helsinki city. *IET Smart Cities*, *3*(4), 201–210. DOI: 10.1049/smc2.12015

Haresamudram, K., Larsson, S., & Heintz, F. (2023). Three levels of AI transparency. *Computer*, *56*(2), 93–100. DOI: 10.1109/MC.2022.3213181

Hartley, K. (2023). Public Perceptions about Smart Cities: Governance and Quality-of-Life in Hong Kong. *Social Indicators Research*, *166*(3), 731–753. DOI: 10.1007/s11205-023-03087-9 PMID: 36999130

Harun, S. N., Hanafiah, M. M., & Noor, N. M. (2022). Rice straw utilisation for bioenergy production: A brief overview. *Energies*, *15*(15), 5542. DOI: 10.3390/en15155542

Hasan, M. M., & Rahman, M. M. (2017). Performance and emission characteristics of biodiesel–diesel blend and environmental and economic impacts of biodiesel production: A review. *Renewable 5and Sustainable Energy Reviews, 74*, 938-948 .DOI: 10.1016/j.rser.2017.03.045

Hasenfratz, D., Saukh, O., Walser, C., Hueglin, C., Fierz, M., & Thiele, L. (2014). Pushing the spatio-temporal resolution limit of urban air pollution maps. In *2014 IEEE International Conference on Pervasive Computing and Communications (PerCom)* (pp. 69–77). IEEE. DOI: 10.1109/PerCom.2014.6813946

Hawkins, C. (2020). The challenges and opportunities of urban planning in the age of artificial intelligence. California Polytechnic State University. https://digitalcommons.calpoly.edu/cgi/viewcontent.cgi?article=1294&context=crpsp

Hernández-Muñoz, J. M. (2011). Smart Cities at the Forefront of the Future Internet. In Lecture Notes in Computer Science: Vol. 6656. *The Future Internet. FIA 2011*. Springer. DOI: 10.1007/978-3-642-20898-0_32

Hoang, T. V. (2024). Impact of integrated artificial intelligence and Internet of Things technologies on smart city transformation. *Journal of Technical Education Science*, *19*(1), 64–73. DOI: 10.54644/jte.2024.1532

Hochreiter, S., & Schmidhuber, J. (1997). Long short-term memory. *Neural Computation*, *9*(8), 1735–1780. DOI: 10.1162/neco.1997.9.8.1735 PMID: 9377276

Holmberg, L., Davidsson, P., & Linde, P. (2020). A feature space focus in machine teaching. In 2020 IEEE International Conference on Pervasive Computing and Communications Workshops (PerCom Workshops), 1–2. DOI: 10.1109/PerComWorkshops48775.2020.9156175

Horgan, D., & Dimitrijević, B. (2019). Frameworks for citizens participation in planning: From conversational to smart tools. *Sustainable Cities and Society*, *48*, 101550. DOI: 10.1016/j.scs.2019.101550

IBM. (n.d.-a). Explainable AI (XAI). https://www.ibm.com/topics/explainable-ai

IBM. (n.d.-b). Internet of Things (IoT). IBM. Retrieved December 15, 2024, from https://www.ibm.com/topics/internet-of-things

IBM. (n.d.-c). Machine learning. IBM. https://www.ibm.com/topics/machine-learning

IBM. (n.d.-d). Phishing. IBM. Retrieved December 7, 2024, from https://www.ibm.com/topics/phishing

IDB. (n.d.). What are the cybersecurity risks for smart cities? Inter-American Development Bank. Retrieved from https://www.idb.org/what-are-the-cybersecurity-risks-for-smart-cities/

IEEE. (2015). Towards a definition of the Internet of Things (IoT). https://iot.ieee.org/images/files/pdf/IEEE_IoT_Towards_Definition_Internet_of_Things_Revision1_27MAY15.pdf

Ionescu, R., Zlati, M. L., & Antohi, V. (2023). Smart cities from low cost to expensive solutions under an optimal analysis. *Financial Innovation*, *9*(1), 60. Advance online publication. DOI: 10.1186/s40854-023-00448-8 PMID: 36883188

Iriyama, Y., Kobayashi, M., Matsubara, T., Nishimura, Y., Nomura, R., & Ishikawa, T. (2005). Design of a fuel vapor-containment system (FVS) to meet zero evaporative emissions requirements in a hybrid electric vehicle. *SAE Transactions*, 1551–1558. DOI: 10.4271/2005-01-3825

Ishwaran, H., & Lu, M. (2019). Standard errors and confidence intervals for variable importance in random forest regression, classification, and survival. *Statistics in Medicine*, *38*(4), 558–582. DOI: 10.1002/sim.7803 PMID: 29869423

ITU. (2015). The Internet of Things: data for Development. https://www.itu.int/en/ITU-D/Statistics/Documents/bigdata/MIS2015_Chapter5.pdf

Jaeger, P. T. (2012). *Disability and the Internet: Confronting a digital divide*. Lynne Rienner Publishers.

Javed, A. R., Ahmed, W., Pandya, S., Maddikunta, P. K. R., Alazab, M., & Gadekallu, T. R. (2023). A survey of Explainable artificial intelligence for smart cities. *Electronics (Basel)*, *12*(4), 1020. DOI: 10.3390/electronics12041020

Jeong, D., Baek, M., Lim, T., Kim, Y., Kim, S., Lee, Y., Jung, W., & Lee, I. (2022). Digital Twin: Technology evolution stages and implementation layers with technology elements. *IEEE Access : Practical Innovations, Open Solutions*, *10*, 52609–52620. DOI: 10.1109/ACCESS.2022.3174220

Jeronen, E. K. (2020). *Economic sustainability*. Summary. In Encyclopedia of Sustainable Management. DOI: 10.1007/978-3-030-02006-4_197-1

Jia, K., Liu, C., Li, S., & Jiang, D. (2023). Modeling and optimization of a hybrid renewable energy system integrated with gas turbine and energy storage. *Energy Conversion and Management*, *279*, 116763. DOI: 10.1016/j.enconman.2023.116763

Joss, S. (2015, February). Smart cities: From concept to practice. Reflections, 9.

Juarez, E. K., & Petersen, M. R. (2021). A comparison of machine learning methods to forecast tropospheric ozone levels in Delhi. *Atmosphere (Basel)*, *13*(1), 46. DOI: 10.3390/atmos13010046

Kalajdjieski, J., Zdravevski, E., Kalajdziski, S., Corizzo, R., Pires, I. M., Lameski, P., Garcia, N. M., & Trajkovik, V. (2020). Air pollution prediction with multi-modal data and deep neural networks. *Sensors (Basel)*, *20*(24), 1–20.

Kalinin, M., Krundyshev, V., & Zegzhda, P. (2021). Cybersecurity risk assessment in smart city infrastructures. *Machines (Basel)*, *9*(4), 78. DOI: 10.3390/machines9040078

Kamiran, F., Karim, A., & Zhang, X. (2012). Decision Theory for Discrimination-Aware Classification. https://doi.org/DOI: 10.1109/ICDM.2012.45

Kamiran, F., & Calders, T. (2011). Data preprocessing techniques for classification without discrimination. *Knowledge and Information Systems, 33*(1), 1–33. DOI: 10.1007/s10115-011-0463-8

Kartal, E. (2023). A comprehensive study on bias in artificial intelligence systems: Biased or unbiased AI, that's the question! *International Journal of Intelligent Information Technologies, 18*(1), 1–15. DOI: 10.4018/IJIIT.309582

Ke, G., Meng, Q., Finley, T., Wang, T., Chen, W., Ma, W., & Liu, T. Y. (2017). Advances in neural information processing systems: Vol. 30. Lightgbm: A highly efficient gradient boosting decision tree. Academic Press.

Khaleel, , Yusupov, , Alfalh, , Güneşer, , & Nassar, , & El-Khozondar. (2024). *Impact of Smart Grid Technologies on Sustainable Urban Development*. Academic Press.

Khan, I. H., Khan, M. I., & Khan, S. (2020b). Challenges of IoT implementation in smart city development. In Lecture notes in civil engineering (pp. 475–486). DOI: 10.1007/978-981-15-2545-2_40

Kim, J. J. (2022). Predictions or validation of assumptions: Predictive policing (Bachelor of Science thesis, School of Engineering, University of Virginia, Charlottesville, VA). Retrieved from https://libraetd.lib.virginia.edu/downloads/pg15bg01b

KIM, S. J. (2022). A Study on the Development Plan of Smart City in Korea. The Journal of Economics. *Marketing and Management, 10*(6), 17–26.

Kirubavathi, G., & Anitha, R. (2014). Botnets: A study and analysis. *Advances in Intelligent Systems and Computing, 246*, 203–214. DOI: 10.1007/978-81-322-1680-3_23

Knight, T., Price, S., Bowler, D., Hookway, A., King, S., Konno, K., & Richter, R. L. (2021). How effective is 'greening' of urban areas in reducing human exposure to ground-level ozone concentrations, UV exposure and the 'urban heat island effect'? An updated systematic review. *Environmental Evidence*, *10*(1), 1–38. DOI: 10.1186/s13750-021-00226-y

Kok, C. H., Azlan, M. A. M., & Ong, S. E. (2020). IoT-based low-cost distributed air quality monitoring system for big data collection. In *2020 10th IEEE International Conference on Control System, Computing and Engineering (ICCSCE)* (pp. 123–130). IEEE. DOI: 10.1109/ICCSCE50387.2020.9204954

Kommineni, M., & Baseer, K. K. (2024). An Architecture and Review of Intelligence Based Traffic Control System for Smart Cities. *EAI Endorsed Transactions on Energy Web*, *11*. Advance online publication. DOI: 10.4108/ew.4964

Komninos, N. (2019). *Smart Cities and Connected Intelligence: Platforms, ecosystems and network effects*. Routledge. DOI: 10.4324/9780367823399

Komninos, N., Kakderi, C., Mora, L., & Sefertzi, E. (2022). Towards high impact smart cities: A universal architecture based on connected intelligence spaces. *Journal of the Knowledge Economy*, *13*(6), 1–29. DOI: 10.1007/s13132-021-00767-0

Kontokosta, C. E., & Hong, B. (2021). Bias in smart city governance: How socio-spatial disparities in 311 complaint behavior impact the fairness of data-driven decisions. *Sustainable Cities and Society*, *64*, 102503. DOI: 10.1016/j.scs.2020.102503

Koriat, A., Lichtenstein, S., & Fischhoff, B. (1980). Reasons for confidence. *Journal of Experimental Psychology. Human Learning and Memory*, *6*(2), 107–118. DOI: 10.1037/0278-7393.6.2.107

Krähmer, K. (2020). Are green cities sustainable? A degrowth critique of sustainable urban development in Copenhagen. *European Planning Studies*, *29*(7), 1272–1289. DOI: 10.1080/09654313.2020.1841119

Kramer, O. (2011). Unsupervised K-nearest neighbor regression. arXiv preprint arXiv:1107.3600. /arXiv.1107.3600DOI: 10.48550

Kuhlman, T., & Farrington, J. (2010). What is Sustainability? *Sustainability (Basel)*, *2*(11), 3436–3448. DOI: 10.3390/su2113436

Kumar, T. M. V., & Dahiya, B. (2016). Smart economy in smart cities. In Advances in 21st century human settlements (pp. 3–76). DOI: 10.1007/978-981-10-1610-3_1

Kumar, G. (2016). Denial of service attacks – An updated perspective. *Systems Science & Control Engineering*, *4*(1), 285–294. DOI: 10.1080/21642583.2016.1241193

Kumar, K., & Pande, B. P. (2023). Air pollution prediction with machine learning: A case study of Indian cities. *International Journal of Environmental Science and Technology*, *20*(5), 5333–5348. DOI: 10.1007/s13762-022-04241-5 PMID: 35603096

Kurinji, L. S., & Kumar, S. (2021). *Is Ex-situ Crop Residue Management a Scalable Solution to Stubble Burning? A Punjab Case Study*. Council on Energy, Environment and Water.

Kusner, M. J., Loftus, J. R., Russell, C., & Silva, R. (2017). Counterfactual fairness. In *Advances in Neural Information Processing Systems*. NIPS.

Laato, S., Tiainen, M., Islam, A. N., & Mäntymäki, M. (2022). How to explain AI systems to end users: A systematic literature review and research agenda. *Internet Research*, *32*(7), 1–31. DOI: 10.1108/INTR-08-2021-0600

Lapenna, S. (2022). What is Internet of Things (IoT)? 139+1 definitions since 1999. https://www.rtsrl.eu/blog/what-is-internet-of-things-iot/

Larsson, S., & Heintz, F. (2020). Transparency in artificial intelligence. *Internet Policy Review*, *9*(2). Advance online publication. DOI: 10.14763/2020.2.1469

Laura, D. V., Chatterton, T., Namdeo, A., Shivanagendra, S. G., Goyal, S., Bell, M., Goodman, P., Longhurst, J., Hayes, E., Kumar, R., Sethi, V., Ramadurai, S. B. G., Majumder, S., Menon, J., Turamari, M. N., & Barnes, J. (2018). Air pollution in Delhi: A review of past and current policy approaches. *Air Pollution.* DOI: 10.2495/AIR180411

Layode, N. O., Naiho, N. H. N. N., Adeleke, N. G. S., Udeh, N. E. O., & Labake, N. T. T. (2024). Data privacy and security challenges in environmental research: Approaches to safeguarding sensitive information. *International Journal of Applied Research in Social Sciences*, *6*(6), 1193–1214. DOI: 10.51594/ijarss.v6i6.1210

Liao, Q. V., & Vaughan, J. W. (2023). AI transparency in the age of LLMs: A human-centered research roadmap. Microsoft Research. https://arxiv.org/abs/2306.01941

Lierow, M. (2014). B2City: the next wave of urban logistics. Academic Press.

Ligozat, A.-L., Bugeau, A., Lefèvre, J., & Combaz, J. (2022). Unraveling the Hidden Environmental Impacts of AI: Life Cycle Assessment of AI Solutions. https://arxiv.org/abs/2110.11822

Li, M., Sun, H., Huang, Y., & Chen, H. (2024). Shapley value: From cooperative game to explainable artificial intelligence. *Autonomous Intelligent Systems*, *4*(1), 2. Advance online publication. DOI: 10.1007/s43684-023-00060-8

Li, Y., Sha, Z., Tang, A., Goulding, K., & Liu, X. (2023). The application of machine learning to air pollution research: A bibliometric analysis. *Ecotoxicology and Environmental Safety*, *257*, 114911. DOI: 10.1016/j.ecoenv.2023.114911 PMID: 37154080

Lyon, D. (2014). Surveillance, Snowden, and Big Data: Capacities, consequences, critique. *Big Data & Society*, *1*(2). Advance online publication. DOI: 10.1177/2053951714541861

Macomber, J. D. (2018, April 4). Smart Cities are Complicated and Costly: Here's How to Build Them. Harvard Business Review. Retrieved from https://hbr.org

Mahajan, V., Muller, E., & Bass, F. M. (1995). Diffusion of new products: Empirical generalizations and managerial uses. *Marketing Science*, *14*(3, supplement), G79–G88. DOI: 10.1287/mksc.14.3.G79

Mahesh, A., & Sandhu, K. S. (2020). A genetic algorithm based improved optimal sizing strategy for solar-wind-battery hybrid system using energy filter algorithm. *Frontiers in Energy*, *14*(1), 139–151. DOI: 10.1007/s11708-017-0484-4

Mahesh, B. (2020b). Machine Learning Algorithms - a review. *International Journal of Science and Research (Raipur, India)*, *9*(1), 381–386. DOI: 10.21275/ART20203995

Mallegowda, M., Kanavalli, A., Verma, Y., Vamsi, S. J. K., Mukesh, T., & Saxena, V. (2021). Prediction of air quality index using machine data learning on atmospheric. *NVEO-Natural Volatiles & Essential Oils Journal,* 7544-7552.

Mallik, A. (2019). Man-in-the-middle attack: Understanding in simple words. *Cyberspace Jurnal Pendidikan Teknologi Informasi*, *2*(2), 109. DOI: 10.22373/cj.v2i2.3453

Mancebo, F. (2019). Smart city strategies: Time to involve people. Comparing Amsterdam, Barcelona and Paris. *Journal of Urbanism*, *13*(2), 133–152. DOI: 10.1080/17549175.2019.1649711

Manisalidis, I., Stavropoulou, E., Stavropoulos, A., & Bezirtzoglou, E. (2020). Environmental and health impacts of air pollution: A review. *Frontiers in Public Health*, *8*, 14. DOI: 10.3389/fpubh.2020.00014 PMID: 32154200

Mansur, T., Nizar, T. M., Ali, R., Baharudin, N., & Ananda-Rao, K. (2021). Performance analysis of smart lighting control system for sustainable campus operation. *International Journal of Advanced Technology and Engineering Exploration.*, *8*(74), 54–63. DOI: 10.19101/IJATEE.2020.S2762179

Margaret, R. (2024). Information and Communication Technology (ICT). https://www.techopedia.com/definition/24152/information-and-communications-technology-ict

Margerum, R. D. (2011). *Beyond consensus: Improving collaborative planning and management.* Mit Press. DOI: 10.7551/mitpress/9780262015813.001.0001

Mavikumbure, H. S., Cobilean, V., Wickramasinghe, C. S., Drake, D., & Manic, M. (2024, July). Generative AI in cyber security of cyber physical systems: Benefits and threats. In 2024 16th International Conference on Human System Interaction (HSI) (pp. 1-8). IEEE.

Ma, Z., Zhang, G., & Wei, D. (2021). Application of Computer Technology in Life under the Background of Big Data. *Journal of Physics: Conference Series*, *1881*(3), 032068. DOI: 10.1088/1742-6596/1881/3/032068

Mbah, T. B. (2010). The Impact of ICT on students study habits. Case study: University of Buea, Cameroon. *International Journal of Science and Technology Education Research*, *1*(5), 107–110.

Mensah, J. (2019). Sustainable development: Meaning, history, principles, pillars, and implications for human action: Literature review. *Cogent Social Sciences*, *5*(1), 1653531. DOI: 10.1080/23311886.2019.1653531

Mera, Z., Matzer, C., Hausberger, S., & Fonseca, N. (2020). Performance of selective catalytic reduction (SCR) system in a diesel passenger car under real-world conditions. *Applied Thermal Engineering*, *181*, 115983. DOI: 10.1016/j.applthermaleng.2020.115983

Mishra, A., Jha, A. V., Appasani, B., Ray, A. K., Gupta, D. K., & Ghazali, A. N. (2023). Emerging technologies and design aspects of next generation cyber physical system with a smart city application perspective. *International Journal of System Assurance Engineering and Management*, *14*(S3, Suppl 3), 699–721. DOI: 10.1007/s13198-021-01523-y

Mitchell, M. (2021). Bias in the vision and language of artificial intelligence. Retrieved from https://web.stanford.edu/class/archive/cs/cs224n/cs224n.1194/slides/cs224n-2019-lecture19-bias.pdf

Mohanty, S. P., Choppali, U., & Kougianos, E. (2016). Everything you wanted to know about smart cities: The Internet of things is the backbone. *IEEE Consumer Electronics Magazine*, *5*(3), 60–70. DOI: 10.1109/MCE.2016.2556879

Moher, D., Liberati, A., Tetzlaff, J., & Altman, D. G.Prisma Group. (2010). Preferred reporting items for systematic reviews and meta-analyses: The PRISMA statement. *International Journal of Surgery*, *8*(5), 336–341. DOI: 10.1016/j.ijsu.2010.02.007 PMID: 20171303

Mora, L., Bolici, R., & Deakin, M. (2017). The first two decades of smart-city research: A bibliometric analysis. *Journal of Urban Technology*, *24*(1), 3–27. DOI: 10.1080/10630732.2017.1285123

Mosavi, A., Ardabili, S., & Varkonyi-Koczy, A. R. (2020). List of deep learning models. In *Engineering for Sustainable Future* (pp. 287–303). Springer. DOI: 10.1007/978-3-030-36841-8_20

Mosqueira-Rey, E., Hernández-Pereira, E., Alonso-Ríos, D., Bobes-Bascarán, J., & Fernández-Leal, Á. (2022). Human-in-the-loop machine learning: A state of the art. *Artificial Intelligence Review*, *56*(4), 3005–3054. DOI: 10.1007/s10462-022-10246-w

Mossberger, K., Tolbert, C. J., & McNeal, R. S. (2007). *Digital Citizenship: The Internet, Society, and Participation*. MIT Press. DOI: 10.7551/mitpress/7428.001.0001

Murray, J. (2011). Cloud network architecture and ICT - Modern Network Architecture. TechTarget =ITKnowledgeExchange.

Nam, T., & Pardo, T. A. (2011). Conceptualizing smart city with dimensions of technology, people, and institutions. *Proceedings of the 12th annual international digital government research conference: digital government innovation in challenging times.* DOI: 10.1145/2037556.2037602

National Development and Reform Commission. (2021). The 14th Five-Year Plan for Economic and Social Development of the People's Republic of China and the Long-Range Objectives Through the Year 2035.

Nickerson, R. S. (1998). Confirmation bias: A ubiquitous phenomenon in many guises. *Review of General Psychology*, *2*(2), 175–220. DOI: 10.1037/1089-2680.2.2.175

Nirwan, N., Siddiqui, A., Kannemadugu, H. B. S., Chauhan, P., & Singh, R. P. (2024). Determining hotspots of gaseous criteria air pollutants in Delhi airshed and its association with stubble burning. *Scientific Reports*, *14*(1), 986. DOI: 10.1038/s41598-023-51140-x PMID: 38200112

Norris, P. (2001). *Digital divide: Civic engagement, information poverty, and the Internet worldwide.* Cambridge University Press. DOI: 10.1017/CBO9781139164887

Northwest Education. (2024). ChatGPT: Revolutionizing the Digital World Impact on Businesses. Author.

Nower, N. (2019). Privacy in IoT: Expectations, causes of concerns, and reasons for concern mitigation. *International Journal of Computer Applications*, *177*(25), 37–42. DOI: 10.5120/ijca2019919718

O'Reilly, T. (2011). Government as a Platform. *Innovations: Technology, Governance, Globalization*, *6*(1), 13–40. DOI: 10.1162/INOV_a_00056

Open, A. I. (n.d.). AI and compute. OpenAI. Retrieved from https://openai.com/index/ai-and-compute/

Ozdamli, F., & Ozdal, H. (2015). Life-long Learning Competence Perceptions of the Teachers and Abilities in Using Information-Communication. Technologies. *Procedia: Social and Behavioral Sciences*, *182*, 718–725. DOI: 10.1016/j.sbspro.2015.04.819

Patil, R. M., Dinde, H. T., & Powar, S. (2020). A literature review on prediction of air quality index and forecasting ambient air pollutants using machine learning algorithms. *International Journal of Innovative Science and Research Technology*, *5*(8), 1234–1240. DOI: 10.38124/IJISRT20AUG683

Penmetsa, V., & Holbert, K. E. (2021). Climate Change Effects on Thermal Power Generation and Projected Losses in Generation and Income in the U.S. for the Period 2020–2050. DOI: 10.1109/NAPS50074.2021.9449688

Perera, C., Qin, Y., Estrella, J. C., Reiff-Marganiec, S., & Vasilakos, A. V. (2017). Fog computing for sustainable smart cities: A survey. *ACM Computing Surveys*, *50*(3), 1–43. DOI: 10.1145/3057266

Phang, S. Y., Phang, S. Y., & Pacey, R. (2018). *Policy innovations for affordable housing in Singapore*. Springer International Publishing. DOI: 10.1007/978-3-319-75349-2

Piqueras, P., Morena, J. D. L., Sanchis, E. J., & Pitarch, R. (2020). Impact of exhaust gas recirculation on gaseous emissions of turbocharged spark-ignition engines. *Applied Sciences (Basel, Switzerland)*, *10*(21), 7634. DOI: 10.3390/app10217634

Prime, G. W. (2022, March 7). Virtual Singapore – Building a 3D-Empowered Smart Nation. Geospatial World. Retrieved from https://www.geospatialworld.net

Prokhorenkova, L., Gusev, G., Vorobev, A., Dorogush, A. V., & Gulin, A. (2018). Advances in neural information processing systems: Vol. 31. CatBoost: unbiased boosting with categorical features. Academic Press.

Puron-Cid, G., & Gil-Garcia, J. R. (2022). Are smart cities too expensive in the long term? Analyzing the effects of ICT infrastructure on municipal financial sustainability. *Sustainability (Basel)*, *14*(10), 6055. DOI: 10.3390/su14106055

Purvis, B., Mao, Y.k & Robinson, D. (2019). Three pillars of sustainability: in search of conceptual origins. Sustainability Science, 14(3), 681–695. DOI: 10.1007/s11625-018-0627-5

Putnam, R. D. (2015). Bowling alone: America's declining social capital. In *The city reader* (pp. 188–196). Routledge.

Radchenko, K. (2023). The economic and social impacts of smart cities: Multi-stakeholder pre-study results. Smart Cities and Regional Development (SCRD). *Journal*, *7*(2), 25–38. DOI: 10.25019/71fq6q53

Ramaiah, M., & Avtar, R. (2019). Urban green spaces and their need in cities of rapidly urbanizing India: A review. *Urban Science (Basel, Switzerland)*, *3*(3), 94. DOI: 10.3390/urbansci3030094

Ramalingam, S., Rajendran, S., & Ganesan, P. (2018). Performance improvement and exhaust emissions reduction in biodiesel operated diesel engine through the use of operating parameters and catalytic converter: A review. *Renewable & Sustainable Energy Reviews*, *81*, 3215–3222. DOI: 10.1016/j.rser.2017.08.069

Ramamoorthy, R., Dutta, P. K., & Akbar, S. A. (2003). Oxygen sensors: Materials, methods, designs and applications. *Journal of Materials Science*, *38*(21), 4271–4282. DOI: 10.1023/A:1026370729205

Ravindiran, G., Hayder, G., Kanagarathinam, K., Alagumalai, A., & Sonne, C. (2023). Air quality prediction by machine learning models: A predictive study on the indian coastal city of Visakhapatnam. *Chemosphere*, *338*, 139518. DOI: 10.1016/j.chemosphere.2023.139518 PMID: 37454985

Ribeiro, M. T., Singh, S., & Guestrin, C. (2016). "Why should I trust you?": explaining the predictions of any classifier. arXiv (Cornell University). DOI: 10.1145/2939672.2939778

Richards, N. M. (2013). The dangers of surveillance. *Harvard Law Review*, *126*(7), 1934–1965. https://harvardlawreview.org/wp-content/uploads/2013/05/vol126_richards.pdf

Risk/Needs Assessment Tools. (n.d.). *Handbook of Correctional Assessment and Treatment* (1st ed.). DOI: 10.1002/9781119184256.ch3

Robles-Lorite, L., Dorado-Vicente, R., Torres-Jiménez, E., Bombek, G., & Lešnik, L. (2023). Recent Advances in the Development of Automotive Catalytic Converters: A Systematic Review. *Energies*, *16*(18), 6425. DOI: 10.3390/en16186425

Roy, P., Ghosh, S., Podder, A., & Sarkar, S. K. (2025). Opportunities and Challenges of Artificial Intelligence (AI) in the Banking and Finance Sector. Shaping Cutting-Edge Technologies and Applications for Digital Banking and Financial Services, 120.

Roy, P., Ghosh, S., Sarkar, S. K., Podder, A., & Paul, S. (2025). AI-Driven Ambient Intelligence Systems for Mental Health Monitoring and Proactive Intervention. *Cuestiones de Fisioterapia*, *54*(3), 2743–2752.

Roy, P., He, J., Zhao, T., & Singh, Y. V. (2022). Recent advances of wind-solar hybrid renewable energy systems for power generation: A review. *IEEE Open Journal of the Industrial Electronics Society*, *3*, 81–104. DOI: 10.1109/OJIES.2022.3144093

Ruhlandt, R. W. S. (2018). The governance of smart cities: A systematic literature review. *Cities (London, England)*, *81*, 1–23. DOI: 10.1016/j.cities.2018.02.014

S&P Global. (2024). The Rise of AI-Powered Smart Cities. https://www.spglobal.com/en/research-insights/special-reports/ai-smart-cities

Sahai, S., Sharma, C., Singh, S. K., & Gupta, P. K. (2011). Assessment of trace gases, carbon and nitrogen emissions from feld burning of agricultural residues in India. *Nutrient Cycling in Agroecosystems*, *89*(2), 143–157. DOI: 10.1007/s10705-010-9384-2

Saheb, T. (2023). Ethically contentious aspects of artificial intelligence surveillance: A social science perspective. *AI and Ethics*, *3*(2), 369–379. DOI: 10.1007/s43681-022-00196-y PMID: 35874304

Salemink, K. (2016). Digital Margins: How spatially and socially marginalized communities deal with digital exclusion. Academic Press.

Salha, R. A., Jawabrah, M. Q., Badawy, U. I., Jarada, A., & Alastal, A. I. (2020). Towards Smart, Sustainable, Accessible and Inclusive City for Persons with Disability by Taking into Account Checklists Tools. *Journal of Geographic Information System*, *12*(04), 348–371. DOI: 10.4236/jgis.2020.124022

Salma, Rahman, & Liyana. (2024). Future of smart cities: integrating health, well-being and productivity in residential building design. https://smart.cidb.gov.my/article/future-of-smart-cities-444

SamSam and the Silent Battle of Atlanta. (2019). In *11th International Conference on Cyber Conflict (CyCon)* (pp. 1-16). DOI: 10.23919/CYCON.2019.8757090

Sanchez, T. W., Brenman, M., & Ye, X. (2024). The ethical Concerns of artificial intelligence in urban planning. *Journal of the American Planning Association*, 1–14. DOI: 10.1080/01944363.2024.2355305

Sarker, I. H. (2021). Deep learning: A comprehensive overview on techniques, taxonomy, applications, and research directions. *SN Computer Science*, *2*(5), 420. Advance online publication. DOI: 10.1007/s42979-021-00815-1 PMID: 34426802

Schryen, G. (2015). Writing qualitative is literature reviews—Guidelines for synthesis, interpretation, and guidance of research. *Communications of the Association for Information Systems*, *37*(1), 12. DOI: 10.17705/1CAIS.03712

Ševčík, M., Chaloupková, M., Zourková, I., & Janošíková, L. (2022). Barriers to the implementation of smart projects in rural areas, small towns, and the city in Brno Metropolitan area. *European Countryside*, *14*(4), 675–695. DOI: 10.2478/euco-2022-0034

Shahbazi, N., Lin, Y., Asudeh, A., & Jagadish, H. V. (2023). Representation bias in data: A survey on identification and resolution techniques. *ACM Computing Surveys*, *293*(13s), 1–39. DOI: 10.1145/3588433

Sharma, A. (2017). India's Smart Cities Mission: Smart for Whom? *Cities (London, England)*, *91*, 70–78.

Shevade, S. K., Keerthi, S. S., Bhattacharyya, C., & Murthy, K. R. K. (2000). Improvements to the SMO algorithm for SVM regression. *IEEE Transactions on Neural Networks*, *11*(5), 1188–1193. DOI: 10.1109/72.870050 PMID: 18249845

Shih, C. F., & Venkatesh, A. (2004). Beyond adoption: Development and application of a use-diffusion model. *Journal of Marketing*, *68*(1), 59–72. DOI: 10.1509/jmkg.68.1.59.24029

Shih, E., Venkatesh, A., Chen, S., & Kruse, E. (2013). Dynamic Use Diffusion Model in a Cross-National Context: A Comparative Study of the United States, Sweden, and India. *Journal of Product Innovation Management*, *30*(1), 4–16. DOI: 10.1111/j.1540-5885.2012.00982.x

Shukla, S. S., Chava, R., Appari, S., Bahurudeen, A., & Kuncharam, B. V. R. (2022). Sustainable use of rice husk for the cleaner production of value-added products. *Journal of Environmental Chemical Engineering*, *10*(1), 106899. DOI: 10.1016/j.jece.2021.106899

Sidek, N., & Ali, N. (2019). Internet of Things-Based Services Implementation and Challenges in Malaysia: An Inquiry. *Test Engineering and Management*, *81*(11–12), 3219–3231.

Siman, E., Abiodun, J., Timothy, G., & Nandom, S. S. (2023). IoT-driven smart cities: Enhancing urban sustainability and quality of life. In 7th International Interdisciplinary Research & Development Conference. Retrieved from https://www.researchgate.net/publication/374090800_IoT-Driven_Smart_Cities_Enhancing_Urban_Sustainability_and_Quality_of_Life

Simonofski, A., Asensio, E. S., De Smedt, J., & Snoeck, M. (2017, July). Citizen participation in smart cities: Evaluation framework proposal. In 2017 IEEE 19th conference on business informatics (CBI) (Vol. 1, pp. 227-236). IEEE.

Singh, A. K., Alagusundaram, K., Kumar, A., Singh, R., Sehgal, V. K., Chahal, V. P., . . . Singh, S. K. (2019). In-Situ Crop Residue Management: Key Outcome and Learning. *Division of Agricultural Extension, ICAR, New Delhi, 30*.

Singh, T., Kaur, A., Katyal, S. K., Walia, S. K., Dhand, G., Sheoran, K., Mohanty, S. N., Khan, M. I., Awwad, F. A., & Ismail, E. A. (2023). Exploring the relationship between air quality index and lung cancer mortality in India: Predictive modeling and impact assessment. *Scientific Reports*, *13*(1), 20256. DOI: 10.1038/s41598-023-47705-5 PMID: 37985855

Smuha, N. A. (2021). From a 'race to AI' to a 'race to AI regulation': Regulatory competition for artificial intelligence. *Law, Innovation and Technology*, *13*(1), 57–84. DOI: 10.1080/17579961.2021.1898300

Soe, R.-M. (2018). Smart cities: From silos to cross-border approach. *International Journal of E-Planning Research*, *7*(2), 70–88. DOI: 10.4018/IJEPR.2018040105

Solutions, A. (n.d.). Breaking barriers: Top female innovators in tech. Retrieved from https://www.apollo-solutions.com/resources/blog/breaking-barriers-top-female-innovators-in-tech/

Stanly, H., Shalinie, M. S., & Paul, R. (n.d.). A review of generative and non-generative adversarial attack on context-rich images. Engineering Applications of Artificial Intelligence. Retrieved from https://www.sciencedirect.com/science/article/pii/S0952197623007790

Steinberg, S., Stepan, A., & Neary, K. (2021). NotPetya: A Columbia University case study. Picker Center Digital Education Group, Columbia's School of International and Public Affairs (SIPA). https://www.sipa.columbia.edu/sipa-education/picker-center-executive-education/case-collection

Stepping, K. M. K. (2019). Environmental sustainability. In Social indicators research series (pp. 187–206). DOI: 10.1007/978-3-030-05023-8_10

Stevens, A., Anisfeld, A., Kuester, B., London, J., Saleiro, P., & Ghani, R. (2018). Aequitas: Bias and fairness audit. Center for Data Science and Public Policy, The University of Chicago. Retrieved from https://github.com/dssg/aequitas

Stone, A. (2024). Virtual Singapore Is More Than Just a 3-D Model, It's an Intelligent Rendering of the City. GovTech. https://www.govtech.com

Sugandha, N., Freestone, R., & Favaro, P. (2022b). The social sustainability of smart cities: A conceptual framework. *City, Culture and Society, 29*, 100460. DOI: 10.1016/j.ccs.2022.100460

Suk, W. A., Ahanchian, H., Asante, K. A., Carpenter, D. O., Diaz-Barriga, F., Ha, E. H., Huo, X., King, M., Ruchirawat, M., da Silva, E. R., Sly, L., Sly, P. D., Stein, R. T., Berg, M. V. D., Zar, H., & Landrigan, P. J. (2016). Environmental pollution: An under-recognized threat to children's health, especially in low-and middle-income countries. *Environmental Health Perspectives, 124*(3), A41–A45. DOI: 10.1289/ehp.1510517 PMID: 26930243

Sun, H., Chen, X., Shi, Q., Hong, M., Fu, X., & Sidiropoulos, N. D. (2017). Learning to optimize: Training deep neural networks for wireless resource management. 2017 IEEE 18th International Workshop on Signal Processing Advances in Wireless Communications (SPAWC), 1–6. DOI: 10.1109/SPAWC.2017.8227766

Suresh, V., Muralidhar, M., & Kiranmayi, R. (2020). Modelling and optimization of an off-grid hybrid renewable energy system for electrification in a rural area. *Energy Reports, 6*, 594–604. DOI: 10.1016/j.egyr.2020.01.013

Swaine, M. R., & Freiberger, P. A. (2024, December 11). ENIAC | History, Computer, Stands For, Machine, & Facts. Encyclopedia Britannica. https://www.britannica.com/technology/ENIAC

Talaminos-Barroso, A., Reina-Tosina, J., & Roa, L. M. (2022). Adaptation and application of the IEEE 2413-2019 standard security mechanisms to IoMT systems. *Measurement. Sensors, 22*, 100375.

Tang, X., Li, X., Ding, Y., Song, M., & Bu, Y. (2020). The pace of artificial intelligence innovations: Speed, talent, and trial-and-error. *Journal of Informetrics, 14*(4), 101094. DOI: 10.1016/j.joi.2020.101094

Tene, O., & Polonetsky, J. (2013). Big data for all: Privacy and user control in the age of analytics. *Northwestern Journal of Technology and Intellectual Property, 11*(5), 239–273.

Townsend, A. M. (2013). *Smart cities: Big data, civic hackers, and the quest for a new utopia*. WW Norton & Company.

Tramer, F., Atlidakis, V., Geambasu, R., Hsu, D., Hubaux, J., Humbert, M., Juels, A., & Lin, H. (2017). FairTest: Discovering Unwarranted Associations in Data-Driven Applications. DOI: 10.1109/EuroSP.2017.29

U.S. Energy Information Administration. (2022). Monthly Energy Review. https://www.eia.gov/totalenergy/data/monthly/

Ucun Ozel, H., Gemici, B. T., Gemici, E., Ozel, H. B., Cetin, M., & Sevik, H. (2020). Application of artificial neural networks to predict the heavy metal contamination in the Bartin *River.Environmental Science and Pollution Research International*, *27*(34), 42495–42512. DOI: 10.1007/s11356-020-10156-w PMID: 32705560

Ullah, A., Anwar, S. M., Li, J., Nadeem, L., Mahmood, T., Rehman, A., & Saba, T. (2023). Smart cities: The role of Internet of Things and machine learning in realizing a data-centric smart environment. *Complex & Intelligent Systems*, *10*(1), 1607–1637. DOI: 10.1007/s40747-023-01175-4

United Nations Environment Programme. (2019, January 24). UN report: Time to seize opportunity, tackle challenge of e-waste. Chemicals & Pollution Action. Retrieved from https://www.unep.org/news-and-stories/press-release/un-report-time-seize-opportunity-tackle-challenge-e-waste

United Nations General Assembly. (1987). Report of the World Commission on Environment and Development: Our Common Future; Transmitted to the General Assembly as an Annex to document A/42/427 – Development and International Co-operation: Environment; Our Common Future, Chapter 2: Towards Sustainable Development; Paragraph 1. United Nations General Assembly.

United Nations. (2022). *The 17 Goals*. Sustainable Development Goals. UN.

Van Dijk, J. (2020). *The Digital Divide*. Polity Press.

van Zoonen, L. (2016). Privacy concerns in smart cities. *Government Information Quarterly*, *33*(3), 472–480. DOI: 10.1016/j.giq.2016.06.004

Vargas-Hernández, J. G., Pallagst, K., & Zdunek-Wielgołaska, J. (2023). Urban green spaces as a component of an ecosystem. In *Sustainable Development and Environmental Stewardship: Global Initiatives Towards Engaged Sustainability* (pp. 165–198). Springer International Publishing. DOI: 10.1007/978-3-031-28885-2_8

Veefkind, J. P., Aben, I., McMullan, K., Förster, H., de Vries, J., Otter, G., Claas, J., Eskes, H. J., de Haan, J. F., Kleipool, Q., van Weele, M., Hasekamp, O., Hoogeveen, R., Landgraf, J., Snel, R., Tol, P., Ingmann, P., Voors, R., Kruizinga, B., & Levelt, P. F. (2012). TROPOMI on the ESA Sentinel-5 Precursor: A GMES mission for global observations of the atmospheric composition for climate, air quality, and ozone layer applications. *Remote Sensing of Environment*, *120*, 70–83. DOI: 10.1016/j.rse.2011.09.027

Venkatesh, V., Thong, J. Y., Chan, F. K., Hu, P. J. H., & Brown, S. A. (2011). Extending the two-stage information systems continuance model: Incorporating UTAUT predictors and the role of context. *Information Systems Journal*, *21*(6), 527–555. DOI: 10.1111/j.1365-2575.2011.00373.x

Vicci, H. (2024). The Impact of IoT on the Modern World A review and evaluation study. SSRN Electronic Journal. https://doi.org/DOI: 10.2139/ssrn.4818308

Villamil, S., Hernandez, C., & Tarazona, G. (2020). An overview of internet of things. *Telkomnika*, *18*(5), 2320. DOI: 10.12928/telkomnika.v18i5.15911

Vovk, V. (2013). Kernel ridge regression. In *Empirical Inference: Festschrift in Honor of Vladimir N. Vapnik* (pp. 105-116). Berlin: Springer Berlin Heidelberg. DOI: 10.1007/978-3-642-41136-6_11

Walczak, R., Koszewski, K., Olszewski, R., Ejsmont, K., & Kálmán, A. (2023). Acceptance of IoT edge-computing-based sensors in smart cities for universal design purposes. *Energies*, *16*(3), 1024. DOI: 10.3390/en16031024

Wang, L., & Chen, X. (2021). Real-time detection of air pollutants using multichannel gas sensors: A review. *Atmospheric Environment, 245*, 118023.

Wang, Q., Luo, S., Zhang, J., & Furuya, K. (2022). Increased attention to smart development in rural areas: A scientometric analysis of Smart Village research. *Land (Basel), 11*(8), 1362. DOI: 10.3390/land11081362

Wang, Y., Li, J., & Zhang, X. (2019). Design and implementation of a low-cost particulate matter sensor for air quality monitoring. *Sensors (Basel), 19*(12), 2765. PMID: 31226728

Wani, A., & Sathiya, R. (2020). Ransomware protection in IoT using software defined networking. *International Journal of Electrical and Computer Engineering, 10*(3), 3166–3175. DOI: 10.11591/ijece.v10i3.pp3166-3175

Warzel, C., & Ngu, A. (n.d.). Google's 4,000-word privacy policy is a secret history of the internet. The Privacy Project. https://www.nytimes.com/interactive/2019/07/10/opinion/google-privacy-policy.html

Yaacoub, E., & Alouini, M. (2020). Efficient fronthaul and backhaul connectivity for IoT traffic in rural areas. *IEEE Internet of Things Magazine, 4*(1), 60–66. DOI: 10.1109/IOTM.0001.1900061

Yigitcanlar, T. (2014). Smart cities: An effective urban development and management model? *Australian Plants, 52*(1), 27–34. DOI: 10.1080/07293682.2015.1019752

Yuan, P. (2024). Artificial intelligence in the Internet of Things: Integrating and optimizing AI algorithms for real-time data processing and decision-making. *Proceedings of the 2nd International Conference on Machine Learning and Automation.* DOI: 10.54254/2755-2721/102/20241015

Yuchi, W., Gombojav, E., Boldbaatar, B., Galsuren, J., Enkhmaa, S., Beejin, B., Naidan, G., Ochir, C., Legtseg, B., Byambaa, T., Barn, P., Henderson, S. B., Janes, C. R., Lanphear, B. P., McCandless, L. C., Takaro, T. K., Venners, S. A., Webster, G. M., & Allen, R. W. (2019). Evaluation of random forest regression and multiple linear regression for predicting indoor fine particulate matter concentrations in a highly polluted city. *Environmental Pollution*, *245*, 746–753. DOI: 10.1016/j.envpol.2018.11.034 PMID: 30500754

Zaidi, T. (2019). An overview: Various attacks in VANET. In 2018 4th International Conference on Computing Communication and Automation (ICCCA), Noida, India. Retrieved from https://www.researchgate.net/publication/334760930_An_Overview_Various_Attacks_in_VANET

Zehlike, M., Castillo, C., Bonchi, F., Hajian, S., & Megahed, M. (2017). Fairness Measures: Datasets and Software for Detecting Algorithmic Discrimination. Retrieved from http://fairness-measures.org/

Zehlike, M., Bonchi, F., Castillo, C., Hajian, S., Megahed, M., & Baeza-Yates, R. (2017). FA*IR. DOI: 10.1145/3132847.3132938

Zhang, D. (2013, July). Inconsistencies in big data. In 2013 12th IEEE International Conference on Cognitive Informatics & Cognitive Computing (ICCICC) (pp. 176–182). IEEE. DOI: 10.1109/ICCI-CC.2013.6622226

Zhang, F. (2023). Urbanization and consumption structure upgrade: Perspectives from China. China City News. Retrieved from https://www.chinadailyhk.com

Zhang, K., Shi, Y., Karnouskos, S., Sauter, T., Fang, H., & Colombo, A. W. (2022). Advancements in industrial cyber-physical systems: An overview and perspectives. *IEEE Transactions on Industrial Informatics*, *19*(1), 716–729.

Zhang, Y., & Liu, H. (2019). Design and implementation of a portable power system for IoT devices. *Journal of Power Sources*, *420*, 1–10. DOI: 10.1016/j.jpowsour.2019.03.100

Zhang, Z., Hong, W. C., & Li, J. (2020). Electric load forecasting by hybrid self-recurrent support vector regression model with variational mode decomposition and improved cuckoo search algorithm. *IEEE Access : Practical Innovations, Open Solutions*, *8*, 14642–14658. DOI: 10.1109/ACCESS.2020.2966712

Zhou, S., Loiacono, E. T., & Kordzadeh, N. (2023). Smart cities for people with disabilities: A systematic literature review and future research directions. *European Journal of Information Systems*, 1–18. DOI: 10.1080/0960085X.2023.2297974

Zoe, R., & Melissa, I. (2024). The Rise of AI-Powered Smart Cities. https://www.spglobal.com/en/research-insights/special-reports/ai-smart-cities

Zou, H., & Hastie, T. (2005). Regularization and variable selection via the elastic net. *Journal of the Royal Statistical Society. Series B, Statistical Methodology*, *67*(2), 301–320. DOI: 10.1111/j.1467-9868.2005.00503.x

Zumbrun, H. (2023, February). Let's talk about bias: Measurement bias. Presented at NCSLI 2023, Orlando, FL. Retrieved from https://mhforce.com/wp-content/uploads/2023/10/ASQ-Lets-Talk-about-Bias-Measurement-Bias.pdf

About the Contributors

Muneer Ahmad is an accomplished academic and researcher with over 20 years of experience in computer science, artificial intelligence (AI), and data science. He holds a Ph.D. in Computer Science from Universiti Teknologi PETRONAS, Malaysia. Dr. Ahmad has worked in prestigious institutions across the globe, including the University of Roehampton in London, Woosong University in South Korea, National University of Sciences and Technology (NUST) in Pakistan, University of Malaya, King Faisal University in Saudi Arabia, and Hazara University in Pakistan. Dr. Ahmad has published over 100 research articles in respected journals, alongside numerous conference papers and book chapters. His research has made significant contributions to AI, data science, automated crop yield estimation, smart farming, and healthcare improvements using deep learning models. He has secured substantial research grants and led more than a dozen major research projects in Malaysia and Saudi Arabia. In addition to his research, Dr. Ahmad is dedicated to teaching and mentoring. He has supervised over 50 students at the Bachelor's, Master's, and Ph.D. levels, providing guidance in their academic and professional development. His innovative teaching methods, including the flipped classroom model, have been highly effective in fostering critical thinking and deep learning. Dr. Ahmad's commitment to professional development is evident through his active participation in scholarly activities and professional organizations. He serves as a guest editor for special issues in esteemed journals and is a member of IEEE and the British Computing Society (BCS). His extensive academic and research experience, leadership roles, and dedication to innovation make him a valuable asset to the educational community.

Rafia Mumtaz, a distinguished scholar, received the NUST Endowment Fund Scholarship for her MS studies (2004-2006) and a scholarship for her Ph.D. studies at the University of Surrey, UK. She is a Professor and Associate Dean of Faculty of Computing at the National University of Sciences and Technology (NUST), Islamabad, Pakistan. She has excelled in academia and research, publishing over 70 papers and earning accolades like HEC Best University Teacher Award (2022), and School Best Researcher Award (2019). Her pioneering work in precision agriculture earned her Women of Wonders Award (2021). Her leadership and IoT lab have secured grants worth Rs. 174 million and created a joint lab with Coventry University, UK with the name NUST-Coventry Internet of Things Lab, the first in NUST's and Coventry University's history. Her applied research in environmental monitoring has yielded patents and high-impact solutions. Her mentorship has guided students to international success, and she remains dedicated to advancing science and engineering.

Muhammad Ajmal Khan is a distinguished academic and professional currently serving as the Professor, Principal, and Dean at the School of Electrical Engineering and Computer Science (SEECS) at the National University of Sciences and Technology (NUST) in Islamabad, Pakistan. Dr. Khan completed his Ph.D. in Electrical Engineering from Michigan State University, USA, in 2008. He holds a Master's degree in Electrical Engineering from NUST, Islamabad, which he obtained in 2004, and a Bachelor's degree in Avionics Engineering from NED University of Engineering & Technology, Karachi, earned in 1991. His research interests span across micro-electronics, image processing, the Internet of Things (IoT), and machine learning. With a robust professional background, Dr. Khan has held various significant positions. Since 2021, he has been the Principal and Dean at SEECS, NUST. Prior to this, he served as the Commandant of CAE at NUST (2020-2021) and Deputy Director General of Crypto R&D in Islamabad (2019-2020). He has also been the Dean at NUST (CAE) from 2018 to 2019 and headed the Avionics Engineering Department at NUST (CAE) during 2016-2017. Additionally, he was the Director of the Crypto Research Centre in Islamabad from 2013 to

2016 and an Associate Professor at NUST (CAE) from 2009 to 2012. His career began as an Avionics Engineer, a role he fulfilled from 1992 to 2002. Dr. Khan is actively involved in several professional organizations. He is a member of the Royal Aeronautical Society in Pakistan and a Professional Engineer accredited by the Pakistan Engineering Council (PEC). His outstanding contributions to academia and engineering have been recognized through several honors and awards.

***

Garima Chanana is currently working as Assistant Professor in Vivekananda Institute of Professional Studies-Technical Campus, Delhi. She received her Ph.D. degree in Physics from University School of Basic and Applied Sciences, Guru Gobind Singh Indraprastha University, Delhi. She obtained her master's and bachelor's degree in Physics from Miranda House, University of Delhi.

Tirth Vishalbhai Dave is an active researcher at Vellore Institute of Technology in the School of Computer Science and Engineering. He is driven by his passion for data analytics and machine learning, specializes in healthcare predictive modelling, with a particular emphasis on breast cancer mass prediction. His research has earned recognition, being prominently featured in book chapter and prestigious conference proceedings. Tirth has also had the honour of presenting his innovative work on enhanced oxygen demand prediction in effluent reactors at a respected conference, further solidifying his reputation as a forward-thinking researcher. Moreover, Tirth holds a Microsoft Azure AI Fundamentals certification, a testament to his unwavering commitment to staying updated and proficient in cutting-edge technologies.

Shivnath Ghosh is a Professor and Head of the Department of Computer Science and Engineering at Brainware University. With 19 years of academic experience, he has made significant contributions to research and development. His work includes 52 research papers, 7 patents, 12 books, and 10 book chapters. He is currently guiding 6 Ph.D. scholars, with 2 having already completed their degrees under his supervision.

Nor Hazlina Hashim (Lina) commenced her Doctor of Philosophy in year 2010 at University of Wollongong (UOW), Australia. Earlier, Lina graduated Masters of Arts in Communication at Universiti Sains Malaysia (USM) in 2003 and Bachelors of Arts (in Public Relations) at Universiti of Techonologi MARA (UiTM) in 1997. Lina also has 4.5 years of working experience as Supply Management Analysts (SMA) at Intel Technology Sdn. Bhd., Penang (1997-2001) and was a senior lecturer for 8 years at School of Communication, USM, Penang (2010-2018). Lina has taught Message and Design, and Digital Marketing for Master in Integrated Marketing Communication (IMC) at USM@KL, Wisma Sejarah, K.Lumpur from 2013 until 2018. Lina went for her Industrial Training at McCann-Erickson (M) Sdn. Bhd. and exposed on advertising and copy writing. Her research interest is on websites and online studies especially Integrated Marketing Communication (IMC), Digital Marketing, Product Development and Innovations and Q-Methodology.

Khizar Imran is an electrical engineer currently working as an E&I engineer at Packages Limited. With a strong foundation in industrial automation and control systems, he is passionate about research and exploring innovative solutions in his field. His research project, AirSense, was a multi-modal air quality monitoring system, showcasing his commitment to addressing real-world challenges. Khizar is particularly interested in advancing his expertise through further studies and contributing to impactful researches that bridge engineering and technology.

Umer Amer Khan is an author and researcher affiliated with the National University of Sciences and Technology (NUST), Pakistan. He holds expertise in embedded systems and Machine Learning and is a member of the SEECS department. With a strong academic background and practical experience, he has contributed to several projects.

Nivedita M. has contributions of research in Image Processing, Computer Architecture. She has been a Professor at Vellore Institute of Technology, Chennai for the past 10 years with major publications in her research.

Aakif Mairaj is an Assistant Professor of Computer Science at Indiana University Kokomo in the School of Sciences. Currently, He teaches courses related to Computer Networks, Operating Systems, and System Analysis and Design. He received his Ph.D. in Computer Science at the University of Toledo in the Summer 2021. His primary area of research is the application of Game Theory for the Security of Unmanned Aerial Systems. His interest in cybersecurity and ad hoc networks began during his master's at VIT University when he was exposed to nature-inspired algorithms for energy efficiency in Wireless Sensor Networks. During his undergrad final year project in the Islamic University of Science and Technology, he worked on the speed control of DC motors using neural adaptive control. He is passionate about teaching and has taught courses such as Artificial Intelligence and Discrete structures. Before Joining IUK he was a lecturer at Purdue University Northwest.

Normalini Md Kassim was a system engineer for Maybank Berhad in year 1999 to 2001. Her experience in banking industry for 3 years handling loan processing programming. She obtained her first degree in Computer Science from University Technology of Malaysia at year 1999. She was joining Hewlett Packard Singapore at end of year 2001 as a Project Manager in Communication System Section. Her experience in communication programming and supporting the system for a few communication companies in a Philipines and Singapore. She completed her Master in Business Administration (MBA) in University Science Malaysia at year 2005. She is a consultant in risk management for AIA Berhad for 4 years which specific to Islamic financial planning. She started her career in lecturing with School of Distance Learning, USM in year 2007. Currently, she is an academic scholar with School of Management, University Science Malaysia on year 2008 and enrolled for Ph.D research program. With experience in banking, manufacturing, communication and financial industry, she would like to collaborate and share her experience in technology management and risk management area.

Mahad Mohtashim is currently enrolled in his Bachelor's degree in Computer Science at NUST, Islamabad. His major interest lies in artificial intelligence, having developed many projects, especially in Generative AI.

Furthermore, he is invested in the emerging field of quantum computing and plans to integrate these skills to contribute to Quantum AI.

Amitava Podder is an assistant professor of computer science engineering department at Brainware University Barasat.

Vikram Ranjan is currently pursuing B.Tech from Vivekananda Institute of Professional Studies–Technical Campus Delhi.

Piyal Roy is an accomplished academician in the field of Computer Science & Engineering. He has completed his BSc in Computer Science, MSc in Computer Science and MTech in Computer Science & Engineering. Currently, he is working as an Assistant Professor at Computer Science & Engineering department at Brainware University, India.

Sajidha S. A. is employed as an Associate Professor (Senior) in the School of Computer Science and Engineering at Vellore Institute of Technology-Chennai. With a vast and varied academic experience of 24 years she does active research in Machine Learning, Deep Learning, Block Chain, Data base management systems. As a complement to her targets she has earned publications in several high impact SCI journal publications in data analytics based unsupervised learning with the highest impact of 6.2, several book chapter in the field of ML/AI in health care, smart manufacturing /Block chain tech, conference papers in the field of ML in agriculture, cybersecurity, spatial insights and well-respected Scopus indexed papers in the field data analytics, cloud Architecture. She has further expanded her research in the direction of video analytics by working on real time consultancy projects such as Human performance evaluation and smart monitoring at assembly line within an automobile Industry.

Saptarshi Kumar Sarkar, an Assistant Professor at Brainware University, is committed to academic excellence. He brings extensive knowledge and experience to his students, with research interests spanning artificial intelligence (AI), machine learning (ML), and social networking. His contributions have significantly advanced these fields.

Syed Shirazi is an Electrical Engineering graduate from the National University of Sciences and Technology (NUST), SEECS. His research interests include IoT, Machine Learning, Real-Time Systems, and Embedded Systems. Currently working as a Sustainability Engineer at Packages Limited, Ali focuses on energy efficiency and sustainable practices. He is passionate about bridging the gap between academia and industry through innovative research and practical applications.

Ramayah Thurasamy has an MBA from Universiti Sains Malaysia (USM). Currently he is a Professor at the School of Management in USM. He teaches mainly courses in Research Methodology and Business Statistics. Apart from teaching, he is an avid researcher, especially in the areas of technology management and adoption in business and education. His publications have appeared in Computers in Human Behavior, Resources Conservation and Recycling, Journal of Educational Technology & Society, Direct Marketing: An International Journal, Information Development, Journal of Project Management (JoPM), Management Research News (MRN), International Journal of Information Management, International Journal of Services and Operations Management (IJSOM), Engineering, Construction and Architectural Management (ECAM) and North American Journal of Psychology. He is constantly invited to serve on the editorial boards and program committees of many international journals and conferences of repute. His profile can be accessed from http://www.ramayah.com.

Kamal Upreti is currently working as an Associate Professor in Department of Computer Science, CHRIST (Deemed to be University), Delhi NCR, Ghaziabad, India. He completed is B. Tech (Hons) Degree from UPTU, M. Tech (Gold Medalist), PGDM(Executive) from IMT Ghaziabad and PhD in Department of Computer Science & Engineering. He has completed Postdoc from National Taipei University of Business, TAIWAN funded by MHRD. He has published 50+ Patents, 32+Magazine issues and 110+ Research papers in in various reputed Journals and international Conferences. His areas of Interest such as Modern Physics, Data Analytics, Cyber Security, Machine Learning, Health Care, Embedded System and Cloud Computing. He has published more than 45+ authored and edited books under CRC Press, IGI Global, Oxford

Press and Arihant Publication. He is having enriched years' experience in corporate and teaching experience in Engineering Colleges.

Jasmine A. L. Yeap is a postdoctoral research fellow at the School of Management in Universiti Sains Malaysia (USM). Her research focuses primarily on the use and impact of technological innovations among individuals and organizations as well as the management of IT-based resources. Apart from that, she has also conducted studies in other areas ranging from consumer behaviour in the retailing industry, exporting to foreign markets, knowledge sharing and service quality to instrument validation. Most of her works have been published in journals and presented at both local and international conferences.

Index

T

U

V

www.ingramcontent.com/pod-product-compliance
Lightning Source LLC
LaVergne TN
LVHW081340300926
849161LV00008B/2029